THE
SAVER
&
INVESTORS
GUIDE

1993–94

If you have money
to save or invest this up-to-date
edition is crammed with facts
and information for you

WISEBUY PUBLICATIONS

November 1993 Budget Update
There will be a second Budget in November 1993 before the next edition of this book. Changes which affect the advice or information given here for the current 1993–94 tax year will be available in a free update. Send a stamped self-addressed envelope to:

UPDATE 1994
Wisebuy Publications
25 West Cottages
London NW6 1RJ.

THE
SAVERS
&
INVESTORS
GUIDE
1993–94

David Lewis

WISEBUY PUBLICATIONS

David Lewis's Guide was published in annual editions from 1982 to 1986 under the title MONEY MAIL SAVERS' GUIDE. This Guide has no connection with the Daily Mail or Money Mail.

First published 1982
Tenth edition 1993

While great care has been taken to ensure that the information in this book was correct at the time of publication, the author and publishers cannot accept legal liability for any loss incurred by anyone relying solely on the information contained in this book, neither can they accept responsibility with regard to the standing of any organisation mentioned in the text although at the time of publication all companies mentioned were believed to be sound.

This book provides information on all types of investments. If you require investment advice you should consult an independent financial adviser as explained in Chapter 2.

Further copies of THE SAVERS & INVESTORS GUIDE can be obtained from most bookshops. In case of difficulty copies can be obtained from Dept SG93, Wisebuy Publicatons, 25 West Cottages, London NW6 1RJ, price £5.99 plus 61p p+p (UK) ie £6.50 or £8 airmail including p+p.

British Library Cataloguing in Publication Data
The Savers & investors guide.
 1993–94
 1. Investments. Great Britain
 332.6'0941

 ISBN 0-9514595-3-8

Printed by
The Guernsey Press Co Ltd, Guernsey, CI.

Contents

PART 2

Foreword

This is the tenth edition of The Savers & Investors Guide with more investments t an ever. In Part 2 there are now 96 separate investment entries compared with 64 in the first edition published in 1982.

As usual a great deal of detail has changed since the last edition. So I repeat the advice I give with each edition. Study the book avidly. First look up the pages for investments you already have. Are they still the best for you and your tax rate? Are you invested with a recommended company? Look at the alternative investments which are suggested under the heading 'How worthwhile'. Then you can assess whether to leave things as they are or to swop your investments around.

Also look again at the explanatory Chapters in Part 1. They have all been checked and brought up to date.

How to use this book

The Savers & Investors Guide is in two parts. Part 1 explains how your tax rate determines the type of investment you need to consider. But tax is not everything.

Almost as important is the length of time you wish to hold your investments. That depends on what you eventually want to do with the money you have invested.

Part 2 lists all the different types of investments you will want to consider. The important points of each investment are detailed on its individual page. An explanation of what the headings mean is given on page 90.

How the companies are chosen

Many pages list the names of individual companies for you to choose from. These have been selected according to individual criteria which vary depending on the particular investment. Building societies, for instance, are those which at the time of going to press, offer the best rate for the particular type of account for the level of investment indicated; where a large society has the same terms than a small one, the small one is not mentioned. These pages also tell you where to get up to date information on the best building societies and other companies when interest rates change.

In many cases eg pensions, life insurance, unit trusts, personal equity plans, offshore funds, only companies with below average charges are included. In some cases eg School Fees Insurance Plan, all companies which offer this type of investment are listed.

'Past performance' is not usually a good indicator for choosing an investment. An exception can be in the very short term when a top performing unit trust or fund in a fashionable sector or market often continues to perform strongly if the market continues to rise. Another possible exception may be 'with-profits' pensions and life insurance contracts; the ones listed here have been chosen on the basis of good past performance.

New entries and changes

New entries in Part 2 this year are Building Society Postal Account, Building Society Permanent Interest Bearing Shares and Building Society Stock Market Guaranteed Bond. Life Insurance Stock Market Guaranteed Bond and Life Insurance With-Profits Bond are included for the first time. There is also the new National Savings FIRST Option Bond. And finally Unit Trust Index Tracker.

Bank Foreign Currency Account has been recategorised as Offshore Bank Foreign Currency Cheque Account as most accounts are in the Isle of Man and Guernsey. And Offshore Bank Cheque Account With Interest no longer has a separate entry but is referred to under Bank Cheque Account With Interest. National Savings Ordinary Account also does not have a full entry this year but is referred to under National Savings Investment Account.

Acknowledgements

My thanks go to Susan Lewis for editing my copy, to Judith Saffron for researching the bank and building society entries and to Duncan Lewis for proof reading and verifying. Also many thanks to the companies named in the text of this book for checking information on the pages on which they are mentioned.

David Lewis, May 1993

1

Your investment and savings strategy

The key to successful and profitable savings and investment is to keep up to date with investment opportunities. If you are in the know, you can take advantage of them. This book describes all the best ways to save and invest – and several which you are warned to avoid.

All savings and investments should be reviewed at least once a year. This year the best time to check your investments is between June and October when the Budget tax proposals are becoming, or have just become, final. This coincides with the publication date of this book.

However from November 1993 the Budget will be in the last week of November with proposals which became effective from 6 April 1994. So from 1994 the best time to make a major review of your investments will be from March to May. For a free update, see page 2.

Some types of investment, however, should be reviewed more frequently. For instance you should check the interest rate on your bank and building society savings every time there is a change in interest rates. They don't all go up and down by the same amount – and even if you are notified of the new rate, you won't be told if their rate has gone down by more than their competitors.

The same applies to risk investments – **especially if you are investing in shares. You have to keep an eye on what they are doing** and make rational decisions about when to buy and sell. A good investment can quickly become a bad one through neglect.

Financial commentators often remain preoccupied with short-term changes and forecasts. Interest rate changes and anticipation of changes hit the headlines frequently. For weeks and sometimes months there is huge pressure for them to go down – which they eventually do in dribs and drabs. Then there is a 'crisis', usually to do with the 'money supply' or the value of the £ abroad and they rise sharply again. The same applies to share prices on the stock exchange. In the short term they may go up and then go down, even if the underlying trend is upwards.

Some people say forget about these short term fluctuations. They say invest long term. **In practice you have to take both a short and long term view about your savings and investments. There is no best investment for all time.**

Savings or investments

What is the difference between savings and investments? The answer is, nowadays, not a lot. Financial institutions which used to specialise are increasingly becoming more alike – and so are the savings and investments which they offer.

Saving is what you do with the money from your income which you don't spend. 'Savings' is a description of the amount you have accumulated. Investment is what you do with your savings. The word 'Savings' has another meaning – it usually refers to a simple place for your money, like a bank or building society account. It sometimes also implies you do it regularly, say each month or year. 'Investment' usually refers to something more sophisticated. But the two words can often be interchanged – and generally for the rest of this book the word investment refers to both savings and investment.

What is your money for?

You may want to accumulate as much money as possible. Everyone feels more secure with more money. But you should really work out what you want your money for.

● Is it to increase your income so that you have more to spend now?
● Is it to pay for obligations you will have in the future like the cost of private education or supporting a student in higher education?
● Is it to give you a higher income when you retire?
● Do you want the money to pay for a holiday?
● Do you want the money to pay for repairs and maintenance to your home – like exterior decorations or a new roof.
● Do you want the money for major home improvements like a new bathroom, kitchen or an extension?
● Do you want to accumulate a lump sum to give you the opportunity to make a large purchase like a new car, a first or larger home or even a yacht or a holiday home?
● Do you need your money to finance your own business? Or have you plans for setting up on your own?
● Will you want to give some of your money away to your children or grandchildren as well as leaving money in your will?

Your time scale

Think about *when* you will want to use your money. If you want to boost your current income, you will want your money now. If you want to replace your car in five years time, you will need your money then. If you want to raise your income when you retire, work out how long it will be from now to your planned retirement date, say 17 years.

How much you need to accumulate

Now we will see whether you are being realistic or dreaming. Write down how much you expect your objective to cost today. For instance if you want to buy a car in five year's time and you think you need £10,000, write that down. If you want to boost your retirement income by £2,000 a year, write down '£2,000 a year'.

Although inflation has fallen in 1991 and 1992 after rising quite sharply from 1988 to 1990, it still can have an effect on the value of money; **over long periods of time it has quite a big effect, even at a relatively low rate like 4% a year**. You can measure the effect of inflation by looking at the four tables in *Appendix 4 How money grows and falls in value*. Take the following examples.

Suppose you want **to buy a car in five years** which would cost you £10,000 today. You can reckon that car prices will rise by 4% a year over the next five years. Look up *Appendix 4* for the figures in *Table 1 How lump sums grow*. At 4% a year and over five years you find £1,000 has become £1,217. To find out how much £5,000 will grow, multiply by ten and you get £12,170 which is how much you will need to buy that car in five years time.

Now what about that £3,000 a year extra income **to boost your pension when you retire in 17 years time**. What will be the average increase in the Retail Prices Index over the next 17 years? Over the past 17 years price rises (inflation) have averaged 8% a year. Over the past five years they have only averaged 5.9% a year. But over the year to January 1993 the rise was 1.7%.

Take a look at the same Table 1 again. Look what happens to £1,000 if price rises average 4% a year over 17 years – the answer is £1,948. So in 17 years time with prices in general rising by 4% a year, an extra income of £3,000 a year in today's money, would have to be three times £1,948 a year which is £5,844 a year, to have the same purchasing power as £3,000 today.

But if inflation is 10% a year, £1,000 becomes £5,054 after 17 years. So the same income has to be £15,162 a year to be equivalent to £3,000 a year now.

How much do you need to save to get that sort of money? Let's look at the car first. Suppose you want to save regularly for the new car. Look at *Appendix 4* again. This time turn to *Table 4 How much you need to save each year*. You first have to decide how much interest or growth you will get on your money – suppose you decide to invest in a building society and expect 4% a year after tax. Look up the figure for five years and 4% and you get the answer £177.53. So if you have to save about £177 a year to accumulate £1,000 after five years, then you have to save about 12 times £177 which is £2,124 a year to save for the £12,170 which you will need to buy the car.

For your retirement income let's assume that inflation is 4% a year. So you need £5,844 a year income in 17 years' time which is worth £3,000 a year in today's money. Assume you can buy a Life Insurance Annuity yielding 10% after tax at the time you retire – that means you need a lump sum in 17 years' time of about £58,000 to give you an income of £5,800 a year then.

For a long term investment through a Pension you can expect to get a return of, say, 8% a year (probably more) as there is no tax to pay and you get tax relief on your contributions (for more details see Chapter 9). Over 17 years at a return of 8% a year to get £1,000 you need to invest a lump sum of £270 now. So to get £58,000 you have to have 58 times £270 which is £15,660. You can calculate how to arrive at the figure of £270 by turning to *Appendix 4* and *Table 3 How much you need now to accumulate for the future*.

Don't worry if you haven't got the lump sum now – you can save towards your retirement income instead. Use another table from *Appendix 4, Table 4 How much you need to invest each year*. At 8% growth and over 17 years to accumulate £1,000 you need to save £27.43 a year. So to save £58,000 you multiply £27.43 by 58 which means you have to save just over £1,590 a year. To work it out monthly you divide by 12 which comes to about £133 a month.

If you are eligible to save through a pension scheme then you get tax relief at 20%, 25% or 40% on your contributions so the actual cost is that much less, that is only £106, £100 or £80 a month respectively.

A rising income

It's all very well working out what you need as an income in today's money when you retire. But what about the value of that income year by year after you retire? Unfortunately inflation will eat into that just as surely as it eats into your investments before retirement. At age 65 a man can expect to live for another 14 years to age 79, a woman three to four years more to 84. And many people live even longer into their late eighties and nineties.

However if you want a rising income to compensate for, say, 4% a year inflation, a Life Insurance Annuity instead of costing £58,000, would cost around 32% more for a man age 65, that's around £77,000, to have the same starting income of £5,800.

There is another, and probably better, way of investing for a rising income. Instead of allowing your pension fund to mature at one fixed date, you arrange for enough to mature to keep you at the standard of living you require at your initial retirement age. The rest you leave invested and as inflation bites into your income, you start to draw a second amount or 'segment' and so on until all your investments have been converted from accumulating ones into income producing ones. The advantage of this is that pension funds accumulate tax free, while income paying ones are usually taxable. For more on 'segments' see page 59.

If your investment return is high compared to the rate of inflation over a period of 17 years, in reality your retirement income may be much higher.

Your attitude towards risk

Different types of investments have different degrees of risk. There are three main types of risk:

● Risk of losing your money because the investment is one where the value is not fixed – like shares, stocks and investments in foreign currency; or investments like investment trusts, unit trusts and offshore funds which are linked to funds of stocks, shares, etc.
● Risk of losing your money because the organisation which you deposit or invest money with (eg a bank or life insurance company) goes bust because of mismanagement or fraud.
● Risk of losing money because the agent or financial adviser who is introducing you to an investment does not pass the money on and goes bust because of mismanagement or fraud.

There is no protection from the first risk. If you don't like the idea, avoid these types of investments although eventually they may turn out to be very profitable. In the case of the other two, you must take care to whom you entrust your money, although in many cases there are compensation schemes to protect you. In Part 2, each different type of investment has the position summarised under the heading *Risk*. The position of agents and financial advisers is considered in Chapter 2.

Your tax rate

Despite the considerable reduction in direct taxes since 1979 and the simplification of rules, investment decisions still depend on your tax position. This is described in *Chapter 3 Keeping down your tax bill* and *Chapter 5 Capital gains tax and inheritance tax.*

Different types of investment are dealt with in different ways for tax and this is explained in *Chapter 4 How different types of investment are taxed.* It is also summarised in Part 2 under the heading *Tax* for each individual type of investment. When describing the plus and minus points of an investment under the heading *How worthwhile* in Part 2, in most cases it states whether an investment is good for basic, higher or non-taxpayers. 20% taxpayers should usually follow the advice for basic rate taxpayers.

Money tied up in your home

One investment which you shouldn't forget is the value of your home. There are four ways with which you can utilise this value:
● If you live in an area which has high property values, you can move or retire to an area with lower values.
● If you live in a large house, when your children leave home or you retire, you can move to a cheaper or smaller one or to a flat.
● You can borrow against the value of your home – as a second mortgage if you still have a mortgage. The loan can often be paid off when you sell or die. The schemes are usually called *equity release*. Most lenders require you to pay interest. A few allow you to accumulate interest; these include the Cheshire and Ipswich building societies.
● You can take out a *Life Insurance Home Income Plan* when you are 65 or older to boost your income. Details are given in the entry in Part 2.

Remember that when you sell an owner occupied home, it is exempt from capital gains tax. If you have more than one home you can choose which one is your 'main residence' which will be exempt. You can back date the choice by up to two years by writing to your tax office. If one or more of the homes are jointly owned, both owners must sign the letter. However if you rent out the home or use it for a business for part of the time, there may be some tax to pay.

A record of your investments

It is always a good idea to keep methodical records of your investments. The cheapest way is to buy a few different coloured envelope files from a newsagent or stationers. Use one file for each different type of investment – ie red for shares and unit trusts, green for bank and building societies, yellow for pension and life policies. Then whenever you want to check out your investments everything should be clear and in order. Always keep copies of letters you send to the organisations which look after your investments, and make a note of any telephone conversations and the date.

Crossing cheques A/C Payee

If you send large sums of money through the post, there is a chance that someone will steal the cheque and pay it into another account. To protect yourself you should use cheques which are crossed and have the words A/C Payee written within the crossing. This stops the cheque being signed over to someone else's account. Many banks have these printed automatically, but if not, you can add two lines across the middle of the cheque and write in A/C Payee yourself. When you send a cheque through the post payable to a building society, an added precaution is to add the name of your account and your number after the name of the society. For instance: Pay C&G Building Society A/C J R Williams No 457772.

2

Best advice and how to get it

The Financial Services Act regulates investments and investment advisers. It was intended to improve the quality of financial advice you are given and to reduce the chance of you losing money through fraud or incompetence by an agent of an investment institution. The Act has been in force since April 1988.

One achievement of the Act is to compile lists of people who are allowed to be financial or investment advisers. Only firms or people on these lists, apart from the media which is in most cases exempt, are allowed to give investment advice to the public. Almost none of the list makers have attempted to judge the competence or qualifications of the advisers although most of the advisers will have been qualified by experience as having given investment advice in the past.

Since 27 August 1988 there has been the Investors Compensation Scheme if an adviser goes bust after that date owing you money. This applies to all authorised UK financial advisers. In some cases if you invested money after 18 December 1986, you will also be covered. The scheme pays 100% compensation on the first £30,000 and 90% on the next £20,000. So the maximum compensation is £48,000 which could be scaled down if total claims exceed £100 million. Some bodies (notably the Law Societies of England and Wales, Scotland and N. Ireland) have a better scheme, see 'The advisers' later in this Chapter.

If you want to check whether an adviser is fully authorised, and by whom, phone the Securities & Investment Board Central Registry on 071-929 3652 and they will tell you over the phone.

Which investment advice

The Financial Services Act does not cover deposits in banks, building societies, co-operative societies or National Savings. So anyone is allowed to give you advice on these types of investment. **Advisers**

registered under the Financial Services Act have strict rules about how they should give advice – but these rules do not apply to advice on deposits in banks etc. So it is possible that you can get bad advice on one of these deposits and have no come back on the adviser.

Banks and building societies which offer deposit based pension schemes (ie additional voluntary contributions or a personal pension) based on their own deposits, as opposed to pension schemes issued by life insurance companies and unit trusts for which they act as agents, are not covered by the Act either.

Which type of adviser

According to the rules an adviser can be one of two types: an *appointed representative* or an *independent financial adviser*. Appointed representatives are only allowed to advise on the products of one single company or group of companies. Independent financial advisers are supposed to choose the companies they use from all the ones available

Independent advisers	Appointed representatives (of company in brackets)
Bradford & Bingley	Abbey National (Abbey National Life)[1]
Clydesdale	Alliance & Leicester (Scottish Amicable)[1]
Co-operative Bank	Bank of Scotland (Standard Life)[1]
Girobank	Barclays Bank (Barclays Life)[1]
Yorkshire Bank	Birmingham Midshires (Sun Life)[1]
Yorkshire Building Society	Bristol & West (Eagle Star)
	Britannia (Britannia Life)[1]
	Chelsea (GRE)
	Cheltenham & Gloucester (Legal & General)
	Coventry (Commercial Union)
	Halifax (Standard Life)[1]
	Leeds & Holbeck (GA Life)
	Leeds Permanent (Norwich Union)[1]
	Lloyds Bank (Black Horse)[1]
	Midland Bank (Midland Life)[1]
	National & Provincial (National & Provincial)[1]
	Nationwide (GRE)[1]
	Nat. West. (Nat. West. Life)[1]
	Northern Rock (Legal & General)[1]
	Portman (Scottish Life)
	Royal Bank of Scotland (Royal Scottish)
	Skipton (GA Life)
	TSB (TSB Life)[1]
	Woolwich (Woolwich Life)[1]

[1] Has independent subsidiary.

and only to recommend the best products for each particular client's circumstances. This rule is called *polarisation*.

Banks and building societies although not covered by the Act for their own deposits are covered when they act as agents for life insurance policies and unit trusts for example. Most banks and building societies are now appointed representatives of one company, many having converted from being independent financial advisers since 1988.

The bigger banks and building societies which are independent financial advisers and those which are appointed representatives, and who for, are given in the box on the previous page. If you want independent advice, you generally have to ask to be referred to a separate subsidiary company. Banks and building societies which are appointed representatives offering this service are listed on the previous page by a footnote.

Best advice

Financial advice is supposed to be *best advice*. That means the adviser is supposed to get detailed financial information from you before he gives you advice. If you are reasonably well informed, as you will be as a reader of this book, you may find this rather tedious. If you don't want to give the adviser confidential information about yourself, you will probably have to sign a form saying so in which case you may not have a come back if the advice turns out to be poor.

Commission

Some independent financial advisers work on a fee basis. They charge, say, £200. Commission on £10,000 invested in a unit trust or lump sum pension could be 2% to 5% which comes to £200 to £500. The difference is refunded to you, usually by enhancing the allocation of your investment. In the example with only 2% commission you don't benefit from paying a fee. But with larger investments, this method can amount to a very effective discount: eg 5% of £20,000 is £1,000 less £200 gives you £800. *Money Management* magazine maintains a register of independent financial advisers which operate on a fee basis. Phone the magazine for the name or names of advisers. The service is free. Bear in mind some may charge fees far in excess of £200 – so find out the basis at the outset. There are also some advisers who split the commission with you.

It may be that you decide you don't want independent financial advice. You may therefore be inclined to deal with the financial institution (eg unit trust group) direct. However if you employ a solicitor or accountant and pay them fees to do other work for you, you would be better off using them as a post box for your application forms. The financial institution will pay the solicitor or accountant commission usually at the same rate as to any other financial adviser. The solicitor or accountant will set this amount as a credit against fees you incur with him for other work he does.

You complete the application form and make the cheque payable to the unit trust group or whatever in the usual way. On the form you will find a space for the 'Stamp' of an independent financial adviser. You can usually just write in the name and address of your solicitor or accountant. Or if you prefer, you can send the cheque and form to your solicitor or accountant and ask them to forward it to the financial institution for you after stamping it with their stamp.

Either way write to the solicitor or accountant saying you are nominating them to receive the commission so that it can be used against fees incurred by yourself or members of your family. If you send the form direct, send the solicitor or accountant a photocopy of the form, so he or she is in the know.

This only really works well if you don't ask for advice; if you do, you can expect the solicitor or accountant to charge a fee for the advice which will use up part or all of the commission. State in your letter to the solicitor or accountant that "I do not require and have not received any financial advice from you and this transaction is on an execution only basis".

If commission is used to offset professional fees in this way, it is possible there is no need for VAT to be incurred on the fees so long as the commission equals or exceeds the fees. That is a further saving.

The advisers

The advisers you are likely to come across are as follows:
● *Stockbrokers* for individual stocks and shares. You can also deal through a bank or building society's stockbroker. Stockbrokers are regulated by The Securities & Futures Authority. Some stockbrokers have subsidiaries which belong to FIMBRA.
● *FIMBRA members* (Financial Intermediaries, Managers and Brokers Regulatory Association) for buying life insurance policies, pensions and unit trusts. With unit trusts you can always go direct to the unit trust company.
● *Insurance brokers* for life insurance policies, pensions and unit trusts. Insurance brokers are regulated by The Insurance Brokers Registration Council. Insurance brokers which specialise in investment advice will also belong to FIMBRA. That does not mean that an insurance broker

may not have a good life insurance and pensions department even though at least 51% of the business of the company is in general insurance.

● *Chartered and certified accountants* for tax avoidance, trust and estate planning, life insurance policies and pensions. They will normally charge you by the hour for advice and if they receive commission on products you invest in, this should be set against the fee. Some chartered accountants may also be members of FIMBRA.

● *Solicitors* for trust and estate planning although some may give personal financial advice. Solicitors will usually charge you a fee for advice given and should set against it any commission they receive on products you invest in. The compensation scheme if you lose money through a solicitor is 100% of what you have lost plus nominal interest with no time limit. Solicitors are regulated by the Law Societies.

● *Consulting actuaries* are mainly used for setting up company pension schemes but some may give personal financial advice.

Other regulatory organisations

As well as the organisations described above which look after independent financial advisers, there are organisations which look after the managers and promoters of the investments themselves. You will only need to get in touch with these organisations if you have a complaint.

● *Lautro* (Life Assurance and Unit Trust Regulatory Organisation) deals with sales and marketing by UK authorised unit trusts and UK authorised life insurance companies.

● *Imro* (Investment Managers Regulatory Organisation) covers UK unit trusts and investment managers and is concerned with the way in which portfolios are managed.

● *SIB* (The Securities and Investment Board) is the organisation which oversees all the other regulatory bodies. Some organisations, mainly the few building societies and banks which act as independent financial advisers, are authorised by SIB instead of FIMBRA.

If you have to complain

If you have a dispute with any financial organisation which is not resolved to your satisfaction by the manager of the department you are dealing with, you should find out the name of the Chief Executive and write with your complaint. If your complaint is still not resolved, you can then try and use one or other of the various 'Ombudsman' schemes listed below. They don't all cover every type of complaint but can award compensation of up to £100,000.

● *Banking Ombudsman*. This scheme excludes anything covered by the Financial Services Act but includes complaints about 'phantom' cash dispenser withdrawals, bank charges, cheque guarantee cards, foreign currency, credit and debit cards, delays and so on. If in doubt, it's worth a try. Most banks belong to it.

● *Building Societies Ombudsman*. The scope of the scheme is wider than the banking one but a building society can reject the findings within 28 days of you accepting it. This only happens occasionally. All building societies belong.

● *Insurance and Unit Trust Ombudsman*. Excludes some major complaints like surrender values. Can consider claims which have been rejected by insurance companies. Most insurance companies belong as do a number of unit trust managers. For those unit trust managers that do not you can complain to the *Investment Ombudsman* (formerly the *Investment Referee*).

● *Pensions Ombudsman*. A new scheme which started in April 1991. Includes job and personal pensions but not the State scheme. There is no maximum on the amount of compensation which can be paid.

Protecting yourself

One of the easiest ways to protect yourself against fraud is always to make your cheque payable to the final institution you want to invest with. This is not possible when buying shares on the stock exchange but it usually is when buying new issues of shares and also with banks, building societies, life insurance companies etc even if you are dealing with an independent financial adviser. Do not be persuaded by the adviser that it is 'easier' to make the cheque payable to his firm. To ensure the cheque can only be paid into the account of the organisation it is payable to, write 'A/C Payee' between the two lines crossing the centre of the cheque if these words are not already printed on it.

3

Keeping down your tax bill

To choose the right investments, you have to invest by the best way for your own personal tax position. This Chapter tells you how to work out whether you are a reduced rate taxpayer, a basic taxpayer, a higher rate taxpayer (or the equivalent of one) or a non-taxpayer. **Before you take any investment decision you need to know which type of taxpayer you are.**

Income tax

Everyone has heard of income tax. Most people would prefer not to pay it. But lots of people pay more than they need, especially on their savings, through not knowing how the system works.

You do not pay tax on all your income. The taxman lets you off paying tax on the first so many pounds. How much depends on whether you are married, single, divorced or widowed and whether you are a one parent family. Elderly people on small incomes also pay less tax. This

		Income tax allowances
Allowance	This tax year 1993–94	Last tax year 1992–93
Personal	£3,445	£3,445
Married[4]	£1,720	£1,720
Additional[1,4]	£1,720	£1,720
Personal age (65–74)[2]	£4,200	£4,200
Personal age (over 75)[2]	£4,370	£4,370
Married age (65–74)[2,4]	£2,465	£2,465
Married age (over 75)[2,4]	£2,505	£2,505
Widow's bereavement[3,4]	£1,720	£1,720
Blind person's[4]	£1,080	£1,080

[1] For one parent families. [2] Applies to modest incomes only – see Chapter 13. [3] See page 73.

income, on which you do not have to pay tax, comes under the heading of 'allowances'. **Everyone is entitled to the 'personal allowance' or 'personal age allowance'. The other allowances are all paid in addition to this.** A full list is given in the table below. Most give tax relief at your highest rate; from 6 April 1994 the allowances indicated by footnote 4 will get tax relief at 20% only.

The taxman also lets you off paying tax if you have certain expenses: mortgage interest, pension contributions for example. These are called 'outgoings' but the amount of relief on outgoings is often restricted.

There are also some forms of income which are exempt from tax: these are listed overleaf. And others which are taxed differently and are explained in Chapter 4.

Having deducted your allowances and allowable outgoings (and ignoring income exempt from tax), the taxman taxes your income up to a certain level at the *reduced rate* of 20%. Then the next slice is taxed at the 25% *basic rate*. If your income is above the basic rate level, you will have to pay tax on the extra amount at the 40% higher rate.

The amount of income tax allowances and the levels at which the higher rate of tax begin to apply are usually changed each year. In theory they are automatically linked to the rise in the official Retail Prices Index in the previous year to September. So if prices go up by 4% from September 1992 to September 1993, then allowances and tax bands should be raised by 4% for the tax year starting on 6 April 1994.

The Government can decline to act on this decision in its annual Budget as it did in March 1993. Or it can raise the allowances and tax bands by more as it has done in past years. Another possibility is to raise some allowances by more, and others just by the rise in the cost of living or not at all. At the same time the Government also announces changes

and income tax rates

	This tax year 1993–94			Last tax year 1992–93		
Reduced rate	first	£2,500	20%	first	£2,000	20%
Basic rate	next	£21,200	25%	next	£21,700	25%
Higher rate	anything more		40%	anything more		40%

Maximum tax payable on reduced rate band
£500   £400

Maximum tax payable on basic rate band
£5,300   £5,425

---

[4] In addition to personal or personal age allowances. Only one married allowance per couple.

Exempt from income tax

Investments

Personal Equity Plan.

TESSA kept going for 5 years.

£70 interest a year on a National Savings Ordinary Account.

National Savings Certificates (including index-linked issues) and Ulster Savings Certificates.

National Savings Children's Bonus Bond.

National Savings Yearly Plan.

Interest on a tax rebate.

Interest awarded by a Court on damages for personal injury or death.

Premium bond prizes; betting winnings.

Save As You Earn (SAYE) bonuses.

Some Friendly Society savings schemes.

Pensions

Christmas bonus for pensioners.

Income support or supplementary pension.

Industrial disablement pensions and allowances paid to the injured person.

Part of the income from an immediate annuity purchased from a life insurance company.

Part of pensions paid to firemen or policemen injured on duty and possibly part of pension payable to others injured at work.

Pensions, pension additions or annuities, to holders of most gallantry medals from the armed forces.

Pensions paid by German or Austrian governments to the victims of Nazi persecution.

War disablement pensions.

War widows and orphans pension and allowances.

Social security benefits and grants

Assisted places grant.

Attendance allowance.

Child and One-parent benefit.

Child's special allowance, industrial death benefit for a child, guardian's allowance.

Family credit or income supplement.

Foreign social security benefits similar to those exempt in UK.

Home improvement and insulation grants.

Home loan scheme grant.

Housing benefit: rent and rate rebates and allowances.

Income support (benefit paid to dependants of strikers instead of basic unemployment benefit is taxable).

Increases for dependent children paid with widow's allowance, widowed mother's allowance, invalid care allowance, retirement pension.

Invalidity pension, invalidity allowance (if paid with invalidity pension), non-contributory invalidity pension.

Mobility allowance.

Sickness benefit and maternity allowance paid directly by the Department of Social Security.

Social fund grant.

Student grants and scholarships.

Training allowance.

Widow's payment of £1,000.

in the tax rates (up or down) and changes in tax rules designed to block up loopholes or to encourage certain types of investment or incentive.

Most people with jobs are basic rate taxpayers. Retired people may not pay tax if their main source of income is the State retirement pension. If you have a large income, you will pay higher rate tax.

What is your tax rate?

What tax rate you pay depends on your income. But when you decide where to invest, also think whether the income from that money will put you into a higher tax band. The tax rates and bands mentioned in the following examples are for the 1993–94 tax year.

Take a married man earning £26,000 a year. The first £3,445 is not taxable because of his *personal allowance*. The next £1,720 is not taxable because of his *married allowance*. Suppose he makes pension contributions of £1,000 a year before tax. This is an outgoing which gains full tax relief. It cuts another slice off his taxable income. The first £2,500 is taxed at 20%. The rest is taxed at the basic rate. Any extra income he receives from investments would also be taxed at the basic rate until the balance of his income (that is his income minus his allowance and outgoings and the 20% reduced rate tax band) exceeds £21,200. So he is called a basic rate taxpayer because any additional income he receives up to £21,200 (ie £3,865) would be taxed at the basic rate.

A wife is treated in exactly the same way for her own income.

There is no higher rate tax relief on mortgage interest to buy one's own or main home. Everyone gets the same tax relief on such a mortgage, whatever rate of tax they pay, and it makes no difference to tax on other income. This relief is equivalent to 25% of interest paid on the first £30,000 of a mortgage in 1993–94 and will be reduced to 20% for 1994–95.

Similarly from 1994–95 the *married allowance* gives the same relief to everyone equivalent to 20% of the allowance or a maximum of £344 per couple.

Now consider a more wealthy set-up. Suppose a couple each have an income of £30,000 a year. Husband and wife each make £1,500 pension contributions. The wife's allowances and outgoings total £4,945. That leaves £25,055 to be taxed. The first £2,500 is taxed at 20%, the next £21,200 is taxed at 25%, the rest, £25,055 minus £2,500 minus £21,200, which is £1,355 is taxed at 40%. So any extra income from investments would be taxed at the higher rate of 40%. Therefore **this wife is a higher rate taxpayer even though most of her income is taxed at the basic rate**.

If your earnings or pension put you close to the limit where tax starts, or the higher tax band starts to bite, then you need to work out carefully whether you are liable for tax on your investments and at what rate. If you are 65 or over during the tax year – see also Chapter 13.

Minimising your tax

Often minimising your tax is the best way of maximising your investment return. Every investment described in this book tells you whether it is suitable for non-taxpayers, basic rate taxpayers or higher rate taxpayers. 20% taxpayers should consider themselves in the same light as basic rate taxpayers.

Sometimes the tax position does not make much difference. Take the example of three similar sorts of investments: building societies where the basic rate tax is deducted from the interest; National Savings Investment Account where no tax is deducted but you pay it later; and National Savings Certificates where the interest is tax free.

If you are a basic rate taxpayer, the fact that the National Savings Investment Account pays, say, 10% interest and a building society account pays, say, 7.5% after tax is of little consequence, as you will have to declare the investment account interest on your tax return and pay basic rate tax on it. This will reduce the National Savings Investment Account interest to 7.5% after tax, the same as the building society pays. National Savings Certificates are exempt from tax but if you are basic rate taxpayer, you may be able to get a better return from another investment which requires you to pay tax on it.

Therefore for basic rate taxpayers it is often as important to consider other factors in addition to the tax saving. These are:

● convenience: whether you want the money back easily or prefer to tie it up for a longer period to obtain a higher return.

● whether you expect interest rates to fall or rise over the period of your investment (if you expect them to fall, you should choose an investment where the interest rate is fixed).

● how secure or risky the investment is.

If you are a higher rate taxpayer, there is extra tax to pay on both building society and National Savings Investment Account interest but none on National Savings Certificates. That extra tax reduces your return in the former cases. How much it reduces it could influence you, as a higher rate taxpayer, in favour of a tax-free investment.

Non-taxpayers should consider investments where tax is not deducted because it saves them the trouble and delay of claiming a rebate from the Inland Revenue.

Free tax leaflets

These leaflets are available free from HM Inspector of Taxes and PAYE Enquiry Offices – see under Inland Revenue in your telephone directory or the Inland Revenue, Public Enquiry Room, West Wing, Somerset House, London WC2R 1LB.

IR1	Extra-statutory concessions (plus supplement)
IR6	Double taxation relief
IR20	Residents and non-residents: liability to tax in the UK
IR24	Class 4 National Insurance contributions plus appendix
IR25	Taxation of foreign earnings and foreign pensions and insert
IR26	Business profits, changes of accounting date
IR28	Starting in business
IR33	Income tax: school leavers
IR34	PAYE
IR37	Appeals
IR40	Conditions for getting a sub-contractor's tax certificate.
IR41	Income tax and the unemployed
IR42	Lay offs and short time work
IR43	Income tax and strikes
IR45	When someone dies
IR46	Clubs, societies and associations
IR52	Your tax office
IR53	Thinking of taking someone on
IR56	Employed or self-employed
IR57	Thinking of working for yourself
IR58	Going to work abroad
IR60	Income tax and students
IR65	Giving to charity (individuals)
IR68	Accrued income scheme
IR69	Expenses forms P11D
IR72	Investigations: the examination of business accounts
IR73	Investigations: how settlements are negotiated
IR77	Maintenance payments
IR78	Personal pensions
IR80	Married couples
IR84	Have you anything to declare?
IR85	Business expansion scheme – private rented housing
IR87	Rooms to let (plus insert)
IR89	Personal equity plans
IR90	Tax allowances and reliefs
IR91	Widows and widowers
IR92	One parent families
IR93	Separation, divorce and maintenance payments
IR95	Profit sharing schemes
IR97	SAYE share options
IR99	Executive share options
IR103	Private medical insurance
IR104	Simple tax accounts
IR105	How profits are taxed
IR106	Capital allowances
IR109	Settlements for PAYE inspections
IR110	A guide for people with savings
IR111	How to claim a repayment of tax on bank and building society interest
IR112	How to claim a repayment of income tax
IR113	Gift aid: a guide for donors and charities
IR114	TESSA
IR115	Tax and childcare
IR119	Tax relief on vocational training
IR120	You and the Inland Revenue
IR121	Tax and pensioners
IR123	Mortgage interest relief
IR127	Are you paying too much tax on savings?
CGT4	Capital gains: owner occupied
CGT11	Capital gains tax and the small businessman
CGT13	Indexation allowance on quoted shares
CGT14	Capital gains tax: an introduction
CGT15	Capital gains tax: married couples
CGT16	Indexation allowance: disposals after 5 April 1988

4

How different types of investments are taxed

Almost all forms of interest and dividends are taxable and should be disclosed to the Inland Revenue on your tax return when you are sent one generally in April each year. Interest credited or accumulated in a bank or savings account or re-invested in a unit trust counts just as much as interest paid out to you.

If you do not receive a tax return for a few years, do not assume you will escape paying tax on interest where tax has not been deducted before you received it. When you have income liable for tax, it is up to you to ask for a tax return if you have not been sent one.

Tax-free investments

Forms of income which are truly tax-free and do not need to be disclosed to the taxman are interest on a Tessa kept going for 5 years, the proceeds of Personal Equity Plans (invested either in shares or in unit trusts), National Savings Certificates (including the Index-Linked Issues), National Savings Yearly Plan, SAYE, Premium Bond winnings, Ulster Savings Certificates (Northern Ireland).

The first £70 interest from a National Savings Bank Ordinary Account is also tax-free. A husband and wife can each get up to £70 tax-free. However if you get a tax return, you should enter the full amount of your interest: but make quite sure you do not pay tax on it.

You can also rent out a room – see *Rents* later in this chapter.

Interest with tax deducted

UK bank, building society, local authority loan and National Savings First Option Bond interest is paid after deduction of the basic rate of income tax. So if the interest rate used is 7% a year, and you have £10,000 invested, your before tax or *gross* interest is £700. With a 25% basic rate of income tax, then 25% is deducted by the building society or whatever, which comes to £175, and you are left with £525 after tax or *net*. The building society, bank or local authority should provide you with a *tax voucher* saying how much interest was paid and how much tax has been deducted although you may have to wait until the end of the tax year to receive it.

If you are not liable to UK tax on this interest, you can reclaim the tax from the Inland Revenue. The Inland Revenue will want you to send them the tax voucher, so keep it in a safe place. If you are not sent a tax voucher, the bank or building society must give you one on request.

If your entire taxable income (excluding any income, pensions or social security payments which are tax exempt – see list on page 26) is less than your personal tax allowances (personal or personal age – see list on page 24), then you can fill in a form which will allow the bank or building society to pay your interest without deduction of tax. You need a separate form for each individual account you have. The form is on the back of Inland Revenue leaflet *IR110 A guide for people with savings* and is available from banks and building societies and the Inland Revenue.

If you have a joint account and only one of you is eligible to have interest paid without deduction of tax, the one who is eligible can have half the interest paid without deduction of tax. Many banks and building societies allow this – check if yours does.

If your income is mainly from investments – for instance if you have retired early and do not receive a job or State pension – or your taxable pensions come to less than your allowances, **but your taxable income in total comes to more than your allowances, you are not eligible to have interest paid without deduction of tax**. You will need to claim a rebate from the Inland Revenue. Details on how to do this are contained in the free leaflet *IR112 How to claim a repayment of income tax* and *IR111 How to claim a repayment of tax on bank and building society interest* both available from Inland Revenue tax offices.

If you are a higher rate taxpayer, you have to pay extra, based on your before tax or *gross* income. You will receive a tax bill from the Inland Revenue separately.

Before 6 April 1991

Interest paid to UK resident individuals on or before 5 April 1991 by UK banks and building societies (other than SAYE) and on local authority fixed term loans normally came 'basic tax paid'. Individual investors who were basic rate taxpayers did not have to pay extra tax but non-taxpayers could not claim the tax back. The taxman set a special rate of tax for these investments called the 'composite rate'. This reflected the average rate of tax which investors paid and included those who were not liable to pay tax.

Local authority loans started before 1984. Fixed term loans started or renewed on or before 18 November 1984 continue to have (reclaimable) basic rate tax deducted until the end of the present term. Local Authority Negotiable (Yearling) Bonds have basic rate tax deducted from the interest which can be reclaimed by a non-taxpayer.

Tax disclosure

Whether or not interest has tax deducted, UK banks, building societies, local authorities and National Savings have to provide details of all interest paid or credited to your account to the Inland Revenue.

Interest not taxed before you get it

Interest from the National Savings Bank Investment and Ordinary Accounts, National Savings Income and Capital Bonds, British Government Stocks bought through the National Savings Stock Register (and War Loan however bought), interest on deposits with co-operative societies and interest from abroad (eg offshore bank accounts including the Channel Islands and the Isle of Man) does not have tax deducted from it. Nor does interest paid to someone with a UK bank account for a fixed term which was opened on or before 5 July 1984, nor on deposits by trustees of a Discretionary or Accumulation Trust (see Chapter 11), nor by someone resident abroad or on certain fixed term deposits over £50,000 with a bank or building society.

If you are not a taxpayer, they are therefore convenient investments because you do not have the trouble of claiming a tax rebate. If you are a taxpayer, however, you have to pay tax on the income from these investments and the income should therefore be included on your tax return.

There are special rules for working out the tax on such interest. The tax year starts on 6 April and ends on 5 April of the following year.

● In the first tax year in which you receive or are credited with interest from this sort of investment you are taxed on the interest you actually receive during that tax year.

● In the second tax year you are taxed on the interest you actually receive in that year.

● In the third and subsequent tax years, you are taxed on the interest you received in the *previous* tax year (ie in the third tax year you are taxed on the amount of interest received in the second tax year; in the fourth tax year you are taxed on the third tax year's interest).

However, in the third tax year only, you have the option to choose to pay tax on the actual interest received (instead of being taxed on the amount received in the second tax year). That is only worth doing if you get less interest in tax year 3 than in tax year 2.

If you already have one investment of this type (eg National Savings Investment Account) and you then invest in another (eg Offshore Bank Notice Account), the taxman will continue on the preceding year basis for the National Savings, whilst using the rules for the early years of a new account for the offshore bank interest.

Tax assessed under these rules is payable in one lump sum on 1 January of the year of assessment.

Where the interest is relatively low compared with your salary or pension from your former job, instead of asking for a lump sum, the taxman will collect the interest from your earnings or job pension by reducing the allowances on your PAYE code number by the amount of the interest.

As when you open an account, there are special rules when you close one. These rules may not always be applied if you have more than one account of each type (eg you hold several Government Stocks bought through the National Savings Stock Register and sell one).

In the last tax year during which you get interest from one particular type of investment, you are taxed on the actual interest you receive in that tax year.

In the last but one year, you are taxed on the interest in the previous tax year. But after you have closed the account, the taxman may revise that tax assessment and tax you on the actual interest for that tax year if it is higher.

It is likely that these rules will be changed from 1996–97 when the option of self-assessment for tax is introduced.

Rents

You pay tax on rents you receive on 1 January of the tax year in which you receive them. That means you may be paying tax on income you have not yet received (on rent payments due from January to March each year). However rent is normally paid quarterly in advance. A quarterly rent payment on 25 March is for the period April to June and would normally be regarded as being due for the next tax year.

The Inland Revenue makes an estimated assessment based on the previous year's rents – and then after you have made your tax return, adjusts the assessment and either gives you a rebate, or asks for more.

You can claim tax relief on various expenses you incur such as legal costs, estate agents charges, insurance, repairs, maintenance and decorations, electricity and other utilities etc. If the tenants reimburse you for all or part, you should add the amount to the rent you declare. You can also claim on interest of a loan to buy a commercial property up to the amount of rent you receive on all your properties. So if your rents do not excede the interest you pay, you won't get full tax relief. Unused tax relief on interest can be claimed in future years provided you don't sell the property on which you incurred the interest.

Rent a room in your home? Since 6 April 1992 you don't have to pay tax if the rent comes to £3,250 or less in the tax year and the room is furnished and in your only or main home. If the rent comes to more than £3,250 you can pay tax on the extra rent over £3,250 or you can pay tax on the whole amount in the normal way (and claim allowances for depreciation on furniture etc). For more details see the Inland Revenue leaflet *IR87 Rooms to let (plus insert)*.

Life insurance policies

Life insurance companies pay tax. But the proceeds of a life insurance policy (endowment, unit-linked, whole life, etc) are normally free of basic rate income tax and capital gains tax. The proceeds are the amount paid out when the policy matures or when you die.

Although you are exempt from capital gains tax on your life policy, the insurance company is not. 'Gains tax' may be deducted before you receive the proceeds of some unit-linked policies – with others the deduction is reflected in the price of the units. The rate of tax for life companies on these policies is 25% for both income and capital gains.

Higher rate taxpayers will usually be liable to pay extra income tax when they receive the proceeds of a single premium life insurance policy (or on death); or when they cash a regular premium policy which has not been going for ten years (or three-quarters of the original term if less) or a regular premium policy which is not a 'qualifying one'.

Single premium policies (investment bonds) often allow the policyholder to draw a 'tax free' income each year. Such a payment does not count as income for tax purposes and up to 5% of the original investment can be drawn for 20 years, even by higher rate taxpayers, without any liability to pay extra tax. If you do not draw 5% in one year, the allowance can be carried forward and used in a subsequent year.

If you make a withdrawal of more than 5% in a year which cannot be set off against unused allowances for withdrawals in previous years, the excess over 5% is taxed at the difference between the basic and the higher rate of tax if you are liable to the higher rate of tax. The amount of tax is 15%, that is 40% minus 25%. The amount of tax may sometimes be reduced by using 'top slicing relief'. Consult an accountant before you cash a large policy.

As mentioned before, a basic rate taxpayer has no liability to pay tax on the proceeds of such insurance policies although a higher rate taxpayer does. The point to watch out for is that a large policy showing a large profit paid out in one tax year could convert a basic rate taxpayer into a higher rate taxpayer whereas without the proceeds being paid he would not be. For this reason such policies are often sold in 'segments' (eg five £5,000 policies instead of one £25,000 policy) to enable you to avoid receiving large amounts in any one tax year, by cashing in each one in a separate tax year.

A large policy being cashed in after you retire could also reduce Age Allowance and so raise your tax bill – for more on this see Chapter 13.

If you save through a regular premium life insurance policy (eg monthly or yearly), and took out the policy on or before 13 March 1984, you are entitled to tax relief on the premiums. Tax relief is not available for single premium policies nor on policies started after this date. The relief is usually allowed by deduction from your premiums. That means the tax relief is already included in the premiums you pay. This relief is currently 12½% and likely to be reduced to 10% eventually.

Dividends and unit trust distributions

Dividends from shares you hold in companies and income distributions from unit trusts come with a tax credit. For the 1992–93 tax year and earlier years this tax credit was at the 25% basic rate of tax. This meant that basic rate taxpayers paid no extra tax, non-taxpayers and 20% taxpayers could claim a rebate and higher rate taxpayers paid 15% extra.

Since 6 April 1993 this tax credit is equivalent to the 20% rate of tax. Basic rate taxpayers do not pay extra tax. Non-taxpayers can claim a rebate. 20% taxpayers cannot claim a rebate. Higher rate taxpayers pay 20% extra. The 20% tax rate for tax credits does not affect the 20% reduced rate band which is available in full to everyone in addition.

Personal pensions and retirement annuities

How pensions are taxed is described in Chapter 9.

Accrued income

If you have invested in Building Society Permanent Interest Bearing

Shares, Stock Government Fixed Interest, Stock Government Index Linked, Stock Debenture and Loan, or Stock Convertible Loan and the total *nominal* value of all stocks of these types you own is more than £5,000, then the *accrued income scheme* applies when you acquire or dispose of any stock of this type.

If you buy or sell stock, the stockbroker (or Department for National Savings if you buy or sell through them) will work out how much *accrued interest* applies and will add it to, or deduct it from your contract note.

When you buy a stock, if accrued interest is added to the amount you pay, you can claim tax relief on this amount against your other income. If accrued interest is deducted, so you pay less, then you have to declare this amount on your tax return and pay tax on it.

When you sell a stock, if accrued interest is added to the amount you receive, you have to declare this amount on your tax return and pay tax on it. If accrued interest is deducted, so you receive less, then you can claim tax relief on this amount against your other income.

There is a free Inland Revenue explanatory leaflet *IR68 Accrued Income Scheme*.

Equalisation on unit trusts

When you buy any kind of unit trust and some offshore funds, your first distribution or dividend will be equal to the amount you would have received had you owned units for the whole period since the last dividend payment even though you have not owned them for the full time. The amount relating to the period before you bought your units is called *equalisation*. This equalisation payment is not liable to income tax – so only the taxable part should be declared on your tax return.

However you should keep a record of any equalisation payments as they count as a return of capital and should be deducted from your purchase cost when you calculate the amount for capital gains tax if this is applicable.

5

Capital gains tax
and inheritance tax

Capital gains tax

When you sell (or give away) an asset for more than you paid (or it is worth more than when you were given it) you have made a capital gain. Most capital gains are liable to capital gains tax but because of the various exemptions and the index-linking provision brought in from March 1982, in future many gains will escape the tax altogether.

You *dispose* of an asset when you sell it or give it away. When you buy an asset or are given one, you *acquire* it.

For assets disposed of on or after 6 April 1988 the original cost is taken as the value of the asset on 31 March 1982 if you acquired it on or before that date, or the actual cost if you acquired it later.

If you incur any expenses while buying or selling an asset (eg stockbrokers' or agents' commission, stamp duty, legal fees) you are allowed to add these to your original cost. If you make a loss when you sell or give away an asset, this loss can be set against any gains you have made on other assets before the tax is levied. If your losses come to more than your gains you can carry forward the losses indefinitely to be set against gains you make in the future.

The first £5,800 of capital gains you make in the 1993–94 and 1992–93 tax years is tax free. The balance is added to your income and taxed at 20%, 25% or 40% depending on your total income and gains for the year. **Since 6 April 1990 husband and wife each have their own limit.** So if an asset is owned equally, husband and wife can each use their own exemption limit. Each child has a separate exemption limit. Most trusts have a separate limit for capital gains tax of £2,900 in 1993–94 and 1992–93. Trusts currently pay tax at 35%.

Exempt   Certain assets are exempt from capital gains tax. These are your main home (if you own more than one, you can choose which one is your main home within two years of buying the second; you can also change your mind, and back date the new choice by up to two years); private cars; National Savings Certificates; SAYE; the proceeds of Personal Equity Plans; betting winnings and Premium Bonds; life insurance policies if you are the original owner. British Government Stock is exempt and so is Stock Debenture and Loan bought after 13 March 1984. Also exempt are shares in Business Expansion Scheme Companies sold for the first time, having been held 5 years, and bought after 18 March 1986. Foreign currency spent on holidays and holiday homes abroad is exempt although currency bought and sold for gain is not. Things like boats and caravans which are not expected to last for more than 50 years are also exempt. Tangible moveable assets (ie personal belongings, furniture, jewellery) worth less than £6,000 at the time of disposal (a set of objects, eg a pair of ear-rings, usually counts as one object) are also exempt. If the proceeds are more than £6,000 from each object, the taxable gain is ⅗rds of the excess over £6,000 if this is less than the actual gain.

There is no capital gains tax payable on your estate on death but see *inheritance tax* below.

Indexation   Capital gains tax takes account of inflation. Instead of deducting the original cost from the sale price, to work out the gain you take that original cost (plus any allowable expenses on purchase) and normally uplift it by an 'indexation allowance' based on the change in the Retail Prices Index from the date of purchase to the date of disposal. This will reduce your gain and possibly eliminate it altogether. There are two Inland Revenue leaflets available on the indexation allowance – *CGT13 Indexation allowance on quoted shares* and *CGT16 Indexation allowance: disposals after 5 April 1988*.

If you acquired the asset before 31 March 1982, the indexation allowance is worked out as if you acquired the asset in March 1982 *and it is based on the value of the asset on 31 March 1982 not what you actually paid*.

If you acquired the asset *after* 31 March 1982, then the indexation allowance is worked out according to the month in which you acquired the asset and the month in which you disposed of it.

Under the index-linking system you can create a tax loss even if you dispose of shares for the same amount as you paid because inflation has reduced their value. You can also increase an actual loss.

Unit Trust Savings Plan or Investment Trust Savings Plan where you save monthly, you don't have to use monthly indexation figures; you can use the indexation allowance for July each year instead.

Gifts and gains tax If you make a gift of an asset you may be liable to pay capital gains tax if the gain is large. So give away cash – or assets which are exempt, see list on the previous page. Gifts to a trust incur gains tax in the same way as gifts to an individual. Gifts between husband and wife and vice-versa are ignored.

Time to pay Where you make a gift of land (eg a house) or a controlling shareholding of a company or a minority holding in an unquoted company, capital gains tax can be paid over ten years, but interest must be paid unless it is agricultural property.

Inheritance tax

Inheritance tax is a tax on what you leave in your will (and on gifts you make in your lifetime to some trusts and companies). It only affects people who are likely to leave more than £150,000.

Where the estate, plus non-exempt gifts which are made up to 7 years before death, come to more than £150,000 then the tax starts to bite at a rate of 40% of the excess. So if your estate is worth £300,000 (after deducting debts like mortgages, bank loans and outstanding bills), then deduct £150,000 which leaves £150,000 and the tax is 40% of £150,000 which is £60,000.

Non-exempt gifts made within 3 years of death are added to the estate. For gifts made between 3 and 7 years of death only part of the gift is added to the estate: 80% for gifts made more than 3 but less than 4 years before death; 60% for gifts made more than 4 but less than 5 years; 40% more than 5 but less than 6 years; 20% more than 6 but less than 7 years.

Exempt gifts which are not added to the estate even if the giver dies within seven years of making them are:

● Any amount to your husband or wife (even if you are not living with them or are separated but *not* divorced) which is also tax free on death.

● In addition £3,000 in any tax year. If you do not use all the allowance in one tax year, you can use the balance in the next one, after you have used up that year's allowance. Husband and wife each have a £3,000 a year allowance. So between the two they could give £6,000 a year – or £12,000 if neither has used up the allowance from the previous tax year.

● In addition, wedding gifts: £5,000 by each parent (including step-parents); £2,500 by each grandparent or great-grandparent and also the bride and groom to each other; and £1,000 by anyone else.

● In addition, money spent on your own child's education or maintenance if he or she is under 18 or still in full-time education; or reasonable provision for the care or maintenance of a 'dependent relative'.

● In addition, 'normal expenditure' gifts which you give out of your after tax income and which do not affect your standard of living, ie you do not have to draw on capital to make them.

● You can also give up to £250 each tax year to any number of different people provided they have not received any other gifts from you (say under the above exemptions) in the same tax year.

Where an estate is less than £125,000, your executors do not normally have to deliver an account for inheritance tax before probate is granted.

A free booklet Inheritance Tax (IHTI) is available from the Capital Taxes Offices of the Inland Revenue in London, Edinburgh and Belfast.

6

Spread your money around

However much money you have, you want to make the most of it. But making the most of your money does not mean ploughing it all into one investment. You need different investments to suit different needs.

Emergency fund

This is the first purpose of having any investment: a sum of money which you can get at immediately without any penalty if something unexpected happens. For people who have little money, an emergency fund may be their only form of investment.

How much you should have in an emergency fund depends on how worried you are about an emergency. People do fall ill, have accidents, lose their jobs unexpectedly, have to carry out major repairs on their homes. It makes life much easier if you have ready cash to pay for some or all of these things should they occur.

A fund of £500 might do for a young single person. A married couple with children might aim for £2,000 to £3,000. If you are more cautious your emergency fund might be as high as £4,000 or £5,000. The higher your income and expenditure, the higher emergency fund you are likely to need as you will not only use it for emergencies but also to help pay for larger items of spending (say holidays or house repairs). People with jobs might think in terms of three months' pay.

An emergency fund of £3,000 will not affect your right to state means tested Income Support or Housing Benefit (formerly called rent rebate) or Council Tax Benefit (formerly called rate rebate). One between £3,000 and £8,000 (£16,000 for Housing Benefit and Council Tax Benefit) will reduce the state benefits but not eliminate them.

However, there is no need to have all your money readily available. If you are particularly worried about running out of funds, you should tie up as much as you can spare so that it becomes available at regular intervals, say, every year or every two years. Then every year or two, you should check whether your emergency fund is large enough and if necessary replenish it. If you have no savings, it is worth making a commitment to save so much each month by a method which does not tie up your money for too long, in order to build up an emergency fund for the future.

Don't tie up your money for too long

Time may pass quickly. But when you find you are short of money or interest rates have changed, time can pass all too slowly for you. So unless you have a great deal of money, do not tie up your money for too long; you are quite likely to want it back early and getting back a long term investment early usually makes it worse value than having left the money immediately available all the time.

Also be warned against tying up your money at a fixed rate of interest for more than two to four years at a time. Unless the rate is very much better than rates available elsewhere, you may find, with the benefit of hindsight, the sacrifice of tying up the money may not have been worth while if other rates rise and offer a better return. You may then find yourself lured into changing your plans and suffer a penalty.

Compensation funds

Even if you invest in a way where your capital does not fluctuate in value, there is always a chance that the body you are investing in will go bust. It may be rare but it should not be forgotten. With some forms of investment there are compensation funds designed to refund some of your money if this happens. The funds are summarised below:

Banks which are licensed by the Bank of England are covered by a compensation scheme for 75% of the first £20,000 of each investor's total deposits with a bank (ie £40,000 for a joint account owned equally by two people). Maximum payment is £15,000 per investor. Deposits for an original term of over 5 years and in currencies other than £ sterling are not included. See also offshore banks below.

Building societies are protected by a scheme which pays 90% of the first £20,000 of each investor's deposits (ie £40,000 for a two person joint account). Maximum payment is £18,000 per investor. Building societies which decide to convert to 'Plc' become banks and from the date of conversion the 'bank' compensation scheme applies.

UK authorised insurance companies are covered by the Policyholders Protection Act which gives a 90% compensation less 'excessive benefits' a concept determined by a Policyholders Protection Board. Overseas insurance companies (Isle of Man, Jersey, Guernsey and Gibraltar count as overseas) *not* authorised by the Department of Trade must say they are *not* authorised in any advertisement or circular; don't invest in them.

Friendly societies   These are covered by the same limits as independent financial advisers – see below.

Co-operative societies are covered by a compensation scheme which has the same limits as for UK banks.

Local authorities do not have a formal compensation scheme but the Government would probably stand behind any authority liable to default on its loans.

Department for National Savings is a government department and therefore has a government guarantee.

Independent financial advisers   Provided the adviser is fully authorised by one of the UK regulatory bodies The Investors Compensation Scheme covers each investor for 100% of losses up to £30,000 and for 90% of the next £20,000 making a maximum payment of £48,000. This applies to investments made no earlier than 18 December 1986. For more on advisers, and higher limits for solicitors, see Chapter 2.

UK authorised unit trusts   These are covered by The Investors Compensation Scheme at the same limits as for *independent financial advisers* (see above). There is no compensation for a fall in unit or share prices, only if there is a loss due to mismanagement or fraud by the managers.

Offshore banks with branches abroad can advertise for deposits in the UK and have representative offices here even though they are not licensed by the Bank of England. They are not covered by the UK bank compensation scheme; nor are branches of UK banks in Guernsey, Jersey, Alderney or the Isle of Man.
● *Isle of Man* banks and UK bank branches in the Isle of Man are covered by a local compensation scheme which has the same limits as the UK one and includes foreign currency deposits as well as £ sterling.
● If you open an account at a bank in the USA you are covered for 100% of up to US$100,000 per person (ie US$200,000 on a joint account or US$400,000 where an account is in four names) if the bank belongs to

the Federal Deposit Insurance Corporation.

Offshore funds   Where the territory in which the fund is located and the fund is 'recognised' by the Securities & Investment Board (eg Isle of Man, Jersey), there are compensation funds with similar limits to the one for UK unit trusts.

● *Isle of Man, Jersey* for 'recognised' funds, limits same as UK.
● *Guernsey* for 'recognised' funds, compensation for each investor of 90% on the first £50,000 and 30% on the next £50,000.
● *Bermuda* for 'recognised' funds 100% on the first US$50,000.

So for a £100,000 investment, in Guernsey the maximum payment would be £60,000 whereas in the UK it would be £48,000. But for £30,000, in the UK, Isle of Man and Jersey the compensation would be £30,000, whereas in Guernsey it would be £27,000. Not all funds in these territories are recognised.

All funds mentioned in this book were 'recognised' at the time the book went to press. The Financial Times lists recognised funds in its prices page and these funds are allowed to be promoted in the same way as UK based unit trusts.

Personal equity plans   As for *UK authorised unit trusts*.

A longer term strategy

If you really want to tie up your money, do not put all your eggs in one basket. Suppose you have £14,000 and you are a basic rate taxpayer. For your emergency fund put £3,000 into a *Building Society Instant Access Account* or *Building Society Postal Account*.

You now have £11,000 to invest. You may be tempted to tie this up for 5 years or even longer – do not. An emergency fund must be available to be spent – and once you have spent it, you will need another one.

So wherever you invest the next £3,000 of your money, make sure you can get it back after two years. Another £4,000 might be tied up for, say, 4 to 5 years. And the remaining £5,000 can be put into long-term investments like *Investment Trust Personal Equity Plan*, or *Unit Trust Personal Equity Plan*. Other long term investments include different types of *Unit Trusts*, *Investment Trusts* and *Shares*. For the more cautious there is *Stock Government Index Linked*.

7

Turning income into capital

You may inherit money or win it on the football pools. But if you can't count on such a windfall and want to build up a capital sum, you will have to do it by turning your income into capital. This Chapter gives you a few hints on how best to go about it.

The investments you choose need to be those which give a good return but are also convenient for your purpose. Building capital requires investments where income and capital gains can accumulate.

In order to build up such a capital sum, you have to save regularly. This is a commitment each month usually by direct debit or standing order or by direct deduction from your pay.

Don't over commit yourself. That is probably the biggest pitfall of regular savers. Only save as much as you can afford when you start and choose a means of saving which allows you to raise your contribution when you are able to.

Once you have accumulated a reasonable amount in your savings account and reached the minimum for an account which pays a higher rate of interest, then you should transfer the balance and either start again with your regular savings plan or continue your savings into the new better paying account if you can.

Borrowing and saving

Before you set about saving for something, think about your borrowing. Saving and borrowing are the reverse of each other. If you are paying high interest on a borrowing, like a credit card bill which you don't pay off in full at the end of each month, you would do better to reduce the amount you are borrowing rather than saving up separately.

The reason is simple: by paying off your credit card bill you may save paying 20% to 30% interest a year whereas your savings may only generate 4% to 7% interest a year. These actual rates may change but rates for lenders and borrowers go up and down together – and it is always the borrowers who end up paying more.

There is another reason to pay off borrowing before you start to save up capital. You generally have to pay income tax on the interest you receive from savings. But you rarely receive tax relief on interest you pay when you have borrowed money.

In general terms the cheapest form of borrowing is a mortgage to buy your own home. The most costly is a credit card from a store or chain of stores. If you are self employed, you can benefit from tax relief on most borrowing for the business including overdraft interest. So borrow for the business and not for yourself.

Saving to buy a home

Mortgages continue to be easy to get. Since the peak in the housing market in 1988, house prices have fallen in many parts of the country. In some areas by as much as 30% to 40% or even more in cases of forced sales where borrowers cannot afford to pay their mortgages any longer. Now may be the time to find a bargain.

It usually takes about two months from seeing a home and deciding to buy it to the *exchange of contracts* where you need to pay over the deposit. You can therefore save your money into a *Building Society 30 Day Notice Account* or a *Building Society 60 Day Notice Account* once you have reached the minimum investment and get higher interest.

Saving towards a mortgage is best done monthly; an amount to aim for might be the payments you expect on your mortgage.

Save to buy a home with:
Building Society Regular Monthly Savings Account
Building Society Instant Access Account
Building Society Postal Account
Building Society 30 Day Notice Account
Building Society 60 Day Notice Account

Saving towards a family

A young couple who are both working need to save as much as possible if they want to start a family. It is very important that this money is not tied up; five years should be the maximum.

Save towards a family with:
Building Society Regular Monthly Savings Account
Building Society Instant Access Account
Building Society Postal Account
Building Society 30 Day Notice Account
Building Society 60 Day Notice Account
Building Society 90 Day Notice Account

For five years only:
Building Society Tessa Account

Saving for holidays

Saving for holidays is usually very short term. Most people will want to go on holiday once a year – and if you go abroad it is likely to be quite costly: £1,500 plus for a family of four might be a typical figure. You will know from last year how much your next holiday is likely to cost you. Most years you can add on a bit for inflation and add or deduct from the cost depending on whether the pound is weak or strong. Unless you are saving for that special big holiday, there is not much point in committing yourself to a regular monthly saving.

Several building societies offer discounts or 'free' spending money on inclusive holidays or air fares booked by customers of certain accounts. This is equivalent to a discount of about 5%. Similar schemes are run for credit card holders like Access and Barclaycard.

Save for a holiday with:
Building Society Cheque Account With Interest
Building Society Instant Access Account
Building Society Postal Account
Building Society 30 Day Notice Account

You might also consider for spending money:
Offshore Bank Foreign Currency Account
Offshore Single Foreign Currency Fund

Saving for a car

Cars wear out. So if you can afford to, it is as well to put aside a regular amount towards the deposit on a new one. If you cannot pay cash, the cheapest way to borrow is from a building society; hire purchase or a loan from a bank will always be more costly. On a new car a bank or building society may require you to put up 10% to 20% in cash. Occasionally you are offered interest-free hire purchase instead of a discount for cash. If you do not have the cash, it is well worth taking.

Save for a car with:
Building Society Instant Access Account
Building Society Postal Account
Building Society 30 Day Notice Account

8

How best to invest in stocks and shares

The aim of making a profit from shares is to buy when they are cheap and to sell when they are expensive. There are two strategies for share buying and selling:

● You can buy the market as a whole – that is invest in a portfolio of say 20 shares and then forget about them using any dividends to boost your income.

● Or you can be an active investor, a speculator even, and buy and sell shares every week or month, seeking to make a profit from the ups and downs of the stockmarket.

Buying new issues

Many people start to build up a portfolio of shares by investing in the Government privatisation share issues. You could have built up quite a wide portfolio consisting of BAA, British Airways, British Aerospace, British Gas, BP, British Telecom, Cable & Wireless, Rolls Royce and the electricity and water companies, if you had gone in for these new offers. You might also have bought other recommended shares which were offered for the first time like Laura Ashley, TSB, Wellcome, Abbey Life and Abbey National.

With these offers it was easy to buy because all you had to do was fill in a form and send off your money. You also had the advantage of not having to pay stockbroker's commission which is now normally a minimum £15 to £20 per transaction (or 1% to 1.9%) and stamp duty of ½%.

There are plans to privatise the railways, coal mines, the rest of British Telecom and possibly the postal service. These may not all come about.

Applying for new issues and holding onto them is not a bad way to accumulate a portfolio of shares, especially if you only have a small amount of money you want to invest.

Building societies

Following the lead of Abbey National other building societies may convert to public limited companies (Plc). **If you want to participate make sure you and your husband or wife each have £100 or more invested in separate accounts in each of the societies you think will convert.** The largest societies are listed in order of size under 'Where from' on page 112. There will be a cut off date, so the earlier you invest the better.

Buying individual shares

You may want to buy individual shares other than on a new issue. Which ones to buy and when to sell is something even the experts don't agree on, so there is an opportunity for individuals to use their judgement and luck to choose shares themselves. There is no shortage of advice. Most newspapers and specialist magazines like *Investors Chronicle* (weekly) and *Money Observer* (monthly), regularly tip share purchases. There are special newsletters like the *IRS Report* which give share tips and stockbrokers often give their clients recommendations.

If you just follow the published advice, you will often find that the share price has risen by the time you get round to buy the shares. That is because whenever a share tip is published, all stockmarket dealers automatically raise the price. If the tip is found to be correct, then the price will probably rise further. But if it is a dud, the price will fall back to the original level, and you can end up paying more for a share than you need have. You can follow the performance of all UK shares in tables published in *Money Observer* each month.

Tipsters are very good at crowing about how well some of their recommendations have performed – and if they can point to a huge profit they may even advise you to sell. But when the advice is not so hot, many, a notable exception is *Money Observer*, conveniently forget about the recommendations which did not come off.

You should have a portfolio or spread of investments in different companies – at least seven but no more than 20 otherwise you can't keep track of them. The minimum of seven is so you do not suffer unduly if a company you invest in goes bust or the shares fall very steeply.

Under £9,000 a year to invest

If you have £9,000 or less a year which you want to invest in the stock market, but still want to invest directly in shares, you might consider doing this through a *Shares Self Select Personal Equity Plan*. **The limit is**

per person – so a husband and wife could invest £18,000 a year between them.

There are two types – one where the managers choose the shares for you, rather like a unit trust but generally with fewer shares, or the Do-It-Yourself type where you can choose the shares. The advantage of a personal equity plan is that you can usually avoid high minimum commission charges when you buy and sell individual shares and your entire investment is tax free (both income and capital gains). Personal equity plans are probably more suited to people who want to buy and hold shares than those who want to trade. Alternatively if you already hold a portfolio of shares, you could put one (or two) which have a high yield into your personal equity plan. Full details are given in the entry in Part 2 under the heading *Shares Self Select Personal Equity Plan*.

Buying and holding

If you decide you want to buy shares and hold on to them for a long time, you may be better off investing in shares through a unit trust or an investment trust. You certainly will be if you have less than £5,000 to invest. The problem with these, especially unit trusts, is that there are almost as many unit trusts to choose from as there are actual shares to invest in.

More details are given in Part 2 under the headings:

Unit Trust Invested in Shares
Unit Trust Personal Equity Plan
Investment Trust Shares
Investment Trust Personal Equity Plan

The share market has passed its *bear* or downward phase. At the time of writing it was in a *bull* or upward stage. If this continues, you may still be able to make money from an investment in a unit or investment trust. By delaying your investment you may have to buy the trust at a higher price.

Regular savings in shares

If you don't want to keep following the share market waiting for the right time to invest, your best bet is to invest on a regular basis month by month. Over the years you will accumulate money in shares through unit or investment trusts but you should wait until share prices are high before you sell. You can invest regularly through the following which have full details given in Part 2:

Investment Trust Personal Equity Plan
Investment Trust Savings Plan

Unit Trust Personal Equity Plan
Unit Trust Savings Plan

You can also link a regular investment to shares through *Life Insurance Unit-Linked Savings Plan* but such plans generally have higher charges and are less flexible than the other alternatives unless you wish to use them for inheritance tax planning with the proceeds on death in trust for someone else.

Finding a good stockbroker

If you want to follow the market and buy and sell shares then you need a good stockbroker who you can deal with direct and who can give you trading buy and sell prices for your shares by phone. When you deal through a bank or building society, they cannot usually give you a trading price at once.

The best way to find a good stockbroker is by recommendation. If you don't know anyone who is pleased with their's the Stock Exchange will send you a list of local brokers willing to take on new private clients – or you can try phoning some local ones from a list published in the back of one of the specialist books telling you about strategy of share buying.

Find out how much they will charge – and if you are likely to buy or sell in amounts of less than £1,500 at a time, what their minimum commission is. The commission rate is likely to be 1% to 1.9% for transactions of £5,000 or less. There is also a 'contract levy' of 10p on each transaction over £5,000.

Some brokers have two levels of service: the ordinary service where they give advice and the *execution only* service where they just do what you tell them – you make up your own mind about which shares to buy and sell, and when. See 'Where from' under *Shares Ordinary Quoted* for names of stockbrokers which offer low cost dealing services.

Fixing the price

When you buy or sell shares, the deal is often not actually made on the phone when you are speaking to your stockbroker. It is therefore very important that you place a *limit* on the transaction. A limit is the minimum price you will sell at, or the maximum price you will buy at.

When you consider the selling price is too low, or the buying price too high, you can ask for the limit to be held for a week or longer or to the end of the current stock exchange *account period*. The stockbroker must then sell shares at the limit price or better if the shares reach the limit within the period stipulated. Some stockbrokers are reluctant to accept limits beyond the same day.

When you make transactions by phone, especially with limits, you should make a note of the conversation and date it. Most stockbrokers now make tape recordings of phone transactions and they may be able to play back the conversation in the event of disagreement over what was intended.

Want to be an active investor?

There is a lot more you can learn about share strategy. A good start is *Shares A Beginners' Guide to Making Money* by Harold Baldwin (Wisebuy £2.95). Other books worth considering are *The Share Game* by Tony Levene (Pan), *Investors Chronicle Beginner's Guide to the Stockmarket* (Penguin) and *How to Make a Killing in Shares* by Michael Walters (Sidgwick & Jackson). You will also want to read the financial pages of a daily and/or Sunday newspaper.

Want to be a speculator?

Consider gambling with traded options. Details are summarised in Part 2 under the heading *Shares Traded Options*. If you are a pessimist you can still make money while share prices crash by using *put* options.

Shareholder perks

Some people buy shares for the fringe benefits. Surveys listing companies which offer perks are published from time to time by *Money Observer* and by stockbrokers Seymour Pierce Butterfield. Check with the company before you buy the shares that they still offer the perks. Ask for the company secretary.

9

Saving towards a pension

Job pensions are optional. You can invest in your own personal pension instead if you want.

Everyone who has earnings from a job or who is self-employed can contribute to a pension scheme with full tax relief on the contributions, subject to certain limits. Once contributions are invested the income and capital gains in the pension fund are tax exempt. And when you take the pension you can normally draw around a quarter of your pension fund as a tax free lump sum. The rest must be in the form of a pension for the rest of your life – and for the rest of your husband's or wife's life too if you want.

Because these tax advantages are good, anyone saving towards retirement should do so through one type of pension scheme or another. Only people not eligible for a pension scheme should consider other types of investments; these are summarised at the end of this Chapter.

The State pension

There are two parts to this. The first is the State flat rate or basic pension which depends on the contributions made by employees and the self-employed. The current pension (for 1993–94) is £2,917 a year for a single person plus an additional £1,693 for an adult dependent or non-working wife who hasn't earned her own pension. The pension rises each year in April in line with increases in the retail prices index to the previous September.

The second part, the State earnings related or additional pension (SERPS) is available to employees only. The Government has made a concerted effort to encourage people to opt out of SERPS through a personal or job pension.

Since 6 April 1993 you should opt out if you are a man under age 41 now or woman under age 36. It could be worth opting out at slightly older ages but the decision is not so clear cut and depends on how well the investments in personal pensions do.

If you are currently in a job pension there are five possibilities:

● You wish to stay in SERPS because of your age (see above).

● Your job pension is already *contracted-out* of SERPS.

● You can contract-out of SERPS by taking out a special personal pension, called a *minimum contribution personal pension*. This minimum contribution personal pension has some restrictions (which do not apply to a *Pension Personal Pension* which is described in Part 2). The minimum contribution personal pension has no lump sum on retirement, retirement age is a minimum of age 60 women, 65 men (compared with 50 for a personal pension) and you have to have a pension which increases each year and pays a pension to your widow or widower.

● You can contract-out of SERPS through *Pension Free Standing Additional Voluntary Contributions* (see below) but this is not recommended as in this particular instance there is no tax relief on all of the contributions.

● You can leave your job pension and take a personal pension instead. This is only worth considering if you are under age 35 and unlikely to remain with your employer until retirement. If you do leave your job pension, you should also contract-out of SERPS. Part of the pension will be a *minimum contribution personal pension* with the restrictions described above and the rest will be an ordinary *Pension Personal Pension* as described in Part 2.

If you are an employee but you are not in a job pension, you can contract-out of SERPS by taking out a personal pension. This will also be part *minimum contributions personal pension* and part *Pension Personal Pension* as described above.

A job pension

Job, company or occupational pensions are optional. That doesn't mean you should always leave. The decision to leave depends on your age, whether you will stay with the company until retirement, and how good the job pension scheme is. You can get free advice on what to do and what your rights are from the Occupational Pensions Advisory Service (OPAS) which is an educational charity.

If you decide to stay with your job pension scheme, you can boost the pension you get on retirement by investing in additional voluntary contributions. There are now two types and these are considered in Part 2 under the headings:

Pension Additional Voluntary Contributions
Pension Free Standing Additional Voluntary Contributions

If you think you are entitled to a pension from a company you used to work for, but the company has moved or gone out of business, you will be able to use the 'Registry' of occupational pensions which is run by the Occupational Pensions Board, a government department. In 1992 the Registry helped over 7,000 people trace their pension scheme.

A personal pension

If your job does not have a pension scheme, if you are self-employed or if you have two jobs and the second does not have a pension scheme, you are allowed to obtain tax relief at your highest rate on contributions to a personal pension issued by a life insurance company, building society, bank or unit trust group.

When the pensions company invests your money in one of these schemes, it is exempt from income tax and capital gains tax on any income or gains it makes. So as well as obtaining tax relief, your money accumulates tax-free. If you are an employee, you get basic tax relief when you pay the contribution; if you are self-employed you have to reclaim all the relief.

However, once you have committed yourself to a personal pension, you cannot get anything back until you are 50. If you are a professional sportsman, the pension can start to be paid at 35 or 40; other special cases will be considered. You can also start to draw your pension under 50 if you become permanently disabled. You cannot continue to pay contributions or start to receive benefits after the age of 75.

The proceeds of the policy come in the form of a pension for life (which counts as earned income) and 25% of the accumulated pension fund can be paid as a lump sum which is tax free.

If you are already age 50 you can get an instant pension provided you still have eligible earnings. Instead of lasting the usual 5 to 20 years, the policy can be for a very short period, say, a month.

Contributions are restricted to 17½% of your *net relevant earnings* (ie earnings which are not counted for an occupational pension scheme) in the tax year if you are 35 or less. The limits are higher the older you are rising from 20% at 36 to 40% at 61 (see table overleaf). Contributions paid in one tax year can be claimed (fully or partly) against your taxable income in the previous tax year instead of the current one provided there was sufficient relief in the previous year (or carried forward to the previous year from earlier years) to cover the contributions carried back. **You can make use of unused relief from previous years for up to 6 years** (7 years if you elect to have the contributions count against your income in the previous tax year).

Although you may not be able to afford the maximum contribution, you can use up past years' relief if you come into a windfall and want to invest it to provide you with a pension from age 50. The schemes accept single contributions as well as regular contributions – both count equally for tax relief. Personal pensions are covered in Part 2 under the heading *Pension Personal Pension*.

Retirement annuity

Until 1 July 1988 a pension similar to personal pension was available but only through life insurance companies called a *retirement annuity*. You cannot take out a new retirement annuity contract after that date. But **if you already have one you can make additional single or regular contributions provided they are under an existing policy number which you already have. Retirement annuities can give a larger lump sum**, up to 37½% of the accumulated pension fund especially if you retire at the maximum age of 75. However if the starting pension is low, perhaps because the pension rises year by year, or you are a woman, or you want to retire at 60 or all three, the maximum lump sum could be lower for a retirement annuity than for a personal pension. The lower lump sum need not worry you as you are allowed to transfer a retirement annuity into a personal pension at any time before you draw the pension. See *Pension Retirement Annuity* in Part 2.

Contribution limits

Contribution limits for personal pensions and retirement annuities are partially interchangeable. For instance if your net relevant earnings are £10,000 and your allowance is 17.5%, then you can get tax relief on £1,750 worth of retirement annuity or personal pension contributions. However at age 37, for example, you are entitled to an allowance of 20% for a personal pension but only 17.5% for a retirement annuity. What you can do is contribute £1,750 to the retirement annuity and a further £250 to a personal pension. Instead of course, you can contribute the full £2,000 to a personal pension or any mixture provided the lower limit for a retirement annuity is not exceeded.

There is also a maximum overall level of net relevant earnings above which there is no further personal pension allowance. This usually rises each year in line with the Retail Prices Index:
- 1989–90   £60,000
- 1990–91   £64,800
- 1991–92   £71,400
- 1992–93 and 1993–94   £75,000

This maximum does not apply to retirement annuities. This means that people with earnings over the limit who are 35 and under can make higher contributions to a retirement annuity (provided they already have one they can add to) than to a personal pension. However for those over age 35 the earnings level at which they can pay higher contributions to a retirement annuity rather than a personal pension is somewhat higher and depends on age. The company which you have your retirement annuity with or your independent financial adviser should be able to tell you the current level.

If you pay more in contributions than your allowances, you don't get tax relief on the contributions. In the case of a retirement annuity you will be allowed to leave the money in the plan to accumulate tax free until you draw the pension. However that part of the pension you draw will then count as investment income (under current tax rules this would not result in more tax but it might do by the time you retire). If you pay more contributions than your allowances to a personal pension, the pensions company will be told to refund you the amount overpaid.

Contributions limits as % of salary

For 1986–87		For 1987–88 and 1988–89	
Year of birth	**%**	**Age at start of tax year**	**%**
1934 or later	17½	50 or under	17½
1916–1933[1]	20	51 to 55	20
		56 to 60	22½
		61 to 74[1]	27½

For 1989–90 to 1993–94			
Personal pensions		**Retirement annuities**	
Age at start of tax year	**%**	**Age at start of tax year**	**%**
35 or under	17½	50 or under	17½
36 to 45	20	51 to 55	20
46 to 50	25	56 to 60	22½
51 to 55	30	61 to 74[1]	27½
56 to 60	35		
61 to 74[1]	40		

[1] You cannot pay contributions once you reach age 75.

Not eligible for a pension

The following investments (in alphabetical order) are worth considering if you are not eligible for a pension scheme because you are not working:

For regular savings:
Bank Tessa Account (5 years)
Building Society Tessa Account (5 years)
Investment Trust Personal Equity Plan
Investment Trust Savings Plan
Life Insurance With-Profits Endowment Policy
Unit Trust Personal Equity Plan
Unit Trust Savings Plan

For lump sums not needed for 10 years or more consider:
Investment Trust Personal Equity Plan
Investment Trust Shares
Life Insurance Mixed Bond
Life Insurance Property Bond
Offshore Managed Currency Fund
Offshore Single Foreign Currency Fund
Offshore Stock and Bond Fund
Property Business Expansion Shares
Property Commercial Direct Investment
Property Enterprise Zone Trust
Property Residential Direct Investment
Shares Ordinary Quoted
Shares Self Select Personal Equity Plan
Stock Government Index-Linked
Stock Private Index-Linked
Unit Trust Index Tracker
Unit Trust Invested in UK Shares
Unit Trust Invested in Overseas Shares
Unit Trust Personal Equity Plan
Unit Trust Stock and Bond Fund

Of the above only *Property Business Expansion Shares* and *Property Enterprise Zone Trust* have tax relief on the contributions. However *Bank Tessa Account*, *Building Society Tessa Account*, *Investment Trust Personal Equity Plan*, *Shares Self Select Personal Equity Plan* and *Unit Trust Personal Equity Plan* are completely exempt from tax on income or gains provided you don't cash too early.

When you need to draw a pension

Personal pensions or retirement annuities are an ideal way of accumulating money towards a pension at a chosen retirement date between age 50 and 75. They are not such a good way of receiving a pension because most of the proceeds must be taken as a pension annuity from a life insurance company.

When you want to draw your pension, you should shop around, using the *open market option*, to reinvest your pension money with the company offering the highest pension annuity rates available at that time. You will probably want to invest the 25% of the accumulated pension fund which you can take as a lump sum separately elsewhere to obtain a better return. Even a *Life Insurance Annuity* gives a better return than a pension annuity as part of the former is regarded as a return of capital and is tax exempt.

Some pensions are issued in *segments*. That means that you don't have to start drawing all your pensions at the same time. If you have several retirement annuities or personal pensions with different companies you can start to receive pensions from them over a period of time. A free booklet *A Guide to Flexible Pensions at Retirement* on how this works is available from financial advisers Towry Law Pensions Services Ltd.

If the option to spread the commencement of your pension is not open to you, then you might want to consider an increasing pension annuity, either by a fixed amount, linked to the Retail Prices Index or on a 'with-profits' basis. The different income you would get from these at different ages are shown in the table on the next page. The actual return of all these types of pension varies depending on the level of interest rates at the time you retire.

Remember to think about inflation and its effect on your pension after you start to draw it, especially if you retire young.

How much yearly pension a £100,000 accumulated fund will buy

Age when you start pension £	Fixed £	Increasing at 4% a year[1] £	Index-linked £	With-profits[2] £
Man				
50	9,335	6,280	5,858	9,917
55	9,978	6,971	6,554	10,547
60	10,785	7,835	7,423	11,339
65	11,825	8,941	8,536	12,362
70	13,157	10,356	9,960	13,674
75	14,790	12,100	11,718	15,283
Woman				
50	8,745	5,641	5,215	9,342
55	9,160	6,125	5,707	9,742
60	9,744	6,775	6,365	10,309
65	10,559	7,656	7,253	11,108
70	11,685	8,852	8,456	12,216
75	13,198	10,451	10,065	13,707
Joint man and woman of same age				
50	8,321	5,242	4,823	8,918
55	8,567	5,598	5,193	9,143
60	8,923	6,070	5,679	9,474
65	9,435	6,703	6,326	9,959
70	10,147	7,546	7,185	10,641
75	11,109	8,654	8,311	11,571

Assumes pension is paid monthly in advance and guaranteed for five years. [1] Figures for pension in first year. [2] If bonus (both declared and final) are at 5.5%, the annuity will remain level. If bonuses are higher than that the payments increase, and if lower the payments will decrease. Source: Equitable Life.

10

Wives' income and investments

A wife's income

Since 6 April 1990 a wife's income has been treated separately from her husband's. A wife has her own personal tax allowance which can be set against investment income as well as earnings. She also gets her own tax return if necessary (not everyone is sent a tax return every year).

Working wives There is no longer any distinction between earnings and investment income as far as tax is concerned. Both types belong to a wife and investment income is no longer added to a husband's income, for instance, for the purpose of working out higher rate tax.

Non-earning or part time earners Where a wife has no earnings, or her earnings are below her personal tax allowance for the year, she will be a non-taxpayer and should be able to avoid tax on income from investments worth up to about £43,000 each year – more if the investments are in shares with a low dividend yield.

Minimising tax on investment income

Both husband and wife each have their own reduced and basic rate tax band as well as their own personal tax allowance. Where a husband pays tax at a higher rate than his wife, it is worthwhile arranging for the wife to receive all or most of any investment income so that it is taxed at a lower rate, if at all.

If a wife doesn't have money of her own, a husband can give her money (or assets such as shares or commercial property with rental income) to enable her to have income which can be tax free up to the amount of her own personal tax allowance.

There is no capital gains tax, inheritance tax or stamp duty to pay on a transfer of money or assets to a wife. Money can simply be taken from bank, building society or other accounts in the husband's or joint names and put it into an account or accounts in the wife's sole name. Income from accounts in a single name will be treated as the income of the person whose name it is in.

If this does not appeal to you, assets (eg shares, unit trusts) can be held jointly and husband and wife can make a declaration that the asset is owned in unequal shares or indeed entirely by one of you (in which case declare that the other is acting as a 'nominee'). This should be done on Form 17 (from the Inland Revenue).

Signing a declaration which says a husband or wife owns, say 95%, of a jointly held asset, legally makes him or her the owner of it. In the event of a separation or divorce, that spouse would be entitled to the money.

The Inland Revenue will not accept a declaration that a bank or building society account is owned in unequal shares.

However it is probably possible for you to own the investments in unequal shares, but for the Inland Revenue to tax you as if they were owned in equal shares. In order to do this husband and wife should type or write the following on a sheet of paper substituting their own names and details of the account: "We Sara Jane Smith and Arthur Peter Smith of 24 Rose Crescent, London SW16 declare that our joint account at ABC Building Society No 89076655 (or all our bank and building society joint accounts) are beneficially owned as tenants in common in the following proportions: Sara Jane Smith 25%, Arthur Peter Smith 75%." The document should be signed and dated and kept by the spouse with the larger ownership; it would only be of any practical significance in the event of subsequent separation, divorce or death.

Payment without deduction of tax

Where one spouse's total income in the tax year is less than his or her tax allowances (single, married, additional personal, age) interest from UK banks and building societies can be paid without deduction of tax. Details are in *IR110 A guide for people with savings* which also has an application form at the back; you need one leaflet and form for each different account. Many banks and building societies allow you to have half the interest on a joint account paid without deduction of tax where only one of the holders is eligible.

However if a wife's income is, say, £4,000 a year (which is above her personal tax allowance) she is not eligible for interest to be paid without deduction of tax, even though most of her income may be not liable for tax. In that case she should invest in an investment where no tax is deducted as follows:

Bank Cheque Account With Interest (at a branch situated in the Isle of Man)
Offshore Bank Instant Access Account
Offshore Bank Notice Account

For amounts mainly under £10,000:
Offshore Sterling Currency Fund
National Savings Investment Account
National Savings Income Bond
Co-operative Society Term Account

Dividends

Where a wife has shares in UK companies which pay dividends, these come with a tax credit. Tax credits paid to a wife on or after 6 April 1990 can be reclaimed if the wife is otherwise not a taxpayer. This even applies to joint holdings – in which case the wife can only claim half the tax credit. Keep the tax vouchers – the counterfoils which come with the cheque – the Inland Revenue will want them as evidence that you have received the tax credit.

Interest with basic rate tax deducted

Most banks, building societies and local authorities deduct *basic rate* tax before you get your interest. This tax can be reclaimed if you are not a taxpayer on part or all of your income. The same applies to *Stock British Government* and *Stock Debenture and Loan*. Keep these vouchers too.

Getting a tax rebate

If tax is deducted from income of any type and a wife has been unable to make use of her personal tax allowance, she can claim a rebate. Details on how to go about this are contained in a free leaflet *IR112 How to claim a repayment of income tax* from any Inland Revenue tax office. You can make a claim for income or interest received since 6 April 1990. But in the period 6 April 1990 to 5 April 1991 you can't get a refund of any tax deducted on a UK bank, building society or local authority fixed term loan.

Husbands with a low income

A husband has a *married couple's* tax allowance as well as his own personal allowance. If his income is not high enough to make full (or any) use of it, he can transfer it to his wife or they can split it between them. This might occur when a husband is disabled and receives tax exempt benefits or he is unemployed and has a very low income.

Mortgage interest

Where a married couple has a mortgage in joint names, it is assumed that the interest is paid in equal shares. If it is in a single name, interest is assumed to be paid by the person whose name it is in. Either way, if you don't want these rules to apply, you can complete and send Form 15 to the Inland Revenue and make an *allocation of interest election*. There are two situations when you might want to do this:

● Where the mortgage is outside the MIRAS scheme and one partner is a non-taxpayer – or whose income after deducting the personal allowance is less than the mortgage interest.

● One of you is over 65 and might be eligible for Age Allowance or more Age Allowance.

Capital gains tax

A wife is completely separately taxed for capital gains tax. Transfers between husband and wife and vice-versa, however, can be made without any penalty or tax in order to utilise the capital gains tax exemption limits. The starting point for working out the gain on an eventual disposal is the date and value of the original acquisition (not the transfer to a spouse).

Husband and wife can only own one main residence between them. If they have more than one they can choose which is to be the main one and it is therefore exempt from capital gains tax. This contrasts with an unmarried couple with two homes who can get two main residence exemptions if they own one home each and each choose the one they own as their main residence.

Wives over age 65

If you are age 65 or over, or your husband is or you both are, turn to Chapter 13. Separate taxation of husband and wife may cut your tax bill by even more.

11

Children's investments

A child's income and tax allowance

Children are children until they reach age 18 as far as the law is concerned. Up to that age you can hold money in your own name (or in your husband's or wife's name or jointly) which legally belongs to your child. At age 18 the child can demand that the money is put in his or her own name unless the money is given under a formal trust which provides for the trustees (which can be you and your husband and wife) to hold on to it for longer.

The way in which a child's investment income is taxed does not depend on whose name the money is in. It can be in the child's own name, a parent's name or a grandparent's name for example. It depends on who gave the money in the first place, whether the income or interest from it is accumulated or spent, and the terms of any trust which the money is subject to.

A child has a personal tax allowance from the day he or she is born. This is the same as anyone else's and is £3,445 for the current 1993–94 tax year. In addition each child also has his or her own reduced rate band (£2,500 in 1993–94, £2,000 in 1992–93 and £3,000 in 1994–95), and his own basic rate tax band (£21,200 in the current 1993–94 tax year). So a child with investment income of up to £3,445 a year can pay £1,378 less tax than an adult who pays higher rate tax with this £3,445 added to his or her income.

Where a child's income is below his or her personal tax allowance, it is best to find an investment where income tax is not deducted, so as to avoid the trouble and delay of obtaining an income tax rebate. For UK bank and building society accounts this can be done by getting one Inland Revenue leaflet *IR110 A guide for people with savings* for each account you want to have this done on. There is a form at the back of the leaflet for you or the child (over age 16) to complete. If a child is not eligible to have this form completed, say, because his or her income is too high or more than £100 comes from a parent (see below) than the child should choose an investment where tax is not deducted at all.

Should a child invest in an account where tax is deducted but not be liable for it, this tax can be reclaimed using a special *Tax Repayment Claim (Form R232)*. This form is sent to a parent's tax office with the relevant *tax deduction certificates* or *tax vouchers* once the child's income for the year is known. Up to 5 April 1991 no repayment is due on bank and building society interest, but rebates can be obtained on tax deducted on unit trust distributions, share dividends, stock interest and trust income belonging to children.

Investments for a child in his or her own name

For money held in a child's own name, the most convenient investments are in banks and building societies, where interest can be paid without deduction of tax using form IR110 described above. In particular children should consider:

Bank Cash Card Account (over age 12 or 13)
Bank Children's Account (better gifts than building societies usually)
Building Society Cash Card Account (over age 14)
Building Society Children's Account
Building Society Instant Access Account
National Savings Investment Account (1 month notice)
National Savings Ordinary Account

Income from money given by parents

The taxman prevents parents from making direct use of a child's tax allowance through giving money to their own children, by counting as a parent's income, any income over £100 a year from money or investments given to your own child (or to a trust for your own child). So if you give your child £1,000 and he or she gets £70 interest on it, that £70 counts as the child's income, and is effectively tax free. However if you give the child £2,000 and the interest is £140, this amount is added to your income and taxed at your rate (40% if you are a higher rate taxpayer). This counting of a child's income as his or her parent's carries on until the child reaches age 18 or gets married over age 16 if earlier.

There is one exception to this rule. Where you give money to a child 'absolutely' and it accumulates in an account (preferably one which does not deduct income tax) until the child is 18 or marries, all the interest counts as the child's. So the child can benefit from a tax free income which accumulates provided it is less than his or her personal tax allowance each year and the child receives the income after age 18 (or marries).

If any money is withdrawn from the account before the child is 18 or marries, that amount is added to the income of the parent who gave the money and is taxable in the tax year in which the withdrawal is made.

This type of arrangement is not very satisfactory except for smallish amounts as the child is entitled to demand the money at age 18. If you want to give more than, say, £5,000 to your child, you should consider setting up a formal trust so you can keep control of the money until age 25 or even longer – see *Trusts* at the end of this Chapter.

Investments suitable for gifts from parents where it is intended that the income is accumulated to age 18 are:

Offshore Bank Notice Account
National Savings Capital Bond (provided child at least 13)
National Savings Investment Account

Investments suitable for gifts from parents who do not want to bother with a formal trust (or in addition or separate from one) but may want to spend some income on the child (eg school fees, holidays) are:

National Savings Capital Bond
National Savings Fixed Issue Certificates
National Savings Index Linked Certificates
National Savings Yearly Plan

The maximum limit for each of these investments can be doubled as investment can be made once up to the maximum in each child's own name, and once in one or both of the parent's name as trustees for each child. These holdings are in addition to any the parents may have of their own (or in trust for each other). As these investments are tax exempt they are especially suitable for higher rate taxpayers – though some issues do not represent good value to basic taxpayers. Investments in the child's own name require his or her signature for withdrawal from age seven.

Income from other money

Where money comes from any source other than a parent, and including money left to a child by a parent who has died, a child is taxed completely separately from his or her parents. So gifts from relatives and grandparents and money from Saturday jobs and newsrounds etc can all be invested and interest received tax free up to the full personal tax allowance.

For money from this source, which can be held in a parent's name as *nominee* or *bare trustee*, consider accounts where tax is not deducted as the form *IR110* does not provide for this situation:

Offshore Bank Notice Account
Offshore Bank Instant Access Account

National Savings Investment Account
Offshore Sterling Currency Fund
Co-operative Society Term Account
Stock Government Fixed Interest (invested through the National Savings stock register).

If you want to invest longer term, consider the following:
Investment Trust Savings Plan
Unit Trust Savings Plan
Investment Trust Shares
Unit Trust Invested In Shares

Also consider investments listed below under the heading *School fees*.

School fees

Private education is extremely expensive and most people are unlikely to be able to pay for it out of their income. Specialists in this field recommend people to start saving schemes when a child is born in order to spread the burden. But because the rise in school fee charges can exceed the return from most saving schemes, people have been disappointed.

One way of lightening the burden of fees is to ask grandparents to contribute. Another way if you have a gifted child and a low income (under around £22,000 a year; fees paid in full at £9,000 a year) is to apply for a grant under the Assisted Places Scheme (details from Independent Schools Information Service, address in Appendix 1).

The investments listed below are suitable for basic and higher rate taxpayers. Non-taxpayers and reduced rate taxpayers are unlikely to be able to afford private education.

Save regularly for school fees with:	Fees needed
Building Society 90 Day Notice Account	*Up to 4 years*
†*Building Society Tessa Account*	*5 years*
†*Bank Tessa Account*	*5 years*
†*Building Society SAYE*	*5 or 7 years*
†*National Savings Yearly Plan*	*5 years onwards*
†*Investment Trust Personal Equity Plan*	*5–17 years*
Investment Trust Savings Plan	*5–17 years*
Unit Trust Savings Plan	*5–17 years*
†*Unit Trust Personal Equity Plan*	*5–17 years*
†*Life Insurance With Profits Endowment*	*10–17 years*
†*Life Insurance Unit Linked Savings Plan*	*10–17 years*

Lump sums for school fees:

Building Society Postal Account	*Up to 4 years*
Building Society 90 Day Notice Account	*Up to 4 years*
Life Insurance Growth Bond	*2–5 years*
†*Building Society Tessa Account*	*5 years*
†*Bank Tessa Account*	*5 years*
Stock Government Fixed Interest	*Up to 6 years*
†*Stock Government Index-Linked*	*8, 9, 13, 15 years*
†*Life Insurance School Fees Educational Trust*	*4–8 years*
Life Insurance Property Bond	*8–17 years*
Life Insurance Mixed Bond	*8–17 years*
†*Investment Trust Personal Equity Plan*	*8–17 years*
†*Shares Self Select Personal Equity Plan*	*8–17 years*
†*Offshore Multicurrency Fund*	*8–17 years*
Unit Trusts	*8–17 years*

† Especially higher rate taxpayers.

Lump sums of more than a year's fees which a parent wishes to earmark for payment of school fees can usually be paid in advance to the school. You should check, however, that there is no penalty if the child later wants to change schools. The lump sum earns interest and when the fees come due, both the lump sum and interest are available to pay them. The tax position is similar to that of a *Life Insurance School Fees Educational Trust* which is explained in Part 2.

Large lump sums intended as payment for school fees and donated by a wealthy grandparent would be best invested through an Accumulation and Maintenance Trust – consult a solicitor or qualified accountant for advice on how to set one up (see also below). Income from money inherited by a child, or received as a gift from anyone other than its parents, is not taxable to the extent of the personal tax allowance; such money should not be invested as above – choose instead investments listed under the heading *Income from other money* on page 67.

Different types of trust

There are three different types of trust – an *Accumulation and Maintenance Trust*, a *Discretionary Trust* and an *Absolute Trust*. Somewhat confusingly an Accumulation and Maintenance Trust is sometimes described as Discretionary, because the trustees usually have discretion to decide whether the income from the trust is accumulated or spent for the benefit of the beneficiaries (or actually paid to them if they are over age 18). Formally constituted absolute trusts are not recommended.

Accumulation and maintenance trust

With an accumulation and maintenance trust a *settlor*, eg a grandparent, gives a sum of money, say £5,000, to a trust for at least one named beneficiary. The trust deed should be from a draft by a solicitor or chartered accountant with experience in drafting such deeds and might cost you £50 to £500. Once the trust is set up, provided the trust says so, anyone else can add money to it (as well as the original settlor) but this should not be a parent – see *Trust income* opposite.

The trust usually gives the trustees discretion to pay the income of the trust for the education, maintenance or benefit of the beneficiary up to the age of 25 at which time the income must be paid to the beneficiary. These trusts usually specify that the capital of the trust can be distributed to the beneficiaries at any date after the youngest beneficiary is age 25. The trust can continue for the whole life of a beneficiary and there are provisions for the wife and children of a beneficiary to receive the income if the beneficiary dies while the trust is still in existence. The trust can end when the beneficiary's children reach age 21.

The *primary beneficiaries* of such a trust are the people named in the trust deed. However they need not yet be born. The deed might specify "my grandson Simon Jones and any other grandchildren". While Simon is the only grandson he is entitled to 100% of the income of the trust – but if later four brothers and sisters and cousins arrive, he will only be entitled to a fifth of the trust.

The trustees have no discretion about who gets income and capital – the share of each beneficiary must be according to the original trust deed. The only discretion is whether to pay out income to a beneficiary; if it is paid out to one beneficiary and not to another, then records have to be kept, showing each beneficiary's share, so that a beneficiary whose share has been accumulated does not get less.

Discretionary trust

With a discretionary trust you don't need to specify who the beneficiaries are. They can be in rather general terms like "any of the descendents of John and Jane Brown". The trustees can choose to whom they pay any income to, and when, and also whether to advance any capital, and when the trust is finally closed down, to whom the money is left. The *settlor* can leave instructions to the trustees on how they should use their *discretion* (for instance they could be told not to pay any income to anyone who spends it on fast cars).

Discretionary trusts have a few snags, however. Whereas there is no inheritance tax on a gift to an accumulation and maintenance trust, there can be where money is given to a *discretionary trust*. It comes into effect once cumulative gifts exceed the inheritance tax threshold, currently £150,000, and is at half the rate on death (ie currently 20% instead of 40%). Discretionary trusts also have to pay inheritance tax once every ten years on the capital value of their assets if they are worth more than the inheritance tax threshold at the time. Currently that tax is not very large but could be raised if there is a change of Government.

It is generally agreed that discretionary trusts should be set up below the inheritance tax threshold. There is nothing to stop a husband setting one up for £150,000 and his wife setting up a separate trust with identical provisions for a further £150,000. Both would remain below their respective thresholds and no inheritance tax would be payable.

Trust income

The whole of the income from a Discretionary Trust or an Accumulation and Maintenance Trust is currently taxed at a rate of 35%. Income paid to a beneficiary is paid with this tax deducted but the beneficiary (even a child) can reclaim all (or part) of the tax if he or she is not liable to pay the full amount deducted.

Income paid to an unmarried child under 18 from a trust set up by a parent usually counts as the parent's income so no tax rebate is due, and it is not usually worth while a parent setting up a such a trust.

The *settlor*, the person who gave the money to set up the trust, must not benefit from it, otherwise there are no tax advantages.

The tax repayment claim when the income counts as the child's is made by the parent on the child's behalf, using Tax Claim Form (R232). The trustees must fill in Form R185E giving details of the amount of trust income paid to the parents or spent, and tax deducted, and give it to the parent who sends it in with the claim.

If parents are trustees, trust income must be spent on education (eg school fees), maintenance (eg clothes) or benefit (eg holidays) to count as having been distributed by the trust and so enable the parent to claim the tax rebate. If the income of the trust is not spent, the 35% tax cannot be reclaimed. But if in a future year, the income is spent (in addition to income in that year) the tax can be reclaimed then provided the child (children) has enough tax allowances in that year.

The Inland Revenue sometimes considers capital as well as income payments from Discretionary, and from Accumulation and Maintenance Trusts, as the *income* of the beneficiary. The payments are deemed to be *after* deduction of 35% tax. This does not apply when the trust is being wound up nor to payments of school fees out of capital which normally do not count as income payments.

12

Change in plan

Redundancy

Redundancy payments do not usually amount to a lot – £2,000 is the average. But if you have worked with the same company for many years, you might get much more. If you have been in a company's pension scheme and are over age 50, you may get a pension plus a lump sum from the pension scheme at the same time as your redundancy money.

Lump sum redundancy payments or pay in lieu of notice are normally tax-free if they currently amount to less than £30,000 and are paid after you have ended your employment; the balance is taxed in full. Lump sums paid as a 'commutation' of pension rights are also tax-free.

However when a company goes into liquidation, liquidators deduct what they call 'tax' from pay in lieu of notice money. This deduction is not tax and is not paid to the Inland Revenue but the House of Lords has ruled that your statutory pay in lieu of notice amounts to take home pay, and as personal tax allowances are usually used up by unemployment benefit, liquidators are correct to make a deduction.

Unemployment benefit is taxable. So while you receive unemployment benefit, part or all of your tax allowances are set against your benefit.

If you remain unemployed for more than a year, after which unemployment benefit ceases, you are likely to be a non-taxpayer and will probably need to spend some of your capital in order to maintain your standard of living.

If you have retired early (ie before 65 for men, before 60 for women) and receive a pension from a former job, your personal tax allowances will be set against part or all of your job pension. Only if your job pension is less than your personal tax allowances and outgoings will you be a non-taxpayer as far as part or all of your investments are concerned. See also advice in Chapter 13.

Unless you regard your unemployment as early retirement, do not tie up your money: you may need it.

Taxpayers and non-taxpayers should invest in:
  Building Society Cheque Account With Interest
  Building Society Instant Access Account
  Building Society Postal Account
  Building Society 30 Day Notice Account

Non-taxpayers should consider:
  Offshore Bank Notice Account
  National Savings Investment Account

Widows under retirement age

Widow's pensions and widowed mother's allowance are taxable. But if they are less than her personal tax allowance and if she has little other income, she may not be a taxpayer. The £1,000 payment made to widows under 60 without children is tax free. If she has children she may get *child addition* paid with her widow's benefit – and this child addition is also tax-free. And as a single parent looking after children she is entitled to the *additional personal tax allowance for children*. Again if she has little additional income she may not be a taxpayer.

On the other hand, if a widow earns, she continues to receive her widow's benefit and will almost certainly be a taxpayer even if the job is only part time. Her personal tax allowances are first set against her widow's benefit and then against her earnings.

The proceeds of life insurance policies on death do not count as income – even the family income benefit policies which pay out monthly, quarterly or half-yearly instalments. But a pension paid to a widow by her former husband's firm does count as income as does a retirement annuity or personal pension which continues.

In the year of a husband's death there may be less tax to pay. The investment income received in the part of the tax year up to the date of death counts as the husband's income (together with his earnings or pension) against which the married man's tax allowances can be set. Investment income received during the remainder of the tax year (ie until the following 5 April) counts as the widow's; she can set her personal tax allowance plus her widow's bereavement tax allowance against this. The widow's bereavement allowance is given in the tax year of the husband's death *and* the following year only. There is a free Inland Revenue leaflet *IR91 A Guide for Widows and Widowers*.

Separated or divorced

Maintenance payments under a court order or an enforceable separation deed made before 15 March 1988 count as income in the hands of the recipient and may be taxable. Such payments paid to a child count as the child's income and are not liable for tax up to the value of the child's personal allowance assuming the child has no other income.

Voluntary payments and payments which started on or after 15 March 1988 do not count as income so there is no tax for the recipient to reclaim or pay but the payer cannot set them against his income. For more information see two free Inland Revenue leaflets *IR92 One Parent Families* and *IR93 Separation, Divorce and Maintenance Payments*.

Living abroad

If you are serving overseas with the armed forces or diplomatic service your pay is taxable in the UK and your tax position is usually the same as anyone else. If you are serving for a fixed term you may have a good idea how long you want to invest your money: you will want it back when you return to the UK.

If you are working overseas continuously for more than a full tax year, you will be non-resident for that tax year. In other cases you may have to wait three years before your non-resident status is agreed by the Inland Revenue. Particularly during those three years, and afterwards, you must be careful about the timing and length of visits to the UK. More information from an Inland Revenue leaflet IR20 *Residents and non-residents: liability to tax in the UK*. While not liable for UK tax – as a non-resident UK banks and building societies can pay you without deduction of tax – you may be liable for tax in the country in which you live or the country where you invest (which need not be the same). Taxmen in different countries swap information about interest paid on bank accounts.

13

Boosting your retirement income

Age allowance

In the tax year in which you have your 65th birthday you can be eligible for higher personal tax allowances called *age allowance*. These are at a higher rate from the tax year when you reach the age of 75.

The way the rules for age allowance work can mean that to get the best after tax return, and thus the highest retirement income, your choice of investments must be divided between those suitable for a non-taxpayer where tax is not deducted, a basic rate taxpayer and a higher rate taxpayer.

If you receive the State retirement pension and no other pension or a very small pension or another pension which is fully or partly exempt from tax (see list on page 26) it is likely that some of your income from investments is not liable to income tax. If you are in this position you may have to claim a rebate of tax deducted from income on your investments.

Age allowance is given instead of the normal personal tax allowance if your income is below a certain level. The *age allowance income limit* for 1993–94 and 1992–93 is £14,200 or less. If your income comes to above this limit, your age allowance is reduced gradually as your income rises until it comes down to the normal personal tax allowance.

There are two scales of age allowance: if you are 65 to 74 the allowance for 1993–94 is £4,200 plus an extra married age allowance of £2,465; if you are 75 or over (or one of you is) the allowance is £4,370 plus an extra married age allowance of £2,505. Only one partner of the married couple gets the married age allowance, the other gets the age allowance only or you can have half each.

Married couples

Separate taxation of a husband and wife's income applies to pensioners as well as earners. **Provided couples can split their income more or less**

equally between them, that can give rise to a considerable tax saving.

If both husband and wife are over age 65, they will each be entitled to age allowance on their own income. A husband and wife can *each* have an income of up to £14,200 and get full age allowance. So a couple both over age 65 can have a combined income of £28,400 this tax year and each get full age allowance.

If a couple has an income of £28,400 which comes mainly from investments and they can arrange matters so that they each have half the income, that is £14,200 each, and they can split the married age allowance between them (half each), their total tax bill will be £563 a year less than compared with the situation before they were 65.

Married couples with large pensions   Pensions count as the income of the person who receives them. So a wife has her personal tax allowance of up to £3,445 set against it if she is under 65 or the personal age allowance of £4,200 (age 65–74) or £4,370 (age 75 or over). The *married age allowance* can now be set against either spouse's pension – or you can have half each.

There is no scope for switching pensions from husband to wife or vice-versa once they have started to be paid. But people planning to retire should aim to try and equalise their pensions in retirement to enable them to pay the least tax under these rules.

Juggling investments

It is quite permissible to transfer money and assets from husband to wife and vice-versa in order to try and equalise your incomes as far as possible. Joint holdings will be taken by the Inland Revenue to be owned half each unless you tell them otherwise by signing a form. Your tactics should be the same as for a wife under retirement age – see Chapter 10.

Tax effective investments

Here is how to work out your most tax effective investment strategy which as mentioned above may mean choosing some investments suitable for non-taxpayers, some suitable for basic taxpayers and even some suitable for higher rate taxpayers.

Taxable pensions less than your total tax allowances?

If that is the case you should invest in the following investments (in alphabetical order) where *tax is not deducted* until the interest on your investments *plus* your taxable pensions reaches your tax allowances. This will save you the trouble of having to claim a tax rebate. However if you don't mind claiming a rebate, use the other investments mentioned later in the Chapter as well.

Bank Cheque Account with Interest (at offshore branch)
Co-operative Society Term Account
National Savings Investment Account
National Savings Income Bond
Offshore Bank Instant Access Account
Offshore Bank Notice Account
Offshore Investment Fund
Offshore Managed Currency Fund
Offshore Single Foreign Currency Fund
Offshore Sterling Currency Fund (Distribution version)
Offshore Stock and Bond Fund
Property Commercial Direct Investment
Property Enterprise Trust
Property Residential Direct Investment

Marginal age allowance

If your income is over £14,200 you lose £1 of age allowance for every £2 by which your income exceeds this figure until the age allowance is reduced to the level of the ordinary personal tax allowance. This *marginal age allowance income limit* for 65 to 74 year olds in 1993–94 comes to an end when a single person's income reaches £15,710; or when one of the married couple's income reaches £17,200 and the other's £15,710. The limits are a shade higher for the over 75's: £16,050 for a single person and £17,620 for one of a married couple.

These income limits refer to before tax or gross income. If part of your income is from dividends or unit trust distributions you must add the *tax credit* to determine whether they fall within the limits.

By losing your age allowance within these income bands, although you are only a basic rate taxpayer, you are in effect being taxed at a higher rate – in fact at a rate of 37½%. If your income falls within these bands you might consider investments suitable for higher rate taxpayers to reduce your taxable income to £14,200. These are:

Life Insurance Mixed Bond
Life Insurance Property Bond
(with the two above income must be 5% or less of original cost to leave age allowance unaffected).
National Savings Fixed Certificates (only issues paying reasonable interest)

National Savings Index-Linked Certificates
Stock Government Index-Linked
More on all these investments in Part 2 under the individual entry.

Alternatively if you think you will be a basic taxpayer after next 6 April but are a marginal age allowance taxpayer this tax year, transfer your building society investments to a society which pays interest once a year instead of monthly or half yearly. Some societies pay annually in April which makes tax planning easier.

Summary

To summarise: if you, or your husband or wife, are over 65 and your or your spouse's total income (from investments and taxable pensions) is below the actual age allowance levels applicable to each of you (ie £4,200 or £4,370 single, £6,665 or £6,875 married) you are a non-taxpayer. Only one married partner gets the married allowance as well, the other gets the single allowance.

If your income is above the age allowance levels but under the £14,200 age allowance income limit you are a basic rate taxpayer on the excess over the age allowance but still a non-taxpayer on any amount below the allowance which is not set against taxable pensions.

If your income is above £14,200 but below the marginal age allowance income limits (£15,710 or £16,050 single, £17,200 or £17,620 married) then extra income between these limits reduces your age allowance *and* is taxed at the basic rate of tax which together is equivalent to a tax rate of 37½%. So your investment strategy for income between these bands is the same as a higher rate taxpayer.

The best income

In retirement you usually want to get the highest income you possibly can from your investments. The income from your investments can be fixed or variable – and the money you invest can also be fixed or variable. The most convenient way to get an income is monthly but if you split up your investments it may be easier to have the income paid half-yearly when you have less than, say, £5,000 to invest.

Fixed income and fixed capital. With these investments you know the return you are going to get at the outset, usually for a fixed period of time called the term, or, with an annuity for the rest of your life.
Building Society Term Account

Co-operative Society Term Account†
Life Insurance Annuity (fixed)
Life Insurance Income Bond
National Savings FIRST Option Bond
National Savings Fixed Issue Certificates*
Local Authority Fixed Term Loan

Variable income and fixed capital. Here your capital does not vary but the income can go up and down. These include:
Bank deposits (most)
Bank Tessa Account
Building Society accounts (most)
Building Society Tessa Account
Life Insurance Annuity (increasing, with profits or index-linked)
National Savings Certificates (on variable extension rate)
National Savings Income Bond†
National Savings Investment Account†
Offshore Bank accounts†
Offshore Sterling Currency Fund†

Fixed income and variable capital. Investments where the income is fixed but where your capital can go up and down in value. Usually there is a maturity date when you get your money back. These include:
Stock Government Fixed Interest († through National Savings)
Stock Debenture and Loan
Building Society Permanent Interest Bearing Shares
Shares Preference

Variable income and variable capital. Where neither the income nor the capital is fixed. These include:
Life Insurance Mixed Bond
Life Insurance Property Bond
(both the above using income withdrawal, scheme).
National Savings Index-Linked Certificates*
Offshore Single Foreign Currency Fund†
Offshore Stock & Bond Fund†
Stock Government Index-Linked († through National Savings)
Stock Private Index-Linked
Stock Unit Trust Invested in Gilts
Unit Trust Stock & Bond Fund

* This investment does not pay out interest but accumulates it. You should spend capital from another account if necessary which you can replenish at the end of the term.   † Tax not deducted from the income.

Riskier investments with variable income and capital. This is really the same as the last category except that they generally have a lower income and less certainty of what you will get. These include:

Investment Trust Shares
Investment Trust Personal Equity Plan
Investment Trust Split Level Shares (income shares)
Life Insurance Equity Bond
Life Insurance International Bond
Offshore Managed Currency Fund
Property Business Expansion Shares (higher rate taxpayers)
Property Commercial Direct
Property Enterprise Zone Trust
Property Residential Direct
Property Ground Rents
Shares Ordinary Quoted
Shares Self Select Personal Equity Plan
Stock Convertible Loan
Unit Trust Invested in Overseas Shares
Unit Trust Invested in UK Shares
Unit Trust Personal Equity Plan

14

Summary of investments

Here is a summary of the different types of investments. There are nine different categories:

- Investments you can get out immediately or within a few days.
- Investments for which you have to wait a week to a month.
- Investments for which you have to wait from a month to a year.
- Investments with money back from 1–7 years.
- Longer term investments suitable for 8 years or more.
- Getting a monthly income.
- Investing in shares.
- Investing in property.
- Index-linked investments (linked to the Retail Prices Index).

Sometimes a long-term investment can make short-term profits – but it can also mean short-term losses. All are listed alphabetically.

Money back at once or in a few days
No penalty
Bank Cash Card Account
Bank Cheque Account With Interest
Bank Children's Account
Bank Higher Interest Deposit Account
Building Society Cash Card Account
Building Society Cheque Account With Interest
Building Society Children's Account
Building Society Instant Access Account
Building Society Postal Account
Building Society Regular Monthly Savings
Building Society Share and Deposit Accounts
Offshore Bank Foreign Currency Account
Offshore Bank Instant Access Account
Offshore Sterling Currency Fund
Unit Trust Cash Trust

Small penalty
Bank 7 Day Account
Building Society 30 Day Notice Account
Building Society 60 Day Notice Account
Building Society 90 Day Notice Account
National Savings Ordinary Account

Money back in a week to a month
No penalty
Bank 7 Day Account
Bank Notice Account
Building Society Monthly Income Account
Building Society 30 Day Notice Account
National Savings Investment Account
National Savings Premium Bond
Offshore Bank Notice Account

Money back in more than a month but less than a year
Bank Notice Account
Bank Term Account
Building Society 60 Day Notice Account
Building Society 90 Day Notice Account
Building Society Term Share
National Savings Income Bond
Offshore Bank Notice Account
Stock Government Fixed-Interest
Stock Government Index-Linked
Stock Private Index-Linked

Money back from 1 to 7 years
See table opposite.

Investments probably suitable for 8 years or longer
Friendly Society Building Society Linked
Gold Coins
Investment Trust Personal Equity Plan
Investment Trust Shares
Investment Trust Savings Plan
Investment Trust Split Level Trust
Life Insurance Equity Bond
Life Insurance International Bond
Life Insurance Mixed Bond
Life Insurance Property Bond

Money back from 1 to 7 years

	1 yr	2 yrs	3 yrs	4 yrs	5 yrs	6 yrs	7 yrs
Bank Tessa Account	□	□	□	□	■		
Building Society Term Share	□	□	□	□	□		
Building Society Tessa Account	□	□	□	□	■		
Building Society Permanent Interest Bearing Share	□	□	□	□	□	□	□
Building Society SAYE					□		□
Building Society Stock Market Bond			□		□		
Co-operative Society Term Account	■	■	■	□	□		
Investment Trust Personal Equity Plan					■	■	■
Investment Trust Zero Coupon	□	□	□	□	□	□	□
Life Insur. Growth/Income Bond	□	■	■	□	□	□	□
Local Authority Fixed Term Loan	□	■	■	□	□	□	□
National Savings Fixed Issue Certificate	□	□	□	□	■		
National Savings Index-Linked Certs.	□	□	□	□	■		
National Savings Capital Bond					■		
National Savings 1st Option Bond	□						
National Savings Income Bond	□						
National Savings Yearly Plan	□				■		
Offshore Stock & Bond Fund	□	□	□	□	■	■	■
Offshore Single Foreign Currency Fund	□	■	■	■	■	■	■
Property Business Expansion Shares					□	□	
Property Ground Rents							■
Shares Business Expansion Fund					□	□	
Shares SAYE Share Option					□		□
Stock Government Fixed Interest	□	□	□	□	□	□	□
Stock Debenture or Loan	□	□	□	□	□	□	□
Stock Unit Trust Invested in Gilts	□	□	□	□	□	□	□
Unit Trust Personal Equity Plan					■	■	■
Unit Trust Stock & Bond Fund	□	□	□	□	□	□	□

■ Recommended investment period □ Under terms of investment

Life Insurance With-Profits Bond
Life Insurance With-Profits Endowment Policy
Life Insurance With-Profits Flexible Policy
Offshore Investment Fund
Offshore Managed Currency Fund
Offshore Single Foreign Currency Fund
Offshore Stock & Bond Fund
Pension Additional Voluntary Contributions
Pension Buy Out Bond
Pension Director's Pension
Pension Free Standing Additional Voluntary Contributions
Pension Personal Pension
Pension Retirement Annuity
Property Business Expansion Shares
Property Commercial Direct Investment
Property Enterprise Zone Trust
Property Residential Direct Investment
Shares Business Expansion Fund
Shares Ordinary Quoted
Shares Self Select Personal Equity Plan
Stock Convertible Loan
Stock Government Index-Linked
Stock Private Index-Linked
Unit Trust Index Tracker
Unit Trust Invested in Overseas Shares
Unit Trust Invested in UK Shares
Unit Trust Personal Equity Plan
Unit Trust Savings Plan
Unit Trust Stock & Bond Fund

Getting a monthly income
Not all the companies under each heading pay income monthly.
Bank Higher Interest Deposit Account
Building Society Monthly Income Account
Life Insurance Annuity
Life Insurance Equity Bond
Life Insurance International Bond
Life Insurance Fixed Interest, Gilt, Money or Convertible Bond
Life Insurance Mixed Bond
Life Insurance Property Bond
Life Insurance With-Profits Bond
National Savings Income Bond
Offshore Bank Notice Account

Unit Trust Cash Trust
Unit Trust Invested in Shares

Investing in shares
Building Society Stock Market Guaranteed Bond
Investment Trust Personal Equity Plan
Investment Trust Shares
Investment Trust Savings Plan
Life Insurance Equity Bond
Life Insurance Guaranteed Stock Market Bond
Life Insurance International Bond
Life Insurance Unit-Linked Savings Plan
Offshore Investment Fund
Pension Buy Out Bond
Pension Director's Pension
Pension Free Standing Additional Voluntary Contributions
Pension Personal Pension
Pension Retirement Annuity
Shares Business Expansion Fund
Shares Ordinary Quoted
Shares SAYE Share Option
Shares Self Select Personal Equity Plan
Shares Traded Options
Shares Unquoted
Stock Convertible Loan
Unit Trust Index Tracker
Unit Trust Invested in Shares
Unit Trust Personal Equity Plan
Unit Trust Savings Plan

Investing in property
Life Insurance Property Bond
Property Business Expansion Shares
Property Commercial Direct Investment
Property Enterprise Zone Trust
Property Ground Rents
Property Residential Direct Investment

Index-linked investments
National Savings Index-Linked Certificates Issues
Stock Government Index-Linked
Stock Private Index-Linked

Lump sum investment table

Type of investment	Quoted rate[6]	After tax if you pay:[1] No tax	20%	25%	40%	Fixed/ varies	See page
Bank	%	%	%	%	%		
Cash Card Deposit £500	4.00	4.0	3.2	3.0	2.4	V	92
Cheque Account With Int.	5.25	5.4	4.3	4.0	3.2	V	93
Higher Int. Dep. £2,500[2]	4.37	4.4	3.5	3.3	2.7	V	95
Notice: 60 day £2,500+	4.75	4.8	3.8	3.6	2.9	V	96
: 90 day £25,000+	6.00	6.1	4.9	4.6	3.7	V	96
Tessa Account	6.27	6.3	**6.3**	**6.3**	**6.3**	V	99
Building Society							
Cash Card Account £500+	4.25	4.3	3.4	3.2	2.6	V	100
Cheque Account £2,500+	6.10	6.1	4.9	4.6	3.7	V	101
£5,000+	6.35	6.4	5.1	4.8	3.8	V	101
£10,000+	6.60	6.6	5.3	5.0	4.0	V	101
£25,000+	7.10	**7.1**	**5.7**	**5.3**	4.3	V	101
£50,000+	7.10	**7.1**	**5.7**	**5.3**	4.3	V	101
Instant Access Acc. £1+	1.00	1.0	0.8	0.8	0.6	V	103
£500+	5.25	5.3	4.2	3.9	3.2	V	103
£1,000+	5.25	5.3	4.2	3.9	3.2	V	103
Postal Account £2,500+	7.05	7.1	**5.6**	**5.3**	4.2	V	109
£10,000+	7.30	**7.3**	**5.8**	**5.5**	4.4	V	109
£25,000+	7.50	**7.5**	**6.0**	**5.6**	4.5	V	109
30 Day Notice £500+	4.10	4.1	3.3	3.1	2.5	V	104
£5,000+	6.00	6.1	4.9	4.6	3.7	V	104
£25,000+	6.75	6.8	5.4	5.1	4.1	V	104
60 Day Notice £500+	5.00	5.0	4.0	3.8	3.0	V	105
£5,000+	5.38	5.5	4.4	4.1	3.3	V	105
£25,000+	7.25	**7.3**	**5.8**	**5.4**	4.4	V	105
90 Day Notice £1,000+	6.30	6.3	5.0	4.7	3.8	V	106
£10,000+	6.95	7.0	5.6	5.2	4.2	V	106
£25,000+	8.05	**8.1**	**6.4**	**6.0**	4.8	V	106
£50,000+	8.30	**8.3**	**6.6**	**6.2**	5.0	V	106
Permanent Int. Shares	10.20	**10.2**	**8.2**	**7.7**	**6.1**	V	108
Tessa Account	7.50	**7.5**	**7.5**	**7.5**	**7.5**	V	115

Best rates in **heavy black. Check the current rate before you invest. Correct at 16 April 1993.**
[1] Includes reinvestment of monthly, quarterly or half-yearly interest; see overleaf for conversion table.   [2] Some pay more for higher amounts.   [3] No tax deducted from interest.   [4] For a woman aged 70 paid monthly guaranteed 5 years.   [5] Assumes inflation 3½% a year.
[6] Quoted rate is before the effect of half-yearly, quarterly or monthly payment of interest.

Lump sums (continued)

Type of investment	Quoted rate[6]	After tax if you pay:[1]				Fixed/ varies	See page
		No tax	20%	25%	40%		
Co-operative Society	%	%	%	%	%		
1 year term £100	7.00	**7.1**[3]	**5.7**	**5.3**	4.3	F	116
3 year term £100	8.00	**8.2**[3]	**6.5**	**6.1**	4.9	F	116
Life Insurance							
Annuity[4]	11.69	**12.3**	**11.0**	**10.7**	**9.7**	F	124
Income Bond: 2 year	5.00	5.0	5.0	5.0	4.3	F	125
5 year	6.30	6.3	**6.3**	**6.3**	**5.4**	F	125
Local Authority							
3–5 year term	7.00	**7.1**	**5.7**	**5.3**	4.3	F	138
National Savings							
Capital Bond 'G'	7.75	**7.8**[3]	**6.2**	**5.8**	4.7	F	139
FIRST Option £1,000+	6.34	6.3	5.1	4.8	3.8	F	141
1 year term £20,000+	6.74	6.7	5.4	5.1	4.0	F	141
Income Bond	7.00	**7.2**[3]	5.8	5.4	4.3	V	142
Investment: 1 month	6.25	**6.3**[3]	5.0	4.7	3.8	V	143
Index-Linked Certs 5 yr[5]	6.75	6.8	**6.8**	**6.8**	**6.8**	V	144
40th Certs: 1 year	4.00	4.0	4.0	4.0	4.0	F	145
40th Certs: 5 years	5.75	5.8	**5.8**	**5.8**	**5.8**	F	145
General extension rate	3.75	3.8	3.8	3.8	3.8	V	205
Offshore							
Instant Access £2,500+	5.25	**5.3**[3]	4.2	3.9	3.2	V	148
£25,000+	7.00	**7.0**[3]	**5.6**	**5.3**	4.2	V	148
Notice 60 or 90 day							
£5,000+	6.20	**6.2**[3]	5.0	4.7	3.7	V	150
£25,000+	7.30	**7.3**[3]	**5.8**	**5.5**	4.4	V	150
Sterling Currency Fund	5.07	**5.1**[3]	4.1	3.8	3.0	V	154
Single Foreign Currency Fund							
US$	1.82	**1.8**[3]	1.5	1.4	1.1	V	153
Yen	1.90	**1.9**[3]	1.5	1.4	1.1	V	153
DM	7.44	**7.4**[3]	**6.0**	**5.6**	4.5	V	153
FF	8.19	**8.2**[3]	**6.6**	**6.1**	4.9	V	153
Stock & Bond Fund	9.21	**9.4**[3]	**7.5**	**7.1**	**5.7**	V	155
Stock – Government Fixed							
2 years	–	5.9	4.7	4.4	3.2	F	168
5 years	–	**7.2**	**5.8**	**5.4**	4.3	F	168
Unit Trust							
Cash Trust	6.10	6.2	5.0	4.6	3.7	V	182
Stock & Bond Fund	9.21	**9.4**	**7.5**	**7.1**	**5.7**	V	189

How much interest

The amount of interest you receive depends not only on the interest rate but also on how often you receive it. That is because with interest paid half way through the year you get the chance to earn interest on the interest as well as on the amount already in the account. For example, some banks and building societies pay interest half-yearly. The National Savings Bank Investment Account pays yearly.

Before you invest, as well as checking the interest rate, also check how often it is paid. The table on the right shows you how much you would get at the end of a year at various interest rates with interest paid and reinvested in the same account for the rest of the year. You can see it becomes less important when interest rates are low. This rate of interest is called the compound annual rate which is sometimes abbreviated as CAR.

Warning: many banks and building societies pay a lower rate for monthly interest compared with annual. But some do not pay the equivalent of the compound annual rate – they pay less. So the society with the best rate for yearly interest may not be the best for monthly.

| Quoted rate | Interest at year end on £100 if paid: | | | |
	Yearly	Half-yearly	Quarterly	Monthly
%	£	£	£	£
3	3.00	3.02	3.03	3.04
3.5	3.50	3.53	3.55	3.56
4	4.00	4.04	4.06	4.07
4.5	4.50	4.55	4.58	4.59
4.75	4.75	4.81	4.84	4.85
5	5.00	5.06	5.09	5.12
5.25	5.25	5.32	5.35	5.38
5.5	5.50	5.58	5.61	5.64
5.75	5.75	5.83	5.88	5.90
6	6.00	6.09	6.14	6.17
6.25	6.25	6.35	6.40	6.43
6.5	6.50	6.61	6.66	6.70
6.75	6.75	6.86	6.92	6.96
7	7.00	7.12	7.19	7.23
7.25	7.25	7.38	7.45	7.50
7.5	7.50	7.64	7.71	7.76
7.75	7.75	7.90	7.98	8.03
8	8.00	8.16	8.24	8.30
8.25	8.25	8.42	8.51	8.57
8.5	8.50	8.68	8.77	8.84
8.75	8.75	8.94	9.04	9.11
9	9.00	9.20	9.31	9.38
9.25	9.25	9.46	9.58	9.65
9.5	9.50	9.73	9.84	9.92
9.75	9.75	9.99	10.11	10.20
10	10.00	10.25	10.38	10.47
10.25	10.25	10.51	10.65	10.75
10.5	10.50	10.78	10.92	11.02
10.75	10.75	11.04	11.19	11.30
11	11.00	11.30	11.46	11.57
12	12.00	12.36	12.55	12.68
13	13.00	13.42	13.65	13.80

PART 2
Ninety six ways
to invest

What the headings mean

Name   This describes the type of investment as it is generally known and is preceded by the type of institution which offers it (eg Bank, Building Society, Life Insurance Company, National Savings) or the general nature of the investment (eg Offshore, Shares, Stock, Unit Trust).

What it is   A summary of the main distinguishing points.

Who can invest   Whether there are any age or other restrictions on the investor.

How worthwhile   Which sort of taxpayer (non, basic or higher) should seek this type of investment. Reduced rate taxpayers (20%) should follow advice for basic rate taxpayers (25%). Cross-references to competing investments.

Minimum   Minimum range of investment allowed by those schemes listed on the page. Higher minimum schemes may be available but have not been included unless they offer better value.

Maximum   Maximum investment which is allowed by a single institution or scheme.

Suitable   Whether suitable for lump sums, regular savings or both.

Money back   How soon you can get your money back. Any penalties like loss of interest or capital.

Interest   Whether the return from the investment is fixed or variable.

Interest paid   How often the interest is paid, eg half-yearly, yearly, quarterly or monthly. Whether interest is accumulated or paid out and if so the method.

BUILDING SOCIETY

90 Day Notice Account

(*Also called Extra Interest, Special, 90 Day Extra*)

An account usually with a minimum investment which can be added to. Withdrawals can be made by giving 90 days or 3 months notice. There is usually an option to withdraw immediately when you lose the equivalent amount of interest. Usually no loss of interest if £10,000 remains. Make sure you get the best interest for the amount you invest.

Who can invest   Anyone.

How worthwhile   Good value if you don't mind waiting to get your money back. Compare with *Building Society 30 Day Notice Account*, *60 Day Notice Account* and *Building Society Term Share*. Non-taxpayers not eligible for interest to be paid with no tax deducted, consider instead *Offshore Bank Notice Account*.

Minimum   Usually £500 or £1,000 (Coventry £1, Lambeth £250).

Maximum   £30,000 to £1m.

Suitable   Lump sums. Regular savings.

Money back   All or part after the notice period, or, often, immediately with loss of interest on amount withdrawn. Usually no loss of interest if £10,000 remains in the account. £5,000 at Halifax, Mansfield.

Interest   Variable. More interest paid for large amounts eg over £5,000, £10,000, £25,000, £50,000, £100,000.

Interest paid   Yearly. Halifax, Lambeth half-yearly. Manchester quarterly. By cheque, direct to a bank account or left to accumulate. Most also pay monthly: see *Building Society Monthly Income Account*.

Tax How the investment is treated for tax in the UK. Whether tax is deducted at source, whether non-taxpayers can reclaim it, whether higher rate taxpayers pay extra and whether the investment is tax exempt.

Fees to pay Charges levied at the outset or regularly by the institution or financial adviser. These charges reduce the return on your investment.

Passbook Whether there is a passbook, certificate, statements or other document issued.

Children Whether the investment is suitable for a child's investment and any special conditions which apply. Child means someone under age 18.

Risk All savings and investments are equally affected by inflation which erodes their real value. This assesses the risk of losing your capital either because the investment fluctuates in value or the institution with which you invest gets into difficulties.

How to invest How to go about finding an institution which offers the scheme and what to do next.

Where from A list of the institutions which, at the time this book went to press, offered the best rates for the type of scheme described at the level of investment quoted. For example, '*Min £50,000*: Halifax' means Halifax is good value for sums over £50,000; the actual minimum for the account may be lower eg £500. Addresses and telephone numbers are given in Appendix 1. Where the best choice is constantly changing, how to find the best buy.

Tax Basic rate tax is deducted from the interest. Non-taxpayers can reclaim the tax from the Inland Revenue (or have interest paid with no deduction). Higher rate taxpayers have to pay extra.

Fees to pay None.

Passbook Or receipt. Statements usually yearly.

Children Suitable for money earmarked for school fees as you know exactly when you need it and therefore when to give notice.

Risk Full value of original investment returned on withdrawal. 90% compensation scheme on the first £20,000 for each investor.

How to invest See surveys in the press; check adverts for latest best buys; subscribe to *Building Society Choice* or *Moneyfacts* (both published monthly); phone or call at the societies listed below.

Where from *Your min. £1*: Coventry. *£500*: Mansfield, Greenwich, City & Metropolitan. *Minimum £1,000*: Teachers, National Counties, Coventry, Scarborough. *Minimum £5,000*: As for £1,000 plus Northern Rock. *Minimum £10,000*: Cheltenham & Gloucester, Northern Rock, Greenwich, National Counties. Also consider Halifax (Premium Extra) and Alliance & Leicester (Bonus 90) which give a bonus if you don't withdraw for a year.

Always leave some of your money invested where you can get at it at once or within a few days without penalty. Only tie up money for as long as you are sure you will not need it.

BANK

Cash Card Account

An account with a low minimum where you can easily pay in at a bank branch or by post, and withdrawals can be made with a plastic card from a cash dispenser.

Who can invest   Anyone. You do not need a bank current (cheque book) account. But to get large amounts out (other than in cash) you need to transfer the money to a cheque book account except at Abbey National and TSB.

How worthwhile   Poor value for large amounts. Convenient if you make many cash transactions. Compare with *Building Society Cash Card Account*. Consider instead *Building Society Cheque Account with Interest* which for larger amounts pays much better interest and has the same cash card.

Minimum   £1.

Maximum   None.

Suitable   Lump sums. Regular savings.

Money back   Immediately from a cash machine £500 a day Midland; £300 a day Royal Bank of Scotland; £250 a day Abbey National; £200 a day Clydesdale, Lloyds, TSB; varies from £50 a week to £250 a day Nat. West. Cash also may be available over the counter.

Interest   Variable. Sometimes higher for larger amounts.

Interest paid   Added to account monthly, quarterly, half-yearly, yearly depending on the bank.

Tax   Basic rate tax is deducted from the interest. Non-taxpayers can reclaim the tax from the Inland Revenue (or have interest paid with no deduction). Higher rate tax payers have to pay extra.

Fees to pay   None.

Passbook   Statements sent.

Children   Over age 12 at Lloyds; 13 at Abbey National, Nat. West.; 14 at Royal Bank of Scotland; 16 at Midland. Barclays over 14, Midland over 13; see under *Bank Children's Account*.

Risk   75% compensation scheme on the first £20,000 for each investor.

How to invest   Call at one of the banks listed below and check the rate offered. Some advertise out of date rates or none at all. Rates published in *Moneyfacts* monthly.

Where from   Abbey National (Instant Saver), Clydesdale (Instant Solution), Lloyds (Instant Savings), Midland (Saver Plus), Nat. West. (First Reserve), Royal Bank of Scotland (Gold Deposit), TSB (Flexible Savings).

Your card can be used in cash machines at other banks and building societies. Abbey National*, AIB*†, Girobank*†, HFC Bank, Western Trust*, Yorkshire Bank use each other's Link machines (for other members and use abroad [* or †] see Building Society Cash Card Account). Barclays, Lloyds, Royal Bank of Scotland, Bank of Scotland (plus Link), can use each other's cash machines. Firstdirect, Midland, Nat. West., TSB, Clydesdale, Northern can use each other's. Visa cards can use each others' machines but if not listed above there may be a charge, eg 1½% where a Lloyds Bank card is used in a Halifax machine. Visa cards can be used abroad

BANK

Cheque Account With Interest

(Also called High Interest Cheque Account, Prime Account, Premier Account)

An account with or without an initial minimum investment where money can be paid in and withdrawn with the cheque book provided, sometimes subject to a minimum withdrawal. Some allow you to overdraw, use direct debits and standing orders, have a cheque guarantee card. Some have a cash machine card.

Who can invest Anyone age 18 or over. Account can be in joint names.

How worthwhile A temporary home for money on its way somewhere else. High Street banks don't usually pay good interest but they pay more than ordinary cheque accounts. Compare with *Building Society Cheque Account With Interest*, *Offshore Bank Multicurrency Account*.

Minimum £1 Lloyds. £1,000 Abbey National, Barclays. £2,000 Citibank, Midland, Western Trust. £2,500 Kleinwort Benson (min. addition £200), Royal Bank of Scotland, Schroder Wagg.

Maximum Usually none.

Suitable Lump sums.

Money back Cheques or cash cards can be used for withdrawals (minimum cheque £100 at Midland and Nat. West.). Visa debit card paid off directly from the account at Save & Prosper.

Interest Variable. Calculated daily. The High Street Banks tend to pay less.

Interest paid Added to account monthly, quarterly, half-yearly depending on the bank. Less or no interest while account balance below £1,000–£2,500.

Tax Basic rate tax is deducted from the interest. Non-taxpayers can reclaim the tax from the Inland Revenue (or have interest paid with no deduction). Higher rate taxpayers have to pay extra. Barclays, Lloyds, Midland, Nat. West., Royal Bank of Scotland offer these accounts in the Isle of Man where no tax is deducted; taxpayers should pay later.

Fees to pay Usually none. 50p at Royal Bank of Scotland (10 free a quarter); 75p Western Trust (2 free a month). Several charge £5 a month if low balance.

Passbook None. Statement issued, monthly or quarterly.

Children Account must be held in an adult's name.

Risk 75% compensation scheme on the first £20,000 for each investor.

How to invest Phone or call at one of the banks listed below. Rates published monthly in *Moneyfacts*.

Where from *High Street Banks*: Abbey National (High Interest Cheque), Barclays (Prime), Midland (High Interest Cheque), Lloyds (High Interest Cheque), Royal Bank of Scotland (Premium). *Other banks*: Citibank (Moneymarket Plus), Kleinwort Benson (High Interest Cheque), Schroder Wagg (Special), Western Trust (High Interest Cheque).

Other cheque accounts which pay interest at High Street banks now pay at an almost non-existent rate of ½% or 1% a year.

BANK

Children's Account

A bank account with free gifts, money boxes, competitions and magazines. Most banks have different gifts for different ages eg under 9, 9–13, 14–17. Barclayplus has Our Price Music Club with discount vouchers. Lloyds 'Headway' has free money guide, camera and cheque book at 16. Midland 'Live cash' £30 shop vouchers and free driving lessons.

Who can invest   Children under 19 Barclays; 11–18 Midland; under 18 Lloyds, Royal Bank of Scotland; under 17 Bank of Scotland; under 13 Abbey National.

How worthwhile   A way to encourage children to save but *Building Society Children's Account* may pay better interest. Unsuitable for large amounts. Older children also consider *Bank Cash Card Account* and *Building Society Cash Card Account*.

Minimum   £1 Abbey National, Barclays, Midland, Bank of Scotland, Royal Bank of Scotland. £5 Lloyds (Young Saver), £10 Lloyds (Headway).

Maximum   None.

Suitable   Lump sums. Regular savings.

Money back   At Barclays 7 days' notice or immediately when you lose 7 days' interest. At Abbey National, Midland, Lloyds, Royal Bank of Scotland immediately with no loss of interest. *Plastic card* for machine withdrawal if age 12 or over at Lloyds (with parent's consent); 13 at Midland; 14 at Royal Bank of Scotland (Route 17), Barclays (Barclayplus). Under 7: parent must sign; over 7 (18 in Scotland): child can withdraw on own signature.

Interest   Variable. Some pay more than others.

Interest paid   Added to account yearly, half-yearly, quarterly, monthly depending on the bank.

Tax   Basic rate tax is deducted from the interest. Non-taxpayers can reclaim the tax from the Inland Revenue (or have interest paid with no deduction). Higher rate taxpayers (eg where the interest counts as a parent's income) have to pay extra. For how a child's income is taxed see Chapter 11.

Fees to pay   None.

Passbook   At Abbey National. Otherwise paying-in books provided. Statements usually sent twice a year or on request; quarterly at Royal Bank; monthly at Lloyds.

Risk   75% compensation scheme on the first £20,000 for each investor.

How to invest   Call at some of the banks listed below and compare what they have to offer.

Where from   Abbey National (Action Savers Club), Bank of Scotland (Supersaver 5, up to 16; Express 12–17), Barclays (Barclayplus Junior up to 10; Barclayplus 11+), Lloyds Bank (Young Savers, Headway), Midland (Livecash), Royal Bank of Scotland (Rainbow 0–8; Cash Club 9–13; Route 17 14–17). See also under *Bank Cash Card Account*.

BANK

Higher Interest Deposit Account

(Also called Gold Deposit, Premium Reserve, Monthly Income)

An account with a minimum investment where you can easily pay in and withdraw by transfer to a cheque account at branches of High Street banks.

Who can invest Anyone. Account can be held in joint names. You need a bank cheque book account with the same bank to operate such accounts conveniently.

How worthwhile Poor value at large banks. Consider instead *Building Society Postal Account.*

Minimum Usually £500. Minimum balance £2,000 at Nat. West. Premium Reserve.

Maximum None.

Suitable Lump sums. Large regular savings.

Money back Usually immediately. Minimum withdrawal £100 at Nat. West; £250 at Royal Bank of Scotland. Nat. West and Barclays allow transfers to and from your cheque account by phone. Maximum withdrawal £200 on Saturdays only at Barclays and telephone transfers to cheque account if at same branch.

Interest Variable. Current rates displayed at bank branches. Less interest if account falls below minimum. Rate rises at £2,000, £10,000, £25,000 at Barclays; at these and also £50,000 at Nat. West.

Interest paid Added to account quarterly. Can be paid into a current account or accumulated.

Tax Basic rate tax is deducted from the interest. Non-taxpayers can reclaim the tax from the Inland Revenue (or have interest paid with no deduction). Higher rate taxpayers have to pay extra.

Fees to pay None.

Passbook None. Paying-in slips provided. Statements sent.

Children Unsuitable.

Risk 75% compensation scheme on the first £20,000 for each investor.

How to invest At a bank branch or by post if you already have an account.

Where from Barclays (Higher Rate Deposit Account), Beneficial Bank (Savings Deposit), HFC Bank (Savings Account), Nat. West. (Premium Reserve). See also Abbey National (Instant Saver), Lloyds (Instant Savings), Royal Bank of Scotland (Gold Deposit) under *Bank Cash Card Account.*

Interest rates on these accounts change frequently. Bank accounts are less competitive when interest rates in general are low.

BANK

Notice Account

(*Also called Investment, Gold Ninety, Crown Reserve*)

An account usually with a minimum investment which can be added to but notice of 60 or 90 days must usually be given to withdraw.

Who can invest   Anyone.

How worthwhile   Compare with *Building Society 60 Day Notice Account* and *Building Society 90 Day Notice Account* which usually give better interest. Non-taxpayers not eligible for interest to be paid with no tax deducted, consider instead *Offshore Bank Notice Account* or *National Savings Investment Account*. 6 or 12 months notice not recommended.

Minimum   £500 to £10,000. Minimum deposit £500 at Abbey National.

Maximum   None   or   £25,000–£50,000.

Suitable   Lump sums.

Money back   All or part after required notice given. Most allow early withdrawal for a charge of 25p (Nat. West) or 50p (Lloyds) or £1 (First Direct) per £100 withdrawn for every month of notice not given. TSB, Royal Bank of Scotland, Lloyds (30 Day only), no loss of interest if £10,000 remains. Abbey National 2 penalty free withdrawals a year (6 if over £10,000 remains). Others incur loss of interest on notice period.

Interest   Variable. Rates usually higher over £10,000, £25,000, £50,000.

Interest paid   Half-yearly, yearly, quarterly or monthly depending on the bank. By cheque (Abbey National, TSB) direct to a bank account, or left to accumulate. Often monthly income option to another account at higher minimum.

Tax   Basic rate tax is deducted from the interest. Non-taxpayers can reclaim the tax from the Inland Revenue (or have interest paid with no deduction). Higher rate taxpayers have to pay extra.

Fees to pay   None.

Passbook   Statements usually sent yearly, half-yearly or quarterly. Passbook at Abbey National; choice at TSB.

Children   Unsuitable.

Risk   75% compensation scheme on the first £20,000 for each investor.

How to invest   Call at or phone the companies listed below; ask for details and compare them.

Where from   *60 day*: First Direct (60 day), TSB (60 day). *90 day:* Abbey National (Investment), Royal Bank of Scotland (Gold Ninety).

Interest rates change and new savings schemes are launched. Keep up to date by reading the family money columns in the newspapers where these are reported. Always keep some money readily available for emergencies.

BANK

7 Day Account

(Also called Deposit Account)

An account where you can easily pay in. You withdraw at 7 days' notice or immediately with a loss of 7 days' interest.

Who can invest Anyone. Account can be held in joint names. You do not need a bank current (cheque book) account except at Girobank.

How worthwhile Poor value. Consider instead *Building Society Postal Account* and *Building Society Cheque Account With Interest*. For small amounts consider instead *Building Society Cash Card Account, Bank Cash Card Account*.

Minimum £1.

Maximum None.

Suitable Lump sums. Regular savings: money can be transferred regularly from a current account.

Money back 7 days' notice or immediately with loss of 7 days' interest. At Girobank deposits and withdrawals must be through a Girobank current (cheque book) account.

Interest Variable. Current rates are usually displayed at bank branches. Changes announced in newspapers.

Interest paid Added to account usually half-yearly in June and December. Lloyds Bank interest is added monthly or yearly.

Tax Basic rate tax is deducted from the interest. Non-taxpayers can reclaim the tax from the Inland Revenue (or have interest paid with no deduction). Higher rate taxpayers have to pay extra.

Fees to pay None.

Passbook Usually none. Paying-in slips provided. Statement sent once or twice a year. Yorkshire Bank has a passbook.

Children Consider instead *Bank Children's Account*.

Risk Full value of original investment returned on withdrawal. There is a 75% compensation scheme on the first £20,000 for each investor.

How to invest At a bank branch or by post if you already have an account.

Where from Most banks.

The established banks may also offer savings accounts and, in Scotland, deposit accounts, which allow immediate withdrawal. These pay the same or lower interest than Bank 7 Day Accounts.

BANK

Term Account

(*Also called Term Deposit Account, Fixed Term Deposits*)

Lump sum invested usually at a fixed rate of interest for a fixed term usually of 1 to 5 years. Usually no additions or withdrawals allowed. Higher rates of interest and different lengths of term can be negotiated for larger sums but usually only for terms under a year.

Who can invest   Anyone.

How worthwhile   Compare with *Life Insurance Growth or Income Bond, Local Authority Fixed-Term Loan, National Savings Fixed Certificates, Stock Government Fixed Interest, Stock Debenture and Loan.* Non-taxpayers not eligible for interest to be . paid with no tax deducted, also compare with *Co-operative Society Term Account, National Savings Capital Bond.* Terms over 5 years not recommended.

Minimum   £200–£5,000.

Maximum   Usually none.

Suitable   Lump sums.

Money back   At end of fixed term when company usually notifies you. Some companies will return your money early if you have a good reason but may reduce the interest rate.

Interest   Usually fixed. With all companies, interest paid monthly is less than the half-yearly or yearly rate.

Interest paid   Half-yearly or monthly (a few companies pay yearly or quarterly): by cheque; direct to a bank account; or left to accumulate. Not all companies pay all these ways.

Tax   Basic rate tax is deducted from the interest. Non-taxpayers can reclaim the tax from the Inland Revenue (or have interest paid with no deduction). Higher rate taxpayers have to pay extra.

Fees to pay   None.

Passbook   None. Statement usually sent half-yearly.

Children   Unsuitable.

Risk   75% compensation scheme on the first £20,000 for each investor.

How to invest   Look for companies offering good interest rates in the newspapers. See *Moneyfacts* published monthly.

Where from   Best rates usually from small less well known banks.

Always leave some of your money invested where you can get at it at once or within a few days without penalty. Only tie up money for as long as you are sure you will not need it.

BANK

Tessa Account

(Also called Tax Exempt Special Savings Account)

An account with a yearly maximum investment and no withdrawals for 5 years to receive interest tax free. You can either let the interest accumulate for 5 years or receive part of it each year. Some banks operate a Tessa Transfer Account which allows you to invest the full amount in one go in another account (not tax free) and the bank then transfers the payments each year into your Tessa.

Who can invest Anyone 18 or over. Joint accounts not allowed.

How worthwhile Good value for taxpayers, especially higher rate taxpayers. Compare with *Building Society Tessa Account*. Non-taxpayers consider instead *Building Society 30, 60 or 90 Day Notice Accounts* or *Offshore Bank Notice Account*.

Minimum £1. You can often invest what you like, when you like, subject to the maximums.

Maximum £3,000 in year 1, £1,800 in years 2–4, £600 in year 5 (or up to £1,800 if less than maximum invested in previous years). You can only have one Tessa.

Suitable Lump sums, regular savings.

Money back After 5 years without penalty. Immediately (Nat. West.) or 28 days' notice (Abbey National). If you withdraw more than an amount equal to what the accumulated interest less basic rate tax would be, the Tessa must be closed, transferred to a taxable account, and any interest earned so far becomes taxable. You can transfer your Tessa to another bank or building society and you won't lose the tax benefits. You may lose bonuses on early closure or a transfer.

Interest Usually variable.

Interest paid Usually added to account yearly (Abbey National) or quarterly (Nat. West.) or half yearly. Part of the interest can usually be paid to another bank account. But the amount of interest equivalent to the basic rate of tax which would be deducted on a normal account must be accumulated for the full 5 years.

Tax Interest is tax free. It does not have to be included on a tax return.

Fees to pay Many banks (not listed here) have charges eg £20, £25 or £50 if you want to move the account to another bank or to a building society, should their interest rate become poor value. Abbey National £20 charge if you don't give 28 days notice. First Direct ¼% charge if don't give 14 days notice.

Passbook Statements usually sent.

Children Not eligible.

Risk Full value of investment returned on withdrawal. There is a 75% compensation scheme on the first £20,000 for each investor.

How to invest Call at, phone or write to one of the banks listed below. It's best to invest as much as you can yearly and let your interest accumulate to benefit from the tax exemption. You need your National Insurance number if you have one for the application form.

Where from Abbey National, First Direct, National Westminster.

Check up from time to time that the interest rate remains competitive; if not transfer to a better Tessa Account at another bank or at a building society.

BUILDING SOCIETY

Cash Card Account

(Also called Cardcash, Cashbase, Cashcentre, Moneylink)

An account where you can easily pay in and withdrawals can be made from a cash dispenser usually 24 hours a day (except Halifax 5am to 2am). Some cards can be used abroad.

Who can invest Anyone 14–18 or over.

How worthwhile Convenient if you make many cash transactions. Compare with *Bank Cash Card Account*. For larger amounts consider *Building Society Cheque Account With Interest*.

Minimum £1–£500.

Maximum Usually none.

Suitable Lump sums, regular savings. Deposits can be made at many machines. Salary can be paid direct at many.

Money back Immediately from cash machine £250 a day (£200–£300 Halifax, £200 Chelsea, £100 Portman). Some machines have maximum single transaction below daily limit. Over the counter at own society.

Interest Variable. Sometimes higher for larger amounts.

Interest paid Usually added to account yearly (half-yearly Halifax).

Tax Basic rate tax is deducted from the interest. Non-taxpayers can reclaim the tax from the Inland Revenue (or have interest paid with no deduction). Higher rate taxpayers have to pay extra.

Fees to pay Halifax charges 60p each time you use the card at a non-Halifax machine.

Passbook Yes or statements sent. Some machines can print statements and print your account balance.

Children Available at age 14 from Alliance & Leicester, Bristol & West, Halifax, National & Provincial, Yorkshire.

Risk 90% compensation scheme on the first £20,000 for each investor.

How to invest Contact one of the societies listed below.

Where from Find an account which pays good interest, see *Building Society Instant Access Account* or *Building Society Cheque Account With Interest* which offers a cash card. The following larger building societies belong to the *Link* network and their cards can be used at each other's machines, Post Offices and at banks' machines which belong to Link (see *Bank Cash Card Account*). Alliance & Leicester, Birmingham Midshires, Bradford & Bingley, Bristol & West, Britannia*†, Chelsea*†, Coventry*, Derbyshire*†, Dunfermline*†, Halifax, Leeds Permanent, National & Provincial, Nationwide, North of England, Northern Rock, Norwich & Peterborough*, Portman*, Woolwich, Yorkshire Building Society*†. Those marked † can also use *4B Network* machines in Spain, *Multibanco* Portugal and *Bancontact Mister* in Belgium. Those marked * can use *Plus* machines in Canada, USA, Puerto Rico, US Virgin Islands, Mexico, Western Australia (Perth), Hong Kong, Singapore, Japan and Guam. To find the nearest machine in the USA phone 1-800-THE-PLUS.

BUILDING SOCIETY

Cheque Account With Interest

(*Also called Asset Reserve, Classic, Current*)

An account with or without an initial minimum investment which can be added to (your salary or pension can be paid in direct) and withdrawals made or bills paid with the cheque book provided or in the ordinary way at a building society branch. Some allow you to overdraw, use direct debits and standing orders, have a cash machine and cheque guarantee card.

Who can invest   Anyone 18 or over.

How worthwhile   An alternative with good interest to a bank current (cheque book) account. With lower interest but possibly more convenience also consider *Bank Cheque Account With Interest*.

Minimum   Initially *£500*: Northern Rock. *£2,500*: Chelsea (by post only), Portman. *£5,000*: Halifax.

Maximum   None or £250,000.

Suitable   Lump sums; regular payments (eg salary or pensions).

Money back   Cheques can be used to pay bills or make withdrawals into other accounts. *Link* cash machine card available at Bristol & West, Chelsea, Northern Rock, Portman.

Interest   Variable. Usually more for larger amounts and poor while account below £2,500.

Interest paid   Monthly at Northern Rock. Quarterly at Halifax. Yearly on 1 January at Portman. Yearly on 1 February at Chelsea. Interest accumulates in the account.

Tax   Basic rate tax is deducted from the interest. Non-taxpayers can reclaim the tax from the Inland Revenue (or have interest paid with no deduction). Higher rate taxpayers have to pay extra.

Fees to pay   None.

Passbook   Statements sent.

Children   Unsuitable.

Risk   Full value of original investment returned on withdrawal. There is a 90% compensation scheme on the first £20,000 for each investor.

How to invest   Phone one of the societies listed below.

Where from   Chelsea (Classic), Halifax (Asset Reserve), Northern Rock (Current), Portman (Prestige Cheque).

These Building Society Cheque Account With Interest Accounts give the best rates of interest for an account with a cheque book. However they do not usually match the best rates overall.

BUILDING SOCIETY

Children's Account

(*Also called Junior Savers, Young Saver, Little Xtra Club*)

Building Society Share Account backed by popular children's characters, money boxes, free comics or magazines, letters, birthday cards and special promotions eg cassette discounts.

Who can invest   Children. Maximum age depends on society. Money can be tied up to age 18.

How worthwhile   Good way to encourage younger children to save. Compare with *Bank Children's Account, Building Society Instant Access Account*. Age 12 and over consider instead *Bank Cash Card Account.*

Minimum   Usually £1.

Maximum   Varies.

Suitable   Lump sums. Regular savings.

Money back   On demand: cash £250; cheque up to £5,000. Under 7 (10 Chelsea; 11 Halifax; 12 Bristol & West; 14 Leeds Permanent) parent must countersign. Over 7 (or when society thinks child responsible) child can withdraw on own signature. In Scotland parents must countersign until the child is 18.

Interest   Variable. Usually poor.

Interest paid   Usually half-yearly to accumulate. Several send birthday cards.

Tax   Basic rate tax is deducted from the interest. Non-taxpayers can reclaim the tax from the Inland Revenue (or have interest paid with no deduction). Higher rate taxpayers (eg where interest counts as a parent's income) have to pay extra. For how a child's income is taxed see also Chapter 11.

Fees to pay   None.

Passbook   Yes: often with a special cover.

Risk   90% compensation scheme on the first £20,000 for each investor.

How to invest   Call at or phone one of the societies listed below.

Where from   Britannia (Brighter Saver, piggy bank, gift cheques), Furness (£2.50 bonus on opening), Halifax (Little Xtra Club 0–11, Quest, added to any account 12–16), Ipswich (Tycoon Racoon, gifts), Loughborough (Penguin money box, gift vouchers), Market Harborough (Environmental outings, posters), Marsden (Acorn, money box), North of England (Save 'n' Grow), Tipton & Coseley, West Bromwich (Mister Money), Woolwich (Henry's Cat).

Older children may be keener on higher interest or a cash dispenser card than low interest and special incentives.

BUILDING SOCIETY

Instant Access Account

(Also called Gold, Sovereign, Premium Access)

An account where you can withdraw immediately like a Building Society Ordinary Share Account but with a higher minimum investment and higher interest. Many accounts pay more when account over £1,000, £2,000, £5,000, £10,000, £20,000, £25,000, £30,000, £40,000, £50,000.

Who can invest   Anyone.

How worthwhile   Fair to good value for readily available money but *Building Society Postal Account* usually pays a better interest rate. *Building Society Cheque Account With Interest* may pay less interest but gives quicker access to your money. See also last paragraph on this page. Non-taxpayers consider also *Offshore Bank Instant Access Account*.

Minimum   £500 to £2,500. £1 Nationwide, Tipton & Coseley. £5 Portman. £10 Alliance & Leicester. Minimum balance £100 at Chelsea.

Maximum   £100,000 to £1 million.

Suitable   Lump sums. Regular savings.

Money back   On demand: Usually at any branch. Cash £250 (£500 Halifax, Britannia, Yorkshire; £300 Leeds & Holbeck). Cheques vary by society, check before you invest; usually £20,000 (up to £100,000 at large societies). Many allow withdrawals from any branch. Remainder usually in a few days but many societies say 1 month's notice in rules.

Interest   Variable. More interest usually paid for large amounts eg over £5,000, £10,000, £25,000, £50,000; None at all if balance less than £100 (C&G); £50 Halifax.

Interest paid   Usually yearly (half-yearly Saffron Walden) by cheque; direct to a bank account; or left to accumulate. Some also pay monthly: see *Building Society Monthly Income Account*.

Tax   Basic rate tax is deducted from the interest. Non-taxpayers can reclaim the tax from the Inland Revenue (or have interest paid with no deduction). Higher rate taxpayers pay extra.

Fees to pay   None.

Passbook   Or receipt. Statement sent yearly or half-yearly.

Children   Under 7: parents must sign. Over 7 (or when society thinks child responsible say 10 or 12): child can withdraw on own signature.

Risk   Full value of original investment on withdrawal. 90% compensation scheme on the first £20,000 for each investor.

How to invest   See surveys in the press; subscribe to *Building Society Choice* or *Moneyfacts* (both monthly); phone or call at the societies listed.

Where from   *Your min. £1*: Monmouthshire (Escalator Instant). *£500*: Portman (Instant), Saffron Walden (Cashbuild), Leeds & Holbeck (Gold Access). *£1,000*: As for £500 plus National Counties (Instant), Tipton & Coseley (Instant). *£5,000*: National Counties, Leeds & Holbeck. *£10,000*: National Counties, Leeds & Holbeck, Alliance & Leicester (Midas), Birmingham Midshires (Quantum Instant), Chelsea (Instant Option). *£40,000*: Coventry (Instant Option), *£50,000*: Birmingham Midshires, Skipton (Sovereign).

If you have over £25,000 you may do better by investing in a Building Society Notice Account which requires no notice so long as the balance does not fall below £5,000: Halifax (90 Day Xtra). Also consider Nationwide (CapitalBuilder) which allows one withdrawal of any amount per calendar year; balance over £10,000, without notice or penalty.

BUILDING SOCIETY

30 Day Notice Account

(*Also called One Month Notice, Special Option*)

An account usually with a minimum investment which can be added to. Withdrawals can be made by giving 28 or 30 days' notice. Some accounts have an option to withdraw immediately when you lose the equivalent amount of interest; a few have no loss of interest if £5,000 or £10,000 remains in account. Make sure you get the best interest for the amount you invest.

Who can invest   Anyone.

How worthwhile   Good value if you don't mind waiting a month to get (some of) your money back. Compare with *Building Society 60 Day Notice Account, Building Society 90 Day Notice Account* and *Building Society Term Share*. Non-taxpayers not eligible for interest to be paid with no tax deducted consider instead *Offshore Bank Notice Account*.

Minimum   Usually £500 or £1,000 Hanley £250.

Maximum   £30,000 to £1m.

Suitable   Lump sums. Regular savings.

Money back   All or part after the notice period, or, often, immediately with loss of interest on amount withdrawn. No loss of interest if £5,000 remains in account at Hanley.

Interest   Variable.   More interest paid for large amounts eg over £10,000, £25,000, £50,000.

Interest paid   Yearly   (half-yearly Hanley) by cheque; direct to a bank account; or left to accumulate. Some also pay monthly: see *Building Society Monthly Income Account*.

Tax   Basic rate tax is deducted from the interest. Non-taxpayers can reclaim the tax from the Inland Revenue (or have interest paid with no deduction). Higher rate taxpayers have to pay extra.

Fees to pay   None.

Passbook   Or receipt. Statements usually yearly.

Children   Suitable for money earmarked for school fees as you know exactly when you need it and therefore when to give notice.

Risk   Full value of original investment returned on withdrawal. 90% compensation scheme on the first £20,000 for each investor.

How to invest   See surveys in the press, check adverts for latest offers; subscribe to *Building Society Choice* or *Moneyfacts* (both monthly); phone or call at the societies listed below.

Where from   *Your min. £250 or £500*: Consider ˜ *Building Society Instant Access Account* instead. *Minimum £2,500*: St. Pancras (Special Yield). *Minimum £5,000*: Hanley Economic (Hi-Rate). *Minimum £10,000*: Monmouthshire (Escator Bonus). *Minimum £25,000*. Consider *Building Society Instant Access Account* and Nottingham (Blue Chip 30), Lougborough (High Yield Shares).

Even 30 days can seem a long time if you need money in a hurry, so always keep some immediately available.

BUILDING SOCIETY

60 Day Notice Account

An account usually with a minimum investment which can be added to. Withdrawals can be made by giving 60 days notice. There is usually an option to withdraw immediately when you lose the equivalent amount of interest. Make sure you get the best interest for the amount you invest.

Who can invest   Anyone.

How worthwhile   Good value if you don't mind waiting to get (some of) your money back. Compare with *Building Society 30 Day Notice Account*, *Building Society 90 Day Notice Account* and *Building Society Term Share*. Non-taxpayers not eligible for interest to be paid with no tax deducted, consider instead *Offshore Bank Notice Account*.

Minimum   Usually £500 or £5,000. £10,000 Leeds Permanent.

Maximum   £100,000 to £500,000.

Suitable   Lump sums. Regular savings.

Money back   All or part after the notice period, or usually immediately with loss of interest on amount withdrawn. Some allow withdrawals with no loss of interest if £10,000 remains in account.

Interest   Variable. More interest paid for large amounts eg over £5,000, £10,000, £25,000, £50,000.

Interest paid   Usually yearly (half yearly Birmingham Midshires) by cheque; direct to a bank account; or left to accumulate. Some also pay monthly: see *Building Society Monthly Income Account*.

Tax   Basic rate tax is deducted from the interest. Non-taxpayers can reclaim the tax from the Inland Revenue (or have interest paid with no deduction). Higher rate taxpayers have to pay extra.

Fees to pay   None.

Passbook   Or receipt. Statements usually yearly.

Children   Suitable for money earmarked for school fees as you know exactly when you need it and therefore when to give notice.

Risk   Full value of original investment returned on withdrawal. 90% compensation scheme on the first £20,000 for each investor.

How to invest   See surveys in the press; check adverts for latest best buys; subscribe to *Building Society Choice* or *Moneyfacts* (both monthly); phone or call at the societies listed below.

Where from   *Your min. £500*: Consider *Building Society Instant Access Account* instead or Northern Rock. *Minimum £5,000*: Birmingham Midshires (Quantum High Interest). *Minimum £10,000 and over*: Leeds Permanent.

Always leave some of your money invested where you can get at it at once or within a few days without penalty. Only tie up money for as long as you are sure you will not need it.

BUILDING SOCIETY

90 Day Notice Account

(Also called Extra Interest, Special, 90 Day Extra)

An account usually with a minimum investment which can be added to. Withdrawals can be made by giving 90 days or 3 months notice. There is usually an option to withdraw immediately when you lose the equivalent amount of interest. Usually no loss of interest if £10,000 remains. Make sure you get the best interest for the amount you invest.

Who can invest Anyone.

How worthwhile Good value if you don't mind waiting to get your money back. Compare with *Building Society 30 Day Notice Account, 60 Day Notice Account* and *Building Society Term Share.* Non-taxpayers not eligible for interest to be paid with no tax deducted, consider instead *Offshore Bank Notice Account.*

Minimum Usually £500 or £1,000 (Coventry £1, Lambeth £250).

Maximum £30,000 to £1m.

Suitable Lump sums. Regular savings.

Money back All or part after the notice period, or, often, immediately with loss of interest on amount withdrawn. Usually no loss of interest if £10,000 remains in the account. £5,000 at Halifax, Mansfield.

Interest Variable. More interest paid for large amounts eg over £5,000, £10,000, £25,000, £50,000, £100,000.

Interest paid Yearly. Halifax, Lambeth half-yearly. Manchester quarterly. By cheque, direct to a bank account or left to accumulate. Most also pay monthly: see *Building Society Monthly Income Account.*

Tax Basic rate tax is deducted from the interest. Non-taxpayers can reclaim the tax from the Inland Revenue (or have interest paid with no deduction). Higher rate taxpayers have to pay extra.

Fees to pay None.

Passbook Or receipt. Statements usually yearly.

Children Suitable for money earmarked for school fees as you know exactly when you need it and therefore when to give notice.

Risk Full value of original investment returned on withdrawal. 90% compensation scheme on the first £20,000 for each investor.

How to invest See surveys in the press; check adverts for latest best buys; subscribe to *Building Society Choice* or *Moneyfacts* (both published monthly); phone or call at the societies listed below.

Where from *Your min. £1*: Coventry. *£500*: Mansfield, Greenwich, City & Metropolitan. *Minimum £1,000*: Teachers, National Counties, Coventry, Scarborough. *Minimum £5,000*: As for £1,000 plus Northern Rock. *Minimum £10,000*: Cheltenham & Gloucester, Northern Rock, Greenwich, National Counties. Also consider Halifax (Premium Extra) and Alliance & Leicester (Bonus 90) which give a bonus if you don't withdraw for a year.

Always leave some of your money invested where you can get at it at once or within a few days without penalty. Only tie up money for as long as you are sure you will not need it.

BUILDING SOCIETY

Monthly Income Account

An account which pays out interest monthly. Rate of interest depends on which type of account the money is invested in. Many societies allow monthly income based on any type of account. But it is better to use *Building Society Postal Accounts, 30 Day, 60 Day* or *90 Day Notice Accounts* and *Term Share*, which offer the best interest. See relevant page for details of each type of account.

Who can invest   Anyone.

How worthwhile   Convenient if you want a monthly income. Choose the society which gives the highest return. Compare the rates for monthly income which are not always equivalent to the yearly rates.

Minimum   Usually £5,000 but £1,000 or £2,500 also available. Often higher than the minimum for the particular type of account where interest is paid yearly or half-yearly.

Maximum   None.

Suitable   Lump sums.

Money back   Same conditions as for yearly or half-yearly interest payments. On *Building Society Instant Access Account* usually 1 month's notice required to close account (ie give notice during January, receive the money 1 March).

Interest   Variable. Rate slightly less than for half-yearly or yearly interest. It should be worth the same because it is paid monthly but some societies pay less than an equivalent rate – see table on page 88.

Interest paid   Monthly: by cheque, direct to a bank account, into another account at the society. Check the society you choose pays the interest where you want. Interest until the end of the first month will be sent out with the following month's interest.

Tax   Basic rate tax is deducted from the interest. Non-taxpayers can reclaim the tax from the Inland Revenue (or have interest paid with no deduction). Higher rate taxpayers have to pay extra.

Fees to pay   None.

Passbook   Or certificate issued. Some societies send statements half-yearly or yearly.

Children   Unsuitable.

Risk   Full value of original investment returned on withdrawal. There is a 90% compensation scheme on the first £20,000 for each investor.

How to invest   See surveys in the press, check adverts for latest offers, subscribe to *Building Society Choice* or *Moneyfacts* which include a table of rates updated each month.

Where from   Many building societies.

If you need to spend your interest, a monthly income account is a convenient way to have it paid to you.

BUILDING SOCIETY

Permanent Interest Bearing Share

(*Also known as PIBS*)

Lump sum invested in special shares issued by about 11 large and medium sized building societies at a fixed interest rate. There is no fixed life for the shares, which may be bought and sold at any time at the market price through a stockbroker. If the building society gets into financial difficulties, it may miss interest payments and you could theoretically lose money as the building societies compensation scheme does not apply. They are more like a Stock than a Share or Building Society Account.

Who can invest   Anyone.

How worthwhile   Good value for non-taxpayers and basic rate taxpayers provided interest rates don't rise after you buy in which case they may become poor value. Compare with *Shares Preference, Stock Debenture and Loan* or *Stock Government Fixed Interest*. Higher rate taxpayers consider instead *Stock Government Fixed Interest*.

Minimum   £1,000 to £50,000 depending on the society.

Maximum   None. But some shares may be in short supply and a £20,000 maximum in any one share would be sensible.

Suitable   Lump sums.

Money back   1–3 weeks. You get the market price at the time you sell plus or minus *accrued interest*, see Chapter 3.

Interest   Fixed. The rate at which the society pays, is called *the coupon*. But the return you get is determined by the price you pay, which sets the *yield* which is your return. When the market price is over 100, the yield is less than the coupon.

Interest paid   Usually half-yearly by cheque; or direct to a bank or building society account.

Tax   Basic rate tax is deducted from the interest. Non-taxpayers can reclaim it from the Inland Revenue. Higher rate taxpayers pay extra.

Fees to pay   Stockbrokers commission when you buy and sell: On first £20,000 ¾% to 1%; less on larger amounts; minimum £17. Some may charge more eg 1½% on first £7,000. Same when you sell.

Passbook   Share certificate issued.

Children   Under 18 shares must be held in an adult's name but can be designated with the child's name.

Risk   There is no compensation scheme. The society can stop or miss interest payments. Possible capital loss if interest rates rise and the market price of your shares falls.

How to invest   Ask a stockbroker or bank which shares offer the best *yield*. If you want to invest a large amount, spread your investment between different societies

Where from   Stockbrokers or banks.

Although these shares pay good interest they could lose you money if interest rates rise.

BUILDING SOCIETY

Postal Account

(Also known as Balmoral, Capital Trust, Edinburgh, First Class instant)

An account which pays a good interest rate and where you can withdraw immediately, generally without notice or penalty but only by post. Deposits also have to be made by post (except at Cheltenham & Gloucester). You lose interest while your cheque is in the post, possibly for up to a week if you receive it before a weekend and can't pay into another account until Monday.

Who can invest   Anyone.

How worthwhile   Good value for readily available money. Better value if you make few transactions. Compare with *Building Society Cheque Account With Interest* (more convenient), and particularly for non-taxpayers *Offshore Instant Access Account* and *Unit Trust Cash Trust* (for small amounts).

Minimum   *£500*: Birmingham Midshires. *£2,000*: Britannia. *£2,500*: North of England. *£10,000*: Bristol & West.

Maximum   £100,000 to £3 million. Some are open for deposits from new customers for limited periods.

Suitable   Lump sums.

Money back   A few days. You fill in a form and post it back to the Society which posts you a cheque by return. Minimum cheque sometimes £50 or £100.

Interest   Variable. Sometimes more interest paid for larger amounts eg. when over £10,000, £25,000, £30,000 or £50,000.

Interest paid   Usually yearly (half-yearly at Birmingham Midshires); direct to a bank account; or left to accumulate. Birmingham Midshires and Bristol & West also pay monthly

but at a lower nominal interest rate and require 30 days notice, see *Building Society Monthly Income Account*.

Tax   Basic rate tax is deducted from the interest. Non-taxpayers can reclaim the tax from the Inland Revenue (or have it paid with no deduction). Higher rate taxpayers pay extra.

Fees to pay   None. At Cheltenham & Gloucester (London Deposit) you lose 7 days interest on every withdrawal.

Passbook   Statement usually sent with each transaction or yearly.

Children   Unsuitable.

Risk   Full value of original investment on withdrawal. 90% compensation scheme on the first £20,000 for each investor.

How to invest   See surveys and adverts in the press. Subscribe to *Building Society Choice* (monthly) or phone one of the societies listed at the special 'By Post' phone number.

Where from   Birmingham Midshires (First Class Instant), Bristol & West (Balmoral), Britannia (Capital Trust), North of England (Edinburgh), Teachers (Bullion).

The rates on these accounts may be excellent when you invest but they don't always stay that way.

BUILDING SOCIETY

Save As You Earn (SAYE)

A commitment to save a fixed amount each month for 5 years, when you are paid a bonus of 14 months' payments tax-free. If you keep the money in for another 2 years the bonus is doubled. If you stop the payments, you may withdraw or leave the money in to receive a lower interest rate. Up to 6 payments may be delayed: your contract is then extended by the same number of months.

Who can invest   Anyone 16 years or over.

How worthwhile   *2nd Issue*: Good value for higher rate taxpayers and, while interest rates remain low, basic rate taxpayers. Compare with *National Savings Yearly Plan*, *Building Society Tessa*. Basic rate taxpayers consider instead *Bank or Building Society Tessa*. Poor value for non-taxpayers.

Minimum   £1 a month.

Maximum   £20 a month. If you are investing in a building society SAYE scheme, a new scheme must be with the society you are already with and the combined total must not exceed this amount.

Suitable   Regular savings.

Money back   In 2 to 3 weeks. No partial withdrawals. During the first year money back with no interest. *2nd Issue*: During years 1 to 5: 6% interest tax free (if you die, 8% tax-free). Completed savings withdrawn between years 5 to 7 will receive the 5-year bonus only.

Interest   Fixed. *2nd Issue*: Equivalent to 8.3% a year over 5 years. If left another 2 years, bonus equivalent to 9% a year for those 2 years is paid. The average return over 7 years is 8.6% a year.

Interest paid   SAYE interest paid when you close the account.

Tax   SAYE interest is tax-free.

Fees to pay   None.

Passbook   Or certificate issued. Some societies send statements.

Children   Not eligible.

Risk   Full value of original investment returned on withdrawal. 90% compensation scheme on first £20,000.

How to invest   At a building society branch. Regular payments usually by a bank standing order.

Where from   *SAYE*: many building societies (eg Bradford & Bingley, Halifax); all offer identical terms.

BUILDING SOCIETY

Regular Monthly Savings Account

A commitment to save a certain amount each month in return for higher interest. Some societies allow you to increase or decrease monthly payment and to miss a number of payments each year. Partial withdrawals may be allowed.

Who can invest Anyone.

How worthwhile Taxpayers consider instead a monthly payment to a *Building Society Tessa Account* or a *Bank Tessa Account*. Higher rate taxpayers consider those and also *National Savings Yearly Plan*. Unsuitable for non-taxpayers. If you already have £250 or £500 saved you may do better to add to a *Building Society Instant Access Account*.

Minimum 10p to £10 a month, usually £1 a month.

Maximum Usually £100 to £250 a month (joint accounts £200 to £500).

Suitable Regular savings. Some societies allow up to 3 months' payments to be made in advance and some months payments to be missed before money is transferred to a Share Account.

Money back If account is closed: immediately or within a few days (sometimes 1 month). Partial withdrawals usually one every 6 or 12 months. If more, interest penalty or account must be closed.

Interest Variable.

Interest paid Yearly or half-yearly to accumulate. Most societies will, if asked, pay interest out to you.

Tax Basic rate tax is deducted from the interest. Non-taxpayers can reclaim the tax from the Inland Revenue (or have interest paid with no deduction). Higher rate taxpayers have to pay extra.

Fees to pay None.

Passbook Sometimes. Statement usually sent once a year.

Children Unsuitable.

Risk Full value of original investment returned on withdrawal. 90% compensation scheme on the first £20,000 for each investor.

How to invest To open an account, call at or phone. Regular payment can then be made by visiting branch, by post, bank standing order or credit transfer.

Where from Smaller building societies.

Building Society Regular Monthly Savings Accounts have been overtaken by better value investments – see 'How worthwhile' above.

BUILDING SOCIETY

Share and Deposit Accounts

Ordinary share accounts are the simplest form of investment in building societies but they pay least interest. Money is easily paid in and withdrawn. Deposit accounts are the same but pay even less interest although theoretically they have more security.

Who can invest   Anyone.

How worthwhile   Poor value. Consider instead *Building Society Cash Card Account* which usually pays the same interest or higher and is more convenient. If you have more than £250–£500 consider instead *Building Society Postal Account.*

Minimum   Usually £1.

Maximum   Usually none.

Suitable   Lump sums. Regular savings.

Money back   On demand: cash £250 to £1,000; cheques usually £20,000 or more. Many societies allow withdrawals from any branch. Remainder usually in a few days but many societies say 1 month's notice in rules.

Interest   Variable. Most societies pay the same rate. Some small societies pay more but may require a few days' withdrawal notice. Many societies pay more for large amounts (see *Building Society Postal Account* or *Building Society Instant Access Account*). There may be no interest on balances under £50 or £100.

Interest paid   Usually half-yearly or yearly by cheque, direct to a bank account, or left to accumulate.

Tax   Basic rate tax is deducted from the interest. Non-taxpayers can reclaim the tax from the Inland Revenue (or have interest paid with no deduction). Higher rate taxpayers have to pay extra.

Fees to pay   None.

Passbook   Yes. Statement usually sent half-yearly or yearly. Some societies do not send statement when balance is small eg less than £100. Halifax sends statements on request or if passbook not updated during year.

Children   Under 7: parents must sign. Over 7 (or when society thinks child responsible say 10 or 12): child can withdraw on own signature. Consider instead *Building Society Children's Account.*

Risk   Full value of original investment returned on withdrawal. 90% compensation scheme on the first £20,000 for each investor.

How to invest   At a building society branch or agency.

Where from   Most societies, although some no longer have 'ordinary shares'. The largest (with assets over £1,000 million as at 31 December 1991) in order of size are: Halifax, Nationwide, Alliance & Leicester, Woolwich, Leeds Permanent, Cheltenham & Gloucester, Bradford & Bingley, National & Provincial, Britannia, Bristol & West, Northern Rock, Yorkshire, Birmingham Midshires, Skipton, Portman, Coventry, Chelsea, Leeds & Holbeck, Derbyshire, Norwich & Peterborough, North of England, Cheshire, Principality, West Bromwich.

Building society share accounts have been overtaken by other sorts of building society accounts. So transfer to a better value account without delay.

BUILDING SOCIETY

Stock Market Guaranteed Bond

(*Also known as Share Index+*)

An account which accumulates interest in line with the growth in value of the FT-SE 100 Share Index for 3 or 5 years. You are guaranteed to get your money back over five years and schemes usually guarantee a minimum interest rate eg 4.5% a year too. If you want your money back early you get less interest but still get all your capital back. The bonds are issued for a limited time and different issues from the same society will have different guarantees.

Who can invest   Anyone.

How worthwhile   Potentially good value if you want to tie your money up for 3 or 5 years. But if the stock market is in the doldrums by the time the bond matures, you get a poor return although no loss of capital; if you stop early you also get a poor return. Higher rate taxpayers consider instead *Unit Trust Index Tracker*. The return counts as taxable interest in the year you cash the bond (your tax rate may also be higher in 5 years' time).

Minimum   Alliance & Leicester £1,000; Northern Rock £2,500; Yorkshire £5,000.

Maximum   Varies.

Suitable   Lump sums.

Money back   After 3 or 5 years depending on the society. Or at 30 days notice, usually on 4 or fewer fixed dates during the year.

Interest   Variable. Linked to the rise in the FT-SE 100 Share Index with a guaranteed minimum.

Interest paid   After 3 or 5 years depending on the society. Or when you cash, if you cash early.

Tax   Basic rate tax is deducted from the accumulated interest which is paid in the year when you cash. Non-taxpayers can reclaim the tax from the Inland Revenue (or have it paid with no deduction). Higher rate taxpayers pay extra at the rate for the year in which they cash. Although the scheme is inefficient taxwise, because you get no indexation allowance nor the capital gains tax free limit, you do not incur the high charges of many unit trust and life insurance schemes.

Fees to pay   None.

Passbook   Statement sent.

Children   Unsuitable.

Risk   Full value of original investment on withdrawal. 90% compensation scheme on the first £20,000 for each investor.

How to invest   See surveys and adverts in the press. Ask for details and compare the guarantees and terms of different societies.

Where from   Alliance & Leicester, Britannia, Newcastle, Northern Rock, Yorkshire and other building societies.

One possible problem with these bonds is the possibility of stockmarket manipulation by traders on the day your bond matures resulting in a fall in your maturity value. This has nothing to do with the building society but could effect the value of your investments.

BUILDING SOCIETY

Term Share

Lump sum invested for a term of 6 months to 5 years. Additions may be allowed. Withdrawals can be made usually at 3 months' notice *and* losing 3 months' interest; some accounts are less restrictive, some more. The interest rate is usually fixed although in the past it was only guaranteed as a rate above the Share rate, known as the *differential*.

Who can invest   Anyone.

How worthwhile   Good value provided you get as good, or nearly as good interest, as with a *Building Society Notice Account* and you expect interest rates to fall or remain the same during the investment term; poor value if they rise. Compare with *Stock Government Fixed Interest*. Taxpayers compare with *Life Insurance Income Bond*, *Local Authority Fixed Term Loan*. Higher rate taxpayers compare with *National Savings Fixed Certificates*, *National Savings Yearly Plan*. Non taxpayers compare with *National Savings Capital Bond*, *Co-operative Society Term Account*. Special limited offers usually better value.

Minimum   Usually £1,000, £2,000, £5,000, £10,000.

Maximum   None or £10,000 to £200,000.

Suitable   Lump sums.

Money back   At end of term or earlier usually at 3 months' notice *and* 3 months' loss of interest. If you die, investment plus full interest up to date paid out.

Interest   Usually fixed for the term.

Interest paid   Usually yearly by cheque; direct to a bank account; into another account, or left to accumu-late. Monthly: into bank or other account, see *Building Society Monthly Income Account*.

Tax   Basic rate tax is deducted from the interest. Non-taxpayers can reclaim the tax from the Inland Revenue (or have interest paid with no deduction). Higher rate taxpayers have to pay extra.

Fees to pay   None.

Passbook   Or certificate issued.

Children   Unsuitable.

Risk   Full value of original investment returned on withdrawal. 90% compensation scheme on the first £20,000 for each investor.

How to invest   Look for advertised special offers in the press. A list is published in *Moneyfacts* each month.

Where from   A number of building societies.

Always leave some of your money invested where you can get at it at once or within a few days without penalty. Only tie up money for as long as you are sure you will not need it.

BUILDING SOCIETY

Tessa Account

(Also called: Tax Exempt Special Savings Account)

An account with a yearly maximum investment and no withdrawals for 5 years to receive interest tax free. You can either let the interest accumulate for 5 years or receive part of it each year. Some societies operate a Tessa 'Transfer' or 'Feeder' Account which allows you to invest the full amount in one go in another account (not tax free) and the society then transfers the payments each year into your Tessa.

Who can invest Anyone 18 or over. Joint accounts not allowed.

How worthwhile Good value for taxpayers, especially higher rate taxpayers. Non-taxpayers consider instead *Building Society 30, 60 or 90 Day Notice Accounts* or *Offshore Bank Notice Account*.

Minimum £1–£3,000.

Maximum £3,000 in year 1, £1,800 in years 2–4, £600 in year 5 (or up to £1,800 if less than maximum invested in previous years). You can only have one Tessa.

Suitable Lump sums, regular savings.

Money back After 5 years without penalty. Immediately or up to 90 days notice depending on the society. If you withdraw more than an amount equal to what the accumulated interest less basic rate tax would be, the Tessa Account must be closed, transferred to a taxable account, and any interest earned so far becomes taxable. You can transfer your Tessa to another bank or building society and you won't lose the tax benefits. You may lose bonuses on early closure or a transfer.

Interest Usually variable.

Interest paid Usually added to account yearly or half yearly. Part of the interest can be paid by cheque or to a bank account. But the amount of interest equivalent to the basic rate of tax which would be deducted on a normal account must be accumulated for the full 5 years.

Tax Interest is tax free. It does not have to be included on a tax return.

Fees to pay Some societies (not listed here) have penalties if you want to move the account to another society or to a bank. With others you can avoid the charge by giving up to 90 days notice.

Passbook Yes or statements sent.

Children Not eligible.

Risk Full value of investment returned on withdrawal. There is a 90% compensation scheme on the first £20,000 for each investor.

How to invest Call at, phone or write to one of the societies listed below or other societies which pay good interest and don't have penalties on transfers elsewhere; or subscribe to *Moneyfacts*. It's best to invest as much as you can yearly and let your interest accumulate to benefit from the tax exemption. You have to put your National Insurance number, if you have one, on the application form.

Where from Lambeth (Elite), Leeds & Holbeck, Market Harborough, Nationwide, North of England, Stroud & Swindon, Yorkshire Building Society. Also consider National Counties which has paid a good return but has a transfer penalty.

Check up from time to time that the interest rate remains competitive; if not transfer to a better account.

CO-OPERATIVE SOCIETY

Term Account

(Called Development Bond, Fixed Term Loan, Investment Bond, Unit Loan)

Lump sum invested at a fixed rate of interest for a term of 1 to 5 years. Interest is paid half-yearly or at the end of the term.

Who can invest   Anyone 18 or over.

How worthwhile   Good value if you consider interest rates will fall or remain the same during the term; poor value if they do not. Compare with *National Savings Capital Bond, Building Society Term Share, Local Authority Fixed Term Loan.* Taxpayers also compare with *Life Insurance Growth or Income Bond, National Savings Fixed Certificates, Stock Government Fixed Interest.*

Minimum   Usually £100. £500 at Oxford. £5,000 at CWS on some accounts.

Maximum   £50,000 for each account. None at CWS.

Suitable   Lump sums.

Money back   At end of term.

Interest   Fixed. Rates vary at different times and between societies.

Interest paid   Half-yearly by cheque or accumulated to end of term (you don't always have a choice).

Tax   Not deducted. Taxpayers are liable to pay income tax on the interest which should be declared on a tax return.

Fees to pay   None.

Passbook   Certificate issued.

Children   Investment must be made by a parent or grandparent on behalf of a child.

Risk   75% compensation scheme on the first £20,000 for each investor. Many small societies which have got into financial difficulties have been taken over by the two largest ones CRS and CWS.

How to invest   Phone the Investment Department of a co-operative society for the current rate and an application form. Subscribe to *Moneyfacts* which publishes a list of societies and interest rates each month.

Where from   CRS (1–2 year terms), CWS (1–5 year terms), Anglia Co-op (1 year), Brighton Co-op (1–5 years), Chelmsford Star (3 years), Coventry & East Mercia (1 year), Leicestershire (1 year), Oxford Swindon & Gloucester (1–3 years).

Having your money tied up for even a year or two can seem a long time if you need that money urgently.

FRIENDLY SOCIETY

Bank Account Linked

A commitment to save a fixed amount, monthly or yearly for 10 years into a life insurance policy which after the deduction of a charge is linked to a tax free investment in a bank. After 10 years you do not have to withdraw and can continue to earn tax free interest.

Who can invest Anyone up to age 70.

How worthwhile Fair value for taxpayers, and higher rate taxpayers, who are sure they can save for 10 years. Unsuitable for non-taxpayers. Consider *Building Society Tessa* instead which has the same tax exemption and interest but lower charges.

Minimum £9 a month; £100 a year.

Maximum £18 a month; £200 a year for each eligible person. A married couple can take £36 a month or £400 a year between them. Limits apply to premiums on all such policies with all Friendly Societies. *Beware of policies with higher premiums; you will not get full tax exemption.*

Suitable Regular savings. You can set up a transfer scheme: a lump sum of £1,650 is invested in a special account and each year the premium is automatically transferred to the friendly society policy. The interest on the decreasing balance in the account is not tax free but over 10 years allows the lump sum to fund the regular savings plan in full (ie 10 premiums of £200).

Money back After 10 years. If you stop saving before then, your return is reduced. Can be left longer to accumulate tax free.

Interest Variable. Interest is accumulated within the policy.

Interest paid When you cash in the policy after 10 years or more. If you die while the policy is in force, the greater of the value of your policy or the guaranteed life cover (usually £1,500 for an £18 a month premium) is paid.

Tax There is no tax on the proceeds nor on the interest accumulated on premiums of up to £200 a year or £18 a month.

Fees to pay Deducted from your investment. Equivalent to a tax rate of around 28% on the interest. Charges are lower if you pay yearly.

Passbook None. Insurance policy issued. Yearly statement.

Children Each child can have its own policy.

Risk Friendly societies are covered by a compensation scheme giving 100% of the first £30,000 of investments if the society goes bust.

How to invest Phone or write for an application form.

Where from Homeowners Friendly Society: Unity Trust Bank (High Growth Savings Plan).

Some versions invest half your money in a unit trust. Avoid them as they sacrifice the flexibility of a Unit Trust Personal Equity Plan which has the same tax exemption. If you are offered a scheme with a premium over £200 a year or £18 a month, the excess does not benefit from the tax exemptions described above.

GOLD

Coins

A convenient means of investing in gold. You hope to make a capital gain by selling for more than you paid but you may end up with a loss by selling for less. The price of gold coins is closely linked to the price of gold but different coins may sell for a different *premium* over the price of gold. The main coins suitable for investment in the UK are 'old' Sovereigns (which contain .2354 of a Troy ounce of pure gold). Other gold coins, like the Britannia, Krugerrand, Maple Leaf, Double Eagle, Nugget and gold bars are less attractive as you normally pay 17½% VAT on the whole cost. Half sovereigns and certain dates of sovereigns sell for much more than the value of their weight because of rarity.

Who can invest   Anyone.

How worthwhile   Potentially good value as a long-term investment for taxpayers if you buy and sell at the right time; poor value if you do not. VAT on the purchase price makes most gold coins unattractive if bought in the UK. With coins over 100 years old, some dealers only pay VAT on the dealer's profit margin; ask the dealer. You can't charge VAT when you sell. Compare with *Unit Trust Invested in Gold Shares* (p.185).

Minimum   The price of one coin. With gold at £229 a Troy ounce, a '100 year old' sovereign might cost £61 including VAT on the dealer's margin, a 'new' sovereign £77.31 including VAT; to sell you would get £56 old, £53 new.

Maximum   None.

Suitable   Lump sums. Regular.

Money back   Immediately at the market price.

Interest   None.

Tax   Profits you make on the sale of coins are liable to capital gains tax, see Chapter 5. If you deal frequently in coins you may have to pay income tax instead.

Fees to pay   None: commission is usually included in the buying and selling price. If coins are delivered to you, postage and insurance. VAT at 17½% on purchase price if you buy from a VAT registered supplier (most dealers are registered) but can be less on '100 year old' coins. You can buy coins in Jersey, Guernsey or Gibraltar where there is no VAT, but you have to leave them there.

Passbook   None. You get the coins.

Children   Suitable as gifts especially from parents. Children's capital gains are not aggregated with their parents.

Risk   High. The value of gold can go down as well as up. Keep the coins in a safe place like a deed box in a bank, and have them insured. If you leave your coins with a dealer abroad, to avoid VAT be sure you can trust him.

How to invest   Check the current price in a daily newspaper. Check with a few dealers how much their coins will cost to buy. When you sell, do the same. When you ask for the price, do not say whether you are buying or selling. Check whether the price quoted includes VAT.

Where from   Spink & Son. A list of other coin dealers can be obtained free from Britannia Section, Royal Mint, Llantrisant, Mid Glamorgan CF7 8YT, or phone 0443-222 111 x382. These dealers may also deal in old sovereigns too.

INVESTMENT TRUST

Shares

Lump sum invested in the shares of a company which employs professional managers to invest its assets in shares. The price of investment trusts moves broadly with the value of its portfolio of shares. Sometimes the portfolio of shares is worth more than the market price, and the investment trust shares are said to be at a *discount* the reverse is known as a *premium*. You usually receive an income and hope to make a capital gain by selling for more than you paid but may end up with a loss by selling for less. There are around 150 investment trusts available. Some trusts specialise in particular types of share (eg Energy); others in certain foreign stockmarkets (eg Europe, Far East, USA or a mixture).

Who can invest   Anyone.

How worthwhile   Potentially good value as a long-term investment for taxpayers if you buy and sell at the right time; poor value if you do not. See also *Investment Trust Personal Equity Plan*. Unsuitable for non-taxpayers.

Minimum   £200 to £500 if you invest directly with managers; £1,000 through a bank or stockbroker because of minimum commission.

Maximum   None.

Suitable   Lump sums. See also *Investment Trust Savings Plan*.

Money back   1–3 weeks. You get the market price at the time you sell.

Interest   Variable. Called *dividend*. The before-tax interest is called the *yield*, trusts with different aims give different yields. Some trusts aim for a rising income.

Interest paid   Usually half-yearly by cheque or direct to a bank account. About 5 weeks before the dividend is paid, the shares go *ex-dividend*; this means the seller gets the next dividend, not the buyer.

Tax   20% tax is deducted from the dividend (called a *tax credit*). Non-taxpayers can reclaim the tax credit from the Inland Revenue. Higher rate taxpayers have to pay extra; basic taxpayers don't. Gains on trust shares are liable to capital gains tax, (but see Chapter 5) though no tax on gains on shares held by the trust.

Fees to pay   When you buy stockbrokers' commission: On first £7,000 1% to 1.9%; then usually 0.5%; minimum £15 to £30. Managers may buy and sell free of charge or for 0.2% to 4%. Stamp duty ½%. When you sell commission only.

Passbook   Share certificate issued.

Children   Under 18 shares must be held in an adult's name but can be *designated* with a child's initials.

Risk   High. The value of shares goes down as well as up but no risk of the trust going bust as there is with the shares of an individual company.

How to invest   Get a copy of the latest Monthly Information Service booklet from the *Association of Investment Trust Companies*. It lists managers, savings schemes, PEPS, performance, trust portfolios, speciality, discounts and gearing. Choose from among the larger trusts of the type you want with the highest discount and gearing. Or ask a specialist stockbroker for advice.

Where from   The trust managers or a stockbroker (list available from *Association of Investment Trust Companies*).

INVESTMENT TRUST

Personal Equity Plan

(Also called Investment Trust PEP)

A means of investing free of all tax up to £6,000 a year in investment trusts with at least 50% of their assets in UK or EC shares. Up to £1,500 can be in 'non-qualifying' trusts where 50% of assets are in shares but not necessarily UK or EC. It's easiest to invest monthly. You usually have a choice of trust and should choose one with a higher income to benefit from the tax exemption.

Who can invest   Anyone 18 or over. Joint plans are not allowed but husband and wife can have one each. In any one tax year you can only invest in a Personal Equity Plan from one manager.

How worthwhile   Good value for taxpayers especially higher rate taxpayers. Higher rate taxpayers also consider a Single Share PEP, see *Shares Self Select Personal Equity Plan*. Unsuitable for non-taxpayers.

Minimum   *£30 a month*: Dunedin. *£50 a month*: Alliance Trust Savings, Ivory & Sime. *£100 a month*: Moorgate, Murray Johnstone.

Maximum   £6,000 a year, £500 a month plus managers' charges.

Suitable   Regular savings. Lump sums sometimes have higher charges.

Money back   You can normally sell the shares when you like. If you die the plan ends and your money is returned.

Interest   Variable. Called *dividend*. The before tax interest is called the *yield* and plans which show the highest yield are most attractive as they make the most use of the tax exemptions.

Interest paid   Dividends can be accumulated within the plan to increase its value by being invested in more shares; or they can be paid by cheque or to a bank account half-yearly or quarterly.

Tax   Income and capital gains are completely tax free and need not be entered on a tax return. Tax deducted from the dividend is reclaimed by the manager on your behalf.

Fees to pay   When you buy stockbrokers' commission from nil to 1.75%; stamp duty ½%. Initial set-up charge nil to 5% (nil to 1.5% for companies listed here) or fixed charge £2 to £60; £30 Dunedin. Yearly management charge 1%–1½%; ½% Dunedin; nil Alliance, Ivory & Sime. When you sell commission only.

Passbook   None. Plan certificate provided. Statements sent, monthly, half-yearly or yearly.

Children   Not allowed.

Risk   High but not as risky as buying individual shares. The value of the share can go down as well as up.

How to invest   Choose a trust or manager which operates a scheme. Choose a high yielding ordinary trust with a high *discount* and high *gearing*. Monthly investment is normally by direct debit or standing order from a bank account. A list of investment trust companies and personal equity plans is available from the *Association of Investment Trust Companies* in its Monthly Information Service booklet.

Where from   Alliance Trust Savings, Dunedin, Ivory & Sime, Moorgate, Murray Johnstone.

An Investment Trust Personal Equity Plan is an excellent investment for a higher rate taxpayer.

INVESTMENT TRUST

Savings Plan

A commitment to save a minimum amount regularly, usually monthly, which is invested in shares in an investment trust (a company investing in shares managed by professionals). The investment trust shares broadly reflect the value of the shares held by the trust but can be less or more. You can make additional lump sum savings in any month or raise or lower the monthly amount. The plan can be stopped at any time; you either sell the shares at the current market price or continue holding the shares as an ordinary investment trust — see *Investment Trust Shares*.

Who can invest Anyone.

How worthwhile Flexible and potentially good value for taxpayers who want to invest regularly in a fund of shares. Compare with *Unit Trust Savings Plan*. If you have less than £500 a month (£6,000 a year) to invest, consider instead *Investment Trust Personal Equity Plan*.

Minimum £20 to £100 a month or £200 to £2,000 lump sum. You can buy more when you feel like it.

Suitable Regular savings.

Maximum None.

Money back Within a couple of weeks. Shares are sold at the current market price. Some companies allow partial withdrawals.

Interest Variable. Called *dividend*.

Interest paid The dividends can be paid by cheque, direct to a bank account or used to buy more shares.

Tax 20% tax is deducted from the dividend (called a *tax credit*). Non-taxpayers can reclaim the tax credit from the Inland Revenue. Higher rate

taxpayers have to pay extra; basic taxpayers don't. Gains on shares may be liable to capital gains tax (see Chapter 5) though the managers pay no capital gains tax when they make gains on shares held within the trust.

Fees to pay When you buy stockbrokers' commission usually nil to ¼%; stamp duty ½%. When you sell commission only. Fees vary between trusts.

Passbook None. Statements of shares and dividends sent half-yearly or monthly.

Children Under 18 shares must be held in an adult's name and can be *designated* with a child's initials.

Risk By buying regularly you even out fluctuations in the market price, eg you buy when prices are high as well as low. You still need to choose the right time to sell. Otherwise the same as *Investment Trust Shares*.

How to invest Choose a trust which operates a scheme. Phone the managers and ask for their literature and an application form.

Where from A list of companies and 36 savings plans is available from the *Association of Investment Trust Companies* in its Monthly Information Service booklet. Dunedin (Income Growth) and Ivory & Sime (British Assets) offer schemes linked to trusts looking for a rising income.

An Investment Trust Savings Plan is a good way of regularly investing in shares. It is more flexible than an Investment Trust Personal Equity Plan. It has lower charges than a Unit Trust Savings Plan and income can be paid out to you or accumulated.

INVESTMENT TRUST

Split Level Trust

(*Also called Dual Capital Trust, Split Capital Trust, Dual Purpose Trust*)

Lump sum invested in a company which employs professionals to invest its assets in shares. Unlike ordinary Investment Trust Shares the shares of a Split Level Investment Trust are (usually) split into two main types: *income shares* and *capital shares*. Income shares receive all the income from the trust all of which is paid out as dividends; capital shares receive no income. Split level trusts have a fixed life, like a Government Stock, at the end of which after 2–15 years, depending on the trust, the income shares are repaid at the price at which the shares were first issued and capital shareholders get the value of the investments in the company.

Who can invest   Anyone.

How worthwhile   *Income shares*: Potentially good value for non-taxpayers and basic rate taxpayers but the high and rising income ceases when the trust comes to an end and you may incur a loss of around half your original investment if you don't sell some time before the end of the term. Higher rate taxpayers might consider investing through *Investment Trust Personal Equity Plan*. *Capital shares*: Potentially good value for higher rate taxpayers but the shares fluctuate a great deal in value.

Minimum   Around £1,000 because of minimum commission.

Maximum   None but some may be in short supply.

Suitable   Lump sums. You can save regularly with some by using *Investment Trust Savings Plan*.

Money back   At the end of the term. Or 1–3 weeks if you sell before then; you get the market price at the time

you sell (which may be more or less than you paid).

Interest   *Income shares*: Variable. Called *dividend*. The before tax interest is called the *yield*. You can expect this to rise year by year. *Capital shares*: None.

Interest paid   Usually half-yearly by cheque or direct to a bank account. About 5 weeks before the dividend is paid, the shares go *ex-dividend*; this means the seller gets the next dividend not the buyer.

Tax   20% rate tax is deducted from the dividend (called *tax credit*). Non-taxpayers can reclaim the tax credit from the Inland Revenue. Higher rate taxpayers pay extra; basic taxpayers don't. Gains on trust shares are liable to capital gains tax (but see Chapter 5) though there is no gains tax on gains on shares held by the trust itself.

Fees to pay   Stamp duty ½% when you buy. When you buy or sell: Stockbrokers' commission: 1% to 1.9% on first £7,000; then usually ½%; minimum £15 to £30. If you buy from the managers, commission can be nil to ¼%.

Passbook   Share certificate issued.

Children   Unsuitable. Shares must be registered in an adult's name but can be *designated* with a child's initials or name.

Risk   Higher than Investment Trust Shares.

How to invest   Get advice and details of the available trusts from a specialist stockbroker.

Where from   The *Association of Investment Trust Companies* has a booklet on Split Level Trusts and can provide the names of specialist stockbrokers.

INVESTMENT TRUST

Zero Coupon Preference Shares

(Also called Zero Dividend Shares)

Shares in an Investment Trust Split Level Trust which receive no income but are repaid at a fixed price at a fixed date in 2–15 years time, depending on the trust. Your return is equivalent to a fixed accumulating rate of interest like a Life Insurance Growth Bond. The return depends on the price you pay (plus commission etc) in relation to the price when the shares are repaid (or when you sell, if you sell before then); it also depends on how much tax you have to pay on your gain. They are more like a stock than a share.

Who can invest   Anyone.

How worthwhile   Potentially good value for basic rate and higher rate taxpayers if the gain continues to be taxed as a capital gain rather than income – see *Tax*. Compare with *Life Insurance Growth Bond*. Non-taxpayers compare with *National Savings Capital Bond*.

Minimum   Around £1,000 because of minimum commission.

Maximum   None but some may be in short supply.

Suitable   Lump sums.

Money back   When the shares are repaid at the redemption date. Or 1–3 weeks if you sell before then; you get the market price at the time you sell (which may be more or less than you paid).

Interest   None.

Interest paid   When the shares are repaid.

Tax   Gains on trust shares are liable to capital gains tax, (but see Chapter 5). It is probable that gains on the shares will be liable to income tax instead of capital gains tax by the

time many shares are repaid. Either way no tax is payable until after the shares are repaid (or you sell).

Fees to pay   Stamp duty ½% when you buy. When you buy or sell: Stockbrokers' commission: 1% to 1.9% on first £7,000; then usually ½%. If you buy from the managers, commission can be nil to 0.2%.

Passbook   Share certificate issued.

Children   Shares must be registered in an adult's name but can be designated with a child's initials. Possibly a suitable investment for an Accumulation Trust.

Risk   Moderate. The investment trust might not have enough money to repay the shares in full – or if you have to sell early, and interest rates have risen since you bought, the price may have fallen.

How to invest   Get advice and details of the available trusts and their *redemption yields* from a specialist stockbroker.

Where from   The *Association of Investment Trust Companies* has a booklet on Split Level Trusts and can provide the names of specialist stockbrokers.

Future tax law changes may make this investment less attractive. There are also Stepped Preference Shares which offer dividends which rise at a predetermined rate plus a fixed redemption value.

LIFE INSURANCE

Annuity

Lump sum invested with a life insurance company which usually cannot be returned. You receive a fixed income until you die. Better returns are paid the older you are. Options, but with lower income, include a joint life annuity where payments continue until both partners die or an annuity guaranteed to pay for at least 5 or 10 years.

Who can invest Anyone but only suitable for the elderly (over age 65 men, 70 women).

How worthwhile Designed to deal with the problem of outliving your capital. But because of inflation they are only worth considering if you are over 70 (men), 75 (women). A combination of an annuity and a life insurance policy can be used to reduce inheritance tax. Compare with *Property Ground Rents* and the income shares of *Investment Trust Split Level Trust*.

Minimum Around £10,000, otherwise charges reduce the return.

Maximum None.

Suitable Lump sums.

Money back Usually not possible. Surrender value if available likely to be much less than the investment.

Interest Fixed or increasing at a fixed rate. Rates vary according to type of annuity. For instance a fixed annuity for a man of 70 might pay £1,400 a year, whereas one rising by 5% a year might initially pay £1,000 a year. Current rates surveyed in magazines, eg *Money Management*.

Interest paid Yearly, half-yearly, quarterly or monthly by cheque or direct into bank account usually in arrears. Less income is paid for more frequent payment.

Tax The annuity payment is regarded as part taxable and part return of capital. The capital part of the payment is not taxable but this amount depends on your age when you buy it. For each £10,000 of purchase price, the capital portion of the payment is:
At age 65: £570 (men), £485 (women)
At age 70: £705 (men), £601 (women)
At age 75: £884 (men), £763 (women)
At age 80: £1,114 (men), £985 (women)
These limits apply to new annuities; pre-1992 ones have a larger capital part. Basic rate tax is deducted from the taxable portion; non-taxpayers can arrange for it to be paid without deduction of tax. Higher rate taxpayers have to pay extra tax on the taxable portion only.

Fees to pay None.

Passbook None. You will get an annuity contract detailing the insurance company's obligations.

Children Unsuitable.

Risk UK authorised life companies are covered by a 90% compensation scheme less 'excessive' benefits. For complete safety use an old established company.

How to invest Get an independent financial adviser to obtain quotations for you; also get your own from Equitable Life and London Life which do not pay commission to brokers. If you want to avoid inheritance tax, ask a chartered accountant, solicitor or other adviser for advice.

Where from Most life companies.

Equitable Life offers unit-linked and 'with-profits' annuities where the income depends on the performance of the underlying investments; the income may go up or down. Annuities linked to the Retail Prices Index are also available, though the initial payment for all three types is lower than with a fixed annuity.

LIFE INSURANCE

Growth or Income Bond

Lump sum invested with an insurance company at a fixed interest rate for terms of from 1 to 10 years. Versions which pay out interest are called *Income Bonds*; those which accumulate income are called *Growth Bonds*. Some bonds consist of more than one insurance policy.

Who can invest Anyone. Usually minimum age 18, 17 or 12; maximum none or 79–85.

How worthwhile Good value for basic rate taxpayers provided you do not expect interest rates to rise during the term of the bond. Some bonds pay better rates the older you are. Terms over 5 years not recommended. Higher rate taxpayers compare with *National Savings Fixed Issue Certificates*, *Stock Government Fixed-Interest*. Non-taxpayers and 20% taxpayers consider instead *Co-operative Society Term Account*, *National Savings Capital Bond*, or *Stock Government Fixed-Interest*.

Minimum £1,000–£10,000.

Maximum None.

Suitable Lump sums.

Money back At end of term or when you die. Some bonds can be cashed early but you lose some of your money.

Interest Fixed. Most companies pay higher rates for larger amounts eg over £5,000, £10,000, £25,000, £50,000.

Interest paid With Income Bonds usually yearly (a few pay half-yearly; or monthly with £5,000 minimum investment); by cheque or direct to a bank account. With Growth Bonds the interest is accumulated.

Tax The interest whether paid out or accumulated usually comes tax paid for basic rate taxpayers. Non-taxpayers cannot reclaim the tax. Higher rate taxpayers have to pay extra, either each year or when the bond matures. The income or proceeds of a Bond may reduce someone's entitlement to Age Allowance.

Fees to pay None.

Passbook None. Insurance policy issued.

Children Unsuitable.

Risk None provided you do not cash the policy early. UK authorised companies are covered by a 90% compensation scheme less 'excessive' benefits. For complete safety, use an old established company but new ones usually give the best value. Do not invest in an Income or Growth Bond offered by an overseas life company which is not authorised in the UK; if the company gets into trouble you could lose all your money.

How to invest Consult page 542 of Channel 4 Teletext; subscribe to *Moneyfacts* which publishes a list of bonds and rates monthly or look in the lists published in the Saturday and Sunday financial pages of the newspapers.

Where from See the National press for advertisements of limited offers; from an independent financial adviser; or direct from a life company.

ALICO and General Portfolio Life have offered Income Bonds with a variable income. Income and Growth Bonds have been offered in the past with a return linked to the Retail Prices Index and denominated in a foreign currency.

LIFE INSURANCE

Home Income Plan

A means by which elderly people can use part of the value of the home they own to borrow money which is used to buy an annuity to give them an income for life. You can get a cash lump sum too. The plans listed here have a fixed interest mortgage.

Who can use it Anyone over age 70 (69 at Carlyle Life) who has an unmortgaged owner-occupied house or purpose-built flat (converted flats not always acceptable). If you are married, your joint ages must be at least 150 (145 at Carlyle Life).

How worthwhile Fair to good value for people not eligible for the means tested Income Support especially single people, widows or widowers and non-taxpayers. Better the older you are. May not be worth doing if you are eligible for State benefits as the income from the plan will reduce your Income Support.

Minimum The value of your home must be at least £21,500 or £43,000, for you to borrow £15,000 or £30,000.

Maximum The maximum loan is usually £30,000; 70% to 75% of the value of your property. At Carlyle for older ages, loans can be greater than £30,000 up to 60%.

Money back None unless you take a plan offering capital protection. When you die, the money you borrowed plus any unpaid interest is taken from the proceeds of the sale of your home so your heirs get less. If you die within 5 years your estate can get some of the money back but the income is lower if you take a 'capital protected' option.

Interest Fixed but see note at bottom of next column.

Interest paid Usually monthly by cheque or direct to a bank or building society account.

Tax You get tax relief (if you are over 65) on the interest you pay on up to £30,000 of the money you have borrowed. The tax relief will usually be given at source which means you pay a lower interest rate and don't have to reclaim the tax relief. The annuity payment is regarded as part income, part return of capital. The capital portion is not taxable but this amount depends on your age when you start the scheme. Basic rate tax is usually deducted from the income portion unless you are a non-taxpayer.

Fees to pay Legal and valuation costs; Carlyle pays £150 plus VAT plus disbursements.

Passbook None. The body which lends the money will take a mortgage on your home and hold the deeds. You get an annuity contract from a life insurance company.

Children Not eligible.

Risk UK life companies are covered by a 90% compensation scheme less 'excessive' benefits.

How to use it Ask a specialist independent financial adviser like Hinton & Wild to get quotes from the companies or do it yourself.

Where from Allchurches Life, Carlyle Life (Mortgage Scheme).

Many building societies will give interest only loans to the over 65's. You can do as you please with the money and the loan is repaid when you die. You don't get tax relief unless an annuity is bought; interest on the loan is variable. A few don't make you pay all or any interest which is added to the loan – see page 16.

LIFE INSURANCE

Equity Bond

Lump sum invested in a single premium life insurance policy linked to units in a fund of mainly UK shares. Some Equity Bonds are linked to a single unit trust or a fund of several trusts. The units reflect the value of the assets held in the fund plus the accumulated income. You can change the investment link between equity, international, fixed-interest, money, property and mixed funds of the same company without cashing the policy.

Who can invest   Anyone.

How worthwhile   Consider *Investment Trust Personal Equity Plan* instead as it has the same type of investment but is tax free. Otherwise consider instead *Unit Trust invested in UK Shares* unless you regularly use up your annual capital gains tax exemption.

Minimum   £500 to £5,000, usually £1,000.

Maximum   None.

Suitable   Lump sums.

Money back   At any time or when you die. You get the current value of the units.

Interest   Income is accumulated.

Interest paid   When you cash the policy or die. You can choose to withdraw a certain amount each half-year; sometimes yearly, quarterly or monthly.

Tax   The life company pays tax on income and capital gains at a rate equal to the basic rate of tax which usually reflect in the price of the units. With bonds linked to individual unit trusts, capital gains tax may be deducted from the proceeds of your policy before you get it, whereas had you invested directly it would usually fall within your individual annual exemption. The proceeds and all withdrawals come tax paid for basic rate taxpayers. Non-taxpayers cannot reclaim the tax. Higher rate taxpayers have to pay extra tax when they cash the policy; and on withdrawals of over 5% a year of original investment or if they go on for more than 20 years.

Fees to pay   Charges deducted from your investment are 5% to 10% (usually 5%) initially and usually ¾% to 1% yearly although trusts which the fund invests in may charge 1% to 1½% a year instead or in addition.

Passbook   None. Insurance policy issued.

Children   Convenient for a trust set up for children to avoid inheritance tax and probate.

Risk   High. The value of the units goes down as well as up. UK life companies are covered by a 90% compensation scheme based on the current value of your units if the company fails.

How to invest   Get details from a few companies and compare what they have to offer or ask an independent financial adviser. The 'past performance' of how the units have risen or fallen are monitored monthly in *Money Management* magazine.

Where from   Many life companies.

It is better to invest in shares through a personal equity plan than through a life insurance policy.

LIFE INSURANCE

Fixed-Interest, Gilt, Money or Convertible Bond

Lump sum invested in a single premium life insurance policy linked to a fund of fixed-interest securities or to a fund invested in bank or other interest-bearing deposits. The units reflect the value of the assets held in the fund plus the accumulated income. You can change the investment link between equity, international, fixed-interest, money, property and mixed funds of the same company without cashing the policy.

Who can invest   Anyone.

How worthwhile   Compare with *Stock Unit Trust Invested in Gilts* and *Stock Government Fixed-Interest.* Compare Money and Convertible Bonds with *Unit Trust Cash Trust* and direct investment in building societies, banks and offshore banks. Unsuitable for non-taxpayers.

Minimum   £500 to £5,000, usually £1,000.

Maximum   None.

Suitable   Lump sums.

Money back   At any time or when you die. You get the current value of the units.

Interest   Income is accumulated.

Interest paid   When you cash in or die. You can choose to withdraw a certain amount each half-year; sometimes yearly, quarterly or monthly.

Tax   The life company pays tax on the accumulated income at a rate equal to the basic rate of tax which usually reflect in the price of the units. Gains on fixed interest stock held by these funds are normally exempt from tax. The proceeds and all withdrawals are tax paid to basic rate taxpayers. Non-taxpayers cannot reclaim the tax. Higher rate taxpayers have to pay extra tax when they cash in; and on withdrawals of over 5% a year of original investment or if they go on for more than 20 years.

Fees to pay   Charges deducted from your investment are 3% to 10% (usually 5%) initially (sometimes less for 'Money' bonds); usually ¾% to 1% yearly.

Passbook   None. Insurance policy issued.

Children   Unsuitable.

Risk   Fixed-Interest or Gilt: medium; the value of the units can go down as well as up. Money and Convertible: none. UK life companies are covered by a 90% compensation scheme based on the current value of your units if the company fails.

How to invest   Get details from a few companies and compare what they have to offer or ask an independent financial adviser. The 'past performance' of how the units have risen or fallen are monitored monthly in *Money Management* magazine.

Where from   Many life companies.

Some companies have launched funds linked to Government Index Linked Stock. You should consider investing directly instead.

LIFE INSURANCE

International Bond

Lump sum invested in a single premium life insurance policy linked to units in a fund of stocks and shares mainly invested overseas. A few, called *Currency Bond*, invest in foreign currency bank accounts or fixed-interest stocks. Some bonds are linked to a single unit trust investing overseas. The units reflect the value of the assets held in the fund plus the accumulated income. You can change the investment link between international, equity, fixed-interest, money, property and mixed funds of the same company without cashing the policy.

Who can invest   Anyone.

How worthwhile   If you do not regularly use your capital gains exemption limit, consider instead *Unit Trust Invested in Overseas Shares* which give you the same investment opportunity but do not automatically deduct tax. Unsuitable for non-taxpayers.

Minimum   £500 to £5,000, usually £1,000.

Maximum   None.

Suitable   Lump sums.

Money back   At any time or when you die. You get the current value of the units.

Interest   Income is accumulated.

Interest paid   When you cash the policy or die. You can choose to withdraw a certain amount each half-year; sometimes yearly, quarterly or monthly.

Tax   The life company pays tax on income and capital gains at a rate equal to the basic rate of tax which usually reflect in the price of the units. With bonds linked to individual unit trusts, capital gains tax may be deducted from the proceeds of your policy before you get it, whereas had you invested directly it would usually fall within your individual annual exemption. The proceeds and all withdrawals come tax paid for basic rate taxpayers. Non-taxpayers cannot reclaim the tax. Higher rate taxpayers have to pay extra tax when they cash the policy; and on withdrawals of over 5% a year or if they go on for more than 20 years.

Fees to pay   Charges deducted from your investment are 5% to 10% (usually 5%) initially and usually ¾% to 1% yearly although unit trusts which the fund invests in may charge 1½% a year instead or in addition.

Passbook   None. Insurance policy issued.

Children   Unsuitable.

Risk   High. The value of the units goes down as well as up. UK life companies are covered by a 90% compensation scheme based on the current value of your units if the company fails.

How to invest   Get details from a few companies and compare what they have to offer or ask an independent financial adviser. The 'past performance' of how the units have risen or fallen are monitored monthly in *Money Management* magazine.

Where from   Many life companies.

Some companies have higher charges on premiums under £2,000, say.

LIFE INSURANCE

Mixed Bond

(*Also called Managed Bond, 3-Way Bond, Multiple Bond, Balanced Bond*)

Lump sum invested in a single premium life insurance policy linked to units in a fund of shares, property and possibly fixed interest stocks and bank deposits managed by professionals who seek to raise your return by choosing the right kind of investment at the right time. The units reflect the value of the assets held in the fund plus any accumulated income. You can change the investment link to a property, equity, international, fixed-interest or bank deposit fund of the same company without cashing the policy. Beware of 'managed' bonds which are really 'equity' bonds and have no property or fixed interest investments.

Who can invest Anyone.

How worthwhile Potentially good value for taxpayers who choose a company which does well. An alternative might be to split your investment between *Unit Trusts* (or *Investment Trusts*), *Life Insurance Property Bond* and *Stock Government Fixed Interest*.

Minimum £500 to £5,000, usually £1,000.

Maximum None.

Suitable Lump sums.

Money back At any time or when you die. You usually get the current value of the units.

Interest Income and rents are accumulated.

Interest paid When you cash the policy or die. You can choose to withdraw a certain amount each half-year; sometimes yearly, quarterly or monthly.

Tax The life company pays tax on income and capital gains at a rate equal to the basic rate of tax which usually reflects in the price of the units. The proceeds and all withdrawals are tax paid for basic rate taxpayers. Non-taxpayers cannot reclaim the tax. Higher rate taxpayers have to pay extra tax when they cash in; and on withdrawals of over 5% a year or if they go on for more than 20 years.

Fees to pay Charges deducted from your investment are usually 5% to 10% (usually 5%) and usually 3/4% to 1% yearly.

Passbook None. Insurance policy issued.

Children Convenient for a trust set up for children to avoid inheritance tax and probate.

Risk Moderate to high. The value of units goes down as well as up. UK authorised insurance companies are covered by a 90% compensation scheme based on the current value of your units.

How to invest Get details from a few companies and compare what they have to offer or ask an independent financial adviser. The 'past performance' of how the units have risen or fallen are monitored monthly in *Money Management* magazine.

Where from Many life companies.

Some companies have higher charges on premiums under £2,000. Others give discounts for large amounts.

LIFE INSURANCE

Property Bond

Lump sum investment in a single premium life insurance policy linked to units in a fund of properties (ie shops, offices, warehouses, factories and property development). The properties are valued regularly by independent valuers and their valuation plus income from rents reflect in the price of the units. You can change the investment link to a mixed, fixed-interest, money, equity or international fund of the same company without cashing the policy. 'Property' funds which invest in property company shares are really 'equity' funds.

Who can invest Anyone.

How worthwhile Potentially fair to good value for taxpayers as a long-term investment (over 5 years). Compare with *Property Commercial Direct Investment.*

Minimum £500 to £5,000, usually £1,000.

Maximum None.

Suitable Lump sums.

Money back At any time or when you die. You get the current value of the units (sometimes a bit more if you die). Most companies can defer payment for up to 6 months if they cannot sell a property.

Interest Rents and other income are accumulated.

Interest paid When you cash the policy or die. You can choose to withdraw a certain amount each half-year; yearly, quarterly or monthly.

Tax The insurance company pays tax on income and capital gains at the basic tax rate which reflects in the unit price. The proceeds and all withdrawals are tax paid for basic rate taxpayers. Non-taxpayers cannot reclaim the tax. Higher rate taxpayers have to pay extra when they cash; and on withdrawals over 5% a year or if they go on for more than 20 years.

Fees to pay Charges deducted from your investment are initially 5% to 10% (5% for companies listed below) ¾% to 1% yearly. Some companies can raise the yearly charge. Maintenance, legal, valuation and rent collection costs are also deducted.

Passbook None. Insurance policy issued.

Children Convenient for a trust set up for children to avoid inheritance tax and probate.

Risk Moderate to high. The value of units can go down as well as up. UK authorised life companies are covered by 90% compensation if the company fails.

How to invest Get details from a few companies and compare them or ask an independent financial adviser. 'Past performance' is monitored monthly in *Money Management* magazine.

Where from Abbey Life, Albany Life, Allied Dunbar, AXA Equity & Law, Barclays Life, Hill Samuel, Legal & General, London Life, NM Financial Management, Refuge, Save & Prosper, Scottish Widows, Standard Life.

Cannon Lincoln, NM Financial Management have property bonds investing in residential furnished property. Allied Dunbar also has an American Property Bond.

LIFE INSURANCE

School Fees Educational Trust

(Also called School Fees Capital Plan, School Fee Trust Plan)

A means of paying school fees in advance. You pay a lump sum into a trust for a child which pays part or all of the fees when they are needed. You have a choice of a fixed return, one linked to a unit fund or 'with-profits'. The fees can be pre-paid for one term or up to 15 years; the payments last for 2 to 10 years. After you have joined the scheme you may be able to change your mind about when and to whom you want the fees paid.

Who can invest   Anyone, eg parents, grandparents, godparents.

How worthwhile   Good value for higher rate taxpaying parents who give the money themselves. Convenient for earmarking gifts from grandparents, etc, especially where the money is not needed for fees for a few years. Compare with the return you might get for paying fees in advance direct to a school and getting a discount (but check if any penalty on change of school).

Minimum   None to £3,000.

Maximum   None.

Suitable   Lump sums. Regular savings at Equitable Life, School Fees Insurance Agency.

Money back   Option for the person who gives the money to get it back before fees start to be paid (there can be a penalty). If the child dies, 90% to 100% of the money is returned plus interest. Fees can usually be paid for a second child, if the first no longer requires them.

Interest   Usually fixed, it is accumulated and then paid out together with capital to pay for school fees. Equitable Life (Plans A and B) offers with-profits or unit-linked investments.

School Fees Insurance Agency has unit-linked plan (Investment Annuity Plan).

Interest paid   Each term to pay school fees. Cheques are usually sent to the parents payable to the chosen school. Parents must pay the balance and for any extras.

Tax   The proceeds and all fees payments are tax paid. Payments to or from the scheme (other than by parents) may be liable to inheritance tax if they exceed the various exemptions – see Chapter 5.

Fees to pay   Charges included in the rate you get. If you change your plans, there may be small extra charges.

Passbook   Copy deed and statement.

Children   Unsuitable for a child to invest in. He or she is the beneficiary of the school fees.

Risk   UK life companies are covered by a 90% compensation scheme.

How to invest   Get details from the companies listed below and compare what they have to offer.

Where from   Equitable Life (School Fee Trust Plan), Save & Prosper (School Fees Capital Plan), School Fees Insurance Agency (Capital Payment Plans).

For other ways of saving for school fees turn to Chapter 11.

LIFE INSURANCE

Stock Market Guaranteed Bond

(Also known as Capital Guarantee Bond; Guaranteed Growth Account)

Lump sum invested in a single premium life insurance policy which rises in line with the growth in value of the FT-SE 100 Share Index for 5 years. You are guaranteed to get your money back over five years and schemes may also guarantee a minimum interest rate eg 2.5% a year too. If you want your money back early you get less interest but you usually still get all your capital back. Some schemes offer more complicated guarantees which offer you the chance of 'locking in' an existing gain. The bonds are issued for a limited time and different issues from the same company will have different guarantees.

Who can invest   Anyone.

How worthwhile   Compare with *Building Society Stock Market Guaranteed Bond* which may offer better guarantees and lower charges. If the stock market is in the doldrums by the time the bond matures, you get a poor return although no loss of capital; if you stop early you also get a poor return. Higher rate taxpayers consider instead *Unit Trust Index Tracker*.

Minimum   £1,000 to £5,000.

Maximum   Varies.

Suitable   Lump sums.

Money back   After 5 years. Or earlier but with some penalty.

Interest   Variable. Linked to the rise in the FT-SE 100 Share Index sometimes with a guaranteed minimum.

Interest paid   After 5 years. Or when you cash, if you cash early.

Tax   The life company pays tax on income and capital gains at a rate equal to the basic rate of tax. The proceeds and any profits are basic rate tax paid for basic rate taxpayers. Non-taxpayers cannot reclaim the tax. Higher rate taxpayers pay extra.

Fees to pay   Charges deducted from your investment are usually 5% initial; 1.5% yearly.

Passbook   Statement sent.

Children   Unsuitable.

Risk   Full value of original investment on withdrawal. 90% compensation scheme.

How to invest   See surveys and adverts in the press. Ask for details and compare the guarantees and terms.

Where from   Life insurance companies.

Building societies also offer this type of investment, generally with lower charges.

LIFE INSURANCE

Unit-Linked Savings Plan

A commitment to save a fixed amount (usually monthly or yearly) usually for 10 years or more. After deduction of the company's charges, the remainder of your money is linked to the price of units in a unit trust or other type of fund (eg property, mixed, fixed-interest) run by the life company.

Who can invest Anyone in good health.

How worthwhile Poor to good value for savings kept going for 10 years or more depending on the policy chosen. Very little basis for predicting in advance whether you will do well or badly. 'Maximum Investment Plans' may give potentially better value. Can be used to avoid inheritance tax if written 'in trust'. Otherwise consider instead *Investment Trust Personal Equity Plan*, *Unit Trust Personal Equity Plan*.

Minimum £10 to £100 a month.

Maximum None.

Suitable Regular savings.

Money back You get the value of the units allocated to you after 10 years, either when you choose or at an 'option' or 'maturity' date; some plans allow you to withdraw a 'tax-free' income after 10 years. On death there is usually a minimum guaranteed sum. You can stop saving at any time and take your money or leave it 'paid up' in the policy; either way in the early years you lose out heavily.

Interest Variable. Income from the investments is accumulated.

Interest paid When you cash the policy or when you die.

Tax The insurance company pays tax on income and capital gains at the basic tax rate which reflects in the price of the units; some deduct gains tax from the proceeds. There is no tax on the proceeds but there can be extra tax for higher rate taxpayers if you cash a policy before 10 years or if it is a 'non-qualifying' one. Make sure you are sold a 'qualifying' policy.

Fees to pay Charges are made by the life company and deducted from your investment. Some companies charge less for higher premiums. It is impossible for a layman to compare charges because they are deducted in different ways.

Passbook None. Insurance policy issued. Unit valuation sent yearly.

Children Policies can be 'in trust' for children to avoid probate and inheritance tax.

Risk Depends on the type of investment to which the policy is linked. The value of units can go down as well as up. UK life companies are covered by a 90% compensation scheme based on the current value of your units.

How to invest Ask an independent financial adviser to recommend a few companies with the lowest charges and good investment managers. Also ask Equitable Life, London Life, Professional Life and Provident Life for a quote.

Where from Many life companies.

Policies issued on or before 13 March 1984 normally get tax relief (at half the basic rate) on the premiums. Keep them going.

LIFE INSURANCE

With Profits Bond

Lump sum invested in a single premium life insurance policy. Your life is insured for about the amount you invest to which profits or 'bonuses' are added every year. The rate of bonus can rise and fall; once a bonus is added to a policy, it is guaranteed but see *Risk*. The fixed sum insured plus bonuses plus a discretionary 'terminal bonus' is paid when you cash the policy or on earlier death. The bonds are likely to be better value, the longer you hold them. They are not always available for investment. And several companies make you take them as part of a 'package' with other investment links.

Who can invest   Anyone.

How worthwhile   A new form of investment without a track record. They have been described as a halfway house between a building society and the stockmarket. Compare with *Building Society Guaranteed Stock Market Bond*. Unsuitable for non-taxpayers.

Minimum   £500 to £5,000.

Maximum   Varies.

Suitable   Lump sums.

Money back   Within a few days but may be subject to a deduction in the early years.

Interest   Variable. Based on bonus rates at the discretion of the life company. When you cash, there may be a deduction called 'market value adjustment factor' but not if you die or at Legal & General, Scottish Provident if you make withdrawals of up to 7½% of the amount invested (ie no adjustment to income drawn).

Interest paid   When you cash or the person insured dies. You can withdraw a fixed amount each half-year; sometimes yearly, quarterly or monthly.

Tax   The life company pays tax on income and capital gains at a rate equal to the basic rate of tax and this is reflected in the bonus rate. The proceeds and any profits are tax paid for basic rate taxpayers. Non-taxpayers cannot reclaim the tax. Higher rate taxpayers pay extra.

Fees to pay   Charges deducted from your investment are usually 5% initial; yearly usually not explicit at the discretion of the life company.

Passbook   Statement sent.

Children   Unsuitable.

Risk   Original investment less initial charge plus value of bonuses on withdrawal but subject to an extra charge called 'market value adjustment factor'. Scottish Provident guarantees no 'market value adjustment' if you cash on any 5th policy anniversary (Legal & General also but only once after 10 years). 90% compensation scheme.

How to invest   See surveys and adverts in the press. Ask for details and compare the companies.

Where from   The following life insurance companies have offered schemes but may not have one available now: AXA Equity & Law, Commercial Union, Eagle Star, Equitable Life, Friends Provident, General Accident, Legal & General, Norwich Union, Scottish Provident.

LIFE INSURANCE

With-Profits Endowment Policy

A commitment to save a fixed amount (usually monthly or yearly) for a fixed term chosen by you of 10 to 25 years or more. In return a life (usually your own) is insured for a fixed amount to which profits called 'reversionary bonuses' are added every year. The rate of bonus can rise and fall but once a bonus has been added to a policy, it is guaranteed. The fixed sum insured plus bonuses, plus with most companies a discretionary 'terminal bonus' are paid when the term ends or on earlier death.

Who can invest Anyone in good health. Better value the younger you are. The insured can be yourself or anyone in whom you have an insurable interest (eg your husband or wife). Joint policies available.

How worthwhile Poor to good value for taxpayers depending on the company chosen, for savings kept going for 10 years or more. Poor value if you give up saving before you complete the term.

Minimum £10–£20 a month.

Maximum None.

Suitable Regular savings.

Money back On maturity or death. You can stop saving at any time and take your money, 'the surrender value'; or leave it 'paid up' in the policy. Either way in the first few years you will lose most if not all your savings; even well into the policy there can be a heavy deduction.

Interest Variable. Based on bonus rate at the discretion of the life company.

Interest paid When policy matures or the person insured dies.

Tax The insurance company pays tax on the income and capital gains it makes which reflects in your bonus rate. There is no tax on the proceeds but there can be extra tax for higher rate taxpayers if you cash a policy before 10 years or if it is a 'non-qualifying' one. Make sure you are sold a 'qualifying' policy.

Fees to pay Premiums may include a policy fee (eg £1 a month) which make a £50 a month policy better value than a £15 a month one.

Passbook None. Insurance policy issued. Bonus statements normally issued yearly.

Children Policies can be 'in trust' for children to avoid probate and inheritance tax.

Risk The 'terminal' bonus may account for about half the proceeds of a 25 year policy which makes 'with-profits' a potentially risky investment as a terminal bonus can disappear overnight if the company decides to reduce or remove it. UK authorised insurance companies are covered by a 90% compensation scheme less 'excessive' benefits.

How to invest Ask an independent financial adviser to find the best company for your age and term based on past performance and the company's financial strength which for a 25 year term should be from one of the companies listed below.

Where from AXA Equity & Law, Clerical Medical, Commercial Union, Eagle Star, Friends Provident, GA Life, Norwich Union, Royal London, Scottish Amicable, Scottish Life, Scottish Widows, Standard Life.

Policies issued on or before 13 March 1984 normally get tax relief (at half the basic rate). Keep them going.

LIFE INSURANCE

With-Profits Flexible Policy

A commitment to save a fixed monthly amount for at least 10 years. In return your life is insured for a fixed sum to which profits called 'reversionary bonuses' are added every year. The rate of bonus can rise and fall but once a bonus has been added to a policy it is guaranteed. The fixed sum insured plus bonuses are paid, plus with some companies a discretionary terminal bonus, if you die or whenever you choose after 10 years. Some policies have to end after 20 to 25 years or when you reach 65.

Who can invest   Anyone in good health usually up to age 50, 55, 60, 65 or 70.

How worthwhile   Fair to good value depending on the company chosen, for savings you think you will need in 10 to 20 years' time. Consider instead a series of *Life Insurance With-Profits Endowment Policies*. Similar policies, called 'whole life' policies can be used 'in trust', to avoid inheritance tax.

Minimum   £10 to £25 a month.

Maximum   None.

Suitable   Regular savings.

Money back   On death or at any time after 10 years. If you stop saving before 10 years there will be a heavy penalty.

Interest   Variable. Based on bonus rate.

Interest paid   When you cash the policy after 10 years or when you die.

Tax   The life company pays tax on the income and capital gains it makes which reflects in your bonus rate. There is extra tax for higher rate taxpayers if you cash a policy before 10 years or if it is a 'non-qualifying' one. Make sure you are sold a 'qualifying' policy.

Fees to pay   The premiums may include a fixed policy fee (eg £1 a month) which make a £50 a month policy better value than a £10 a month one.

Passbook   None. Insurance policy issued. Bonus statements normally issued yearly.

Children   Policies can be 'in trust' for children to avoid probate and inheritance tax.

Risk   A cut in 'terminal bonus' can seriously erode the return from your policy. UK authorised insurance companies are covered by a 90% compensation scheme less 'excessive' benefits. For complete safety use an old established company.

How to invest   Ask an independent financial adviser to get details of 'past performance' (not future projections) from the best companies for your age, and to advise you on which companies are the strongest financially.

Where from   Consider the companies listed under *Life Insurance With-Profits Endowment*. Some only issue 'whole life' policies which are designed to pay out the best return on death, not if you cash them in.

With life insurance you get better value by choosing the company rather than letting the company choose you.

LOCAL AUTHORITY

Fixed Term Loan

Lump sum invested for a fixed term of 1 to 7 years at a fixed rate of interest. Some local authorities offer short-term loans for from 7 to 364 days but usually for amounts over £100,000. No additions or withdrawals allowed.

Who can invest   Anyone 18 or over.

How worthwhile   Taxpayers compare with *Life Insurance Growth* or *Income Bond, National Savings Fixed Issue Certificate*. Non-taxpayers and taxpayers compare with *National Savings Capital Bond, Co-operative Society Term Account*. Terms over 5 years not recommended. Also compare with *Stock Government Fixed Interest, Stock Debenture and Loan*.

Minimum   £500–£1,000.

Maximum   Varies.

Suitable   Lump sums.

Money back   At end of term.

Interest   Fixed. Rates vary between different local authorities and depend on the length of term and minimum allowed. Larger sums (eg over £5,000) may earn higher interest.

Interest paid   Usually half-yearly. Sometimes at end of term. Some short-term loans pay monthly.

Tax   Since 6 April 1991 (and before 6 April 1986) basic rate tax is deducted from the interest. Non-taxpayers can reclaim the tax from the Inland Revenue (or have interest paid with no deduction). Higher rate taxpayers have to pay extra. See also Chapter 4.

Fees to pay   None.

Passbook   None. Certificate issued.

Children   The investment must be held in an adult's name.

Risk   None.

How to invest   Subscribe to *Moneyfacts* which includes a table of rates updated each month. Phone the treasurer of the local authority you choose, check the rate, and ask for an application form; or agree terms by phone and send a cheque with a letter confirming the details.

Where from   Local authorities.

You can also invest in a local authority through Negotiable (Yearling) Bonds. These are issued by a number of local authorities every Tuesday for 1, 2 year or longer periods. The interest rate for all bonds issued on the same day is the same eg 1 year 6½%, 2 years 6% and is fixed for the term of the bond. Bonds can also be bought and sold on the stockmarket. If you buy for less than the redemption value you can make a capital gain which is exempt from capital gains tax.

NATIONAL SAVINGS

Capital Bond

A lump sum investment which accumulates interest at a fixed rate and should be held the full 5 years. You can get your money back early but you will receive lower interest.

Who can invest Anyone.

How worthwhile Series G good value, especially for non-taxpayers who want to accumulate interest. Taxpayers compare with *Life Insurance Growth Bond, Local Authority Fixed Term Loan, Stock Government Fixed Interest, Stock Loan and Debenture.* Higher rate taxpayers consider instead *National Savings Fixed Issue Certificate.*

Minimum £100. Larger purchases and additions must be in multiples of £100.

Maximum £250,000 for Series B to G.

Money back About 2 weeks, in multiples of £100 provided £100 remains; otherwise whole investment must be cashed. There is always an interest penalty if you cash early. Ask for a repayment form and post paid envelope at a post office.

Interest Fixed for each series. Series G pays equivalent of 7.75% a year. For current rate at post offices, on Channel 4 Teletext page 543 or phone 071-605 9483 or 9484.

Interest paid Yearly, added to the bond on anniversary of purchase.

Tax Not deducted. Taxpayers are liable to pay income tax on the interest which should be declared on a tax return. Interest is credited at an increasing rate, so the tax bill grows year by year; it is approximately twice as high in year 5 as in year 1.

Fees to pay None.

Passbook Certificate issued and you get a yearly interest statement.

Children Suitable, especially for money given by a parent which is intended to accumulate until the child is 18 (see Chapter 11); money repaid to parent or guardian designated at outset if bond matures under age 7. If you invest as a trustee on the application write 'as trustee for' and the name of the beneficiary in brackets after your name; do the same after your signature. Maximum 2 trustees and 2 beneficiaries for each trust.

Risk None.

How to invest Ask for an application at a post office. Pay over the counter. If you prefer you can invest by post (ask for a post paid envelope too).

Where from Post offices.

If you give money to a child you don't have to put the money in the child's own name. It can be held by the parents, for instance, as trustees. Any tax advantages apply regardless of whose name the account is in. For more details see Chapters 4 and 11.

NATIONAL SAVINGS

Children's Bonus Bond

A lump sum investment made for a child by a parent, grandparent or friend which accumulates interest at a fixed tax exempt rate and has a bonus after 5 years. The money can be held in the bond until the child is 21 under extension terms which will be announced from time to time.

Who can invest   Anyone aged over 16 for a child under 16.

How worthwhile   Good value for taxpayer donors. Unsuitable for non-taxpayers.

Minimum   £25. And then in £25 units.

Maximum   £1,000 for all Issues combined.

Suitable   Lump sums. Regular savings.

Money back   You will lose the bonus and there will be an interest penalty if you cash early.

Interest   5% a year fixed plus, for *Issue E*: bonus of 18.28% of purchase price after 5 years equivalent to 7.85% a year. For current rate, see Channel 4 Teletext page 543 or phone 071-605 9483 or 9484. Bonuses for previous issues are as follows: *Issue A* 47.36%, equivalent to 11.84% a year; *Issue B* 40.12%, equivalent to 10.9% a year; *Issue C* 34.16%, equivalent to 10.1% a year; *Issue D* 26.96%, equivalent to 9.1% a year.

Interest   paid   Accumulated to increase its value.

Tax   Interest and bonus are tax free and need not be entered on a tax return.

Fees to pay   None.

Passbook   None. Plan certificate provided.

Children   Designed as a gift to the child.

Risk   None.

How to invest   Get an application from a post office. You can either pay over the counter or send the money to National Savings (ask for a post paid envelope).

Where from   Post offices.

The only snag about this investment is that the child has complete control of the money invested from the age of 16 onward.

NATIONAL SAVINGS

FIRST Option Bond

A lump sum investment which accumulates interest at a fixed rate determined at the outset for 12 months. After 12 months you can withdraw or leave your money for another 12 months at the then current fixed rate plus a bonus for sums over £20,000. If you want to withdraw before 12 months, you get no interest; if you want to withdraw at any other time, you get interest at half the agreed rate since the last anniversary date.

Who can invest   Anyone over age 16. Joint accounts for 2 people are allowed.

How worthwhile   Fair value for basic rate taxpayer and non-taxpayers who expect interest rates to remain the same or fall over the 12 month period. Better value for small amounts (ie under £10,000) or between £20,000 and £25,000. Compare with *Building Society Term Share, Co-operative Society Term Account, Stock Government Fixed Interest*. Higher rate taxpayers also compare with *Life Insurance Growth Bond*.

Minimum   £1,000.

Maximum   £250,000.

Suitable   Lump sums.

Money back   A few days. Ask for post paid envelope and a form at a post office. There is no interest if you cash early in the first 12 months and interest is paid at half the rate since the last anniversary with no bonus if you cash other than at an anniversary.

Interest   Fixed. 0.4% more interest before tax paid for amounts over £20,000.

Interest paid   Added to your investment at the end of each 12 month period or when you withdraw.

Tax   Basic rate tax is deducted from the interest. Non-taxpayers can reclaim the tax from the Inland Revenue. Higher rate taxpayers pay extra.

Fees to pay   None but see *Money back*.

Passbook   Statement sent with each transaction or yearly.

Children   Over age 16 only or held in trust for up to 2 beneficiaries of any age.

Risk   Full value of original investment on withdrawal.

How to invest   Ask for a form and post paid envelope at a post office.

Where from   Send the completed form to FIRST Option Bonds, Glasgow G58 1SB.

Value for money on this investment depends on how the interest rate turns out compared to a variable interest rate at a building society.

NATIONAL SAVINGS

Income Bond

An investment which pays out monthly interest suitable for people who can tie up their money for at least a year. You can get your money back in full by giving 3 months' notice to expire after the end of the first 12 months you have held the bond. You can get your money back within the first 12 months but interest will be paid at half the usual rate.

Who can invest　Anyone.

How worthwhile　Compare with *Building Society Monthly Income Account* or *Offshore Bank Notice Account* paying interest monthly.

Minimum　£2,000. Larger purchases and additions must be in multiples of £1,000.

Maximum　£250,000 for individual or joint accounts.

Suitable　Lump sums.

Money back　At 3 months notice in multiples of £1,000 provided at least £2,000 remains; otherwise whole investment must be cashed. If end of notice period is after the end of the first year there is no penalty; if it is within the first year interest is reduced to half. Ask for a repayment form and post-paid envelope at a post office.

Interest　Variable. Changes announced 6 weeks in advance. Current rate at post offices, on Channel 4 Teletext page 543 or phone 071-605 9483.

Interest paid　Monthly on the 5th direct to a bank, building society, or National Savings account. The first payment is made on the next interest date after you have held the bond 6 weeks and will include all interest from the date of purchase.

Tax　Not deducted. Taxpayers are liable to pay income tax on the interest which should be declared on a tax return.

Fees to pay　None.

Passbook　Certificate issued.

Children　Unsuitable. Consider *National Savings Capital Bond* or *Investment Account* instead. Income bonds are suitable for investment by the trustees of a formally constituted trust with children as the beneficiaries. Maximum 2 beneficiaries for each trust.

Risk　None.

How to invest　Ask for an application form and post-paid envelope at a post office.

Where from　Send the completed application to National Savings, Blackpool, FY3 9YP.

Always leave some of your money invested where you can get at it at once or within a few days without penalty. Only tie up money for as long as you are sure you will not need it.

NATIONAL SAVINGS

Investment Account

An account into which you can pay at any post office. To withdraw you must give 1 month's notice.

Who can invest   Anyone. Accounts can be held jointly.

How worthwhile   Good value for small amounts. Otherwise consider instead *Building Society 30 Day Notice Account* or *Offshore Bank Notice Account.*

Minimum   £20 each time you make a deposit.

Maximum   £100,000, plus accumulated interest for all National Savings Investment Accounts.

Suitable   Lump sums. Regular savings.

Money back   Any amount at 1 month's notice from the day the withdrawal application reaches National Savings in Glasgow. Ask for a repayment form and post-paid envelope at a post office. It can be paid in cash at a post office or by cheque.

Interest   Variable. Current rate at post offices, on Channel 4 Teletext page 543 or phone 071-605 9483 or 9484.

Interest paid   Yearly added to account on 31 December.

Tax   Not deducted. Taxpayers are liable to pay income tax on the interest which should be declared on a tax return.

Fees to pay   None.

Passbook   Yes, called a bank book.

Children   Suitable. Under 7 a relative or friend can open an account in a child's name where withdrawals may be made by the child's parent or guardian. At age 7 the child can withdraw on his or her own signature; use application form DNS26B (with a brown stripe on the edge). An account can be opened by anyone as trustees for money belonging to a child. Maximum 2 trustees and 2 beneficiaries for each trust; to open such a trust account you should write to National Savings, Glasgow G58 1SB.

Risk   None. Full value of original investment returned on withdrawal.

How to invest   At a post office or by post.

Where from   Any post office or write to National Savings Bank, Glasgow G58 1SB.

National Savings Ordinary Account allows you to pay in and withdraw up to £100 in cash at any post office. Interest is 3.75% if you have more than £500 in the account for the whole calendar year; otherwise it is 2.5%. No interest on deposit or withdrawal during the calendar month in which it is made. Interest up to £70 a year per person is tax exempt. Minimum £10 each deposit; maximum £10,000 overall. Otherwise similar to National Savings Investment Account. From age 7, a child can operate the account itself.

NATIONAL SAVINGS

Index-Linked Certificates

(*Formerly known as Grannybonds*)

A way of linking your investment to the Retail Prices Index. On top you get a fixed interest rate, which is lower if you stop before 5 years. Interest, once added, is index-linked too. For how the Retail Prices Index has risen in the past see Appendix 2.

Who can invest   Anyone.

How worthwhile   Good value for taxpayers, especially higher rate taxpayers. Poor value for non-taxpayers.

Minimum   £100 (four units).

Maximum   £10,000 (400 units) and you can also reinvest a further £20,000 from other fixed or index-linked issues which are more than 5 years old. You may hold more if you inherit them. Single maximum applies to joint holdings. Certificates may also be held in trust thus doubling the maximum investment. You may buy these in addition to previous issues of Index-Linked Certificates.

Suitable   Lump sums. Regular savings.

Money back   About 2 weeks. Ask for a repayment form and post-paid envelope at a post office or bank. Any number of £25 units may be cashed. During first year: your original investment returned. After first year: index-linking and interest added.

Interest   Variable. For the *6th Issue*: If held for the full 5 years you get index-linking of your initial investment *and* 1½% in year 1; 2% in year 2; 2¾% in year 3; 3¾% in year 4 and 6.32% in year 5. This is equivalent to 3.25% a year. For current rate phone 071-605 9483 or 9484.

Interest paid   When certificates cashed.

Tax   All increases in the value of the certificates are tax-free. It need not be declared on a tax return.

Fees to pay   None.

Passbook   None. You get a certificate. If you do not have a holder's number card, you will be given one. This covers all issues of National Savings Certificates. Its number should be quoted if you withdraw or buy more certificates. You should have a separate holder's card for a trust holding.

Children   Convenient for gifts. Certificates in the name of a child under 7 can normally be cashed by a parent or guardian.

Risk   None. Full value of original investment returned on withdrawal.

How to invest   Pay by cash or cheque. You will be asked to fill in a form and sent the certificates by post. If you are buying for the whole family you may need a separate cheque for each holding.

Where from   Post offices and most banks.

Previous issues of Index-Linked Certificates were called 2nd Index-Linked Issue and Retirement Issue Certificates. These receive a bonus of 4% of the 5 year value payable after 10 years when they should be re-invested elsewhere. Details of the 3rd, 4th, 5th and 6th issues are given in Appendix 3.

NATIONAL SAVINGS

Fixed Issue Certificates

A lump sum which accumulates interest at a fixed rate and which should be held for 5 years to gain full interest.

Who can invest Anyone.

How worthwhile Good value for higher rate taxpayers provided interest rates don't rise over 5 years, in which case might be poor value; see also *National Savings Yearly Plan*. Poor value for non-taxpayers who should consider instead *National Savings Capital Bond*. Basic rate taxpayers compare with *Life Insurance Growth or Income Bond* or *Local Authority Fixed Term Loan*.

Minimum £100. Then certificates are issued in multiples of £25.

Maximum *40th Issue*: £10,000 but you can also reinvest a further £20,000 from other fixed or index-linked issues you hold which are more than 5 years old (see Appendix 3). You may hold more if you inherit them. Single maximum applies to joint holdings. Certificates may also be held in trust thus doubling the maximum investment. You may buy these in addition to other issues of National Savings Certificates.

Suitable Lump sums.

Money back About 2 weeks. In cash at a post office or by cheque. Ask for a repayment form and post-paid envelope at a post office or bank. Any number of £25 units may be cashed.

Interest Fixed. For the *40th Issue*: No interest until the end of year 1 when 4% is added. It is then added every 3 months at the following yearly rate: 2nd year 4.4%; 3rd 5.75%; 4th 6.75%; 5th 7.9%. This works out at 5.75% a year if certificates are held for 5 years. For current rate phone 071-605 9483 or 9484.

Interest paid When certificates cashed. You can draw a yearly 'income' by cashing some of your £25 units but it is better to spend capital, equivalent to the interest, from another investment eg a building society account.

Tax Interest is tax-free. It need not be declared on a tax return.

Fees to pay None.

Passbook None. You get a certificate. If you do not have a holder's number card, you will be given one. This card covers all issues of National Savings Certificates. Its number should be quoted if you withdraw or buy more certificates. You should have a separate holder's card for a trust holding.

Children Consider *National Savings Children's Bonus Bond* and *National Savings Capital Bond* instead. Certificates in the name of a child under 7 can normally be cashed by a parent or guardian.

Risk None. Full value of original investment returned on withdrawal.

How to invest Pay by cash or cheque. You will be asked to fill in a form and sent the certificates by post. If you are buying for the whole family, you may need a separate cheque for each holding.

Where from Post offices and banks.

Many past issues of National Savings Certificates pay very poor interest even for higher rate taxpayers. If you hold them, you should re-invest elsewhere. To see whether other issues are worth keeping see Appendix 3.

NATIONAL SAVINGS

Premium Bond

Once a month ERNIE (Electronic Random Number Indicator Equipment) selects £1 bond numbers, at random, to win prizes totalling about £10 million. Monthly prizes include £50, £100, £500, £1,000, £5,000, £10,000 and one prize of £250,000. In addition each week a prize of £25,000, £50,000 and £100,000 is won. Winning numbers of the big prizes are published in the newspapers but you will also be notified individually if you win.

Who can invest Anyone. Joint holdings not allowed. Parents and grandparents can buy bonds for children.

How worthwhile If you are lucky and enjoy a gamble, you may win a prize, but you may *not*. The odds on a £1 bond winning a prize are now 15,000 to 1. Worth considering only if you are a higher rate taxpayer. On average you can expect to win a prize a year with £1,250 invested. With £20,000 you can expect 16 prizes a year — though most will be £50 and you may win fewer or none at all.

Minimum £100; then in multiples of £10. Each unit is still £1, so £100 gives 100 chances of winning. Bonds become eligible to win 3 clear calendar months after the month of purchase.

Maximum £20,000.

Suitable Lump sums.

Money back About 2 weeks. Ask for a repayment form and post-paid envelope at a post office. A partial withdrawal of a multiple bond is allowed. By cheque or in cash at a post office.

Interest None.

Tax Prizes are free of income tax and capital gains tax. They need not be declared on a tax return.

Fees to pay None.

Passbook None. You are issued with a bond which is individually numbered for each £1 unit and a holder's number card — this number should be quoted if you withdraw or buy more bonds.

Children Under age 16: bonds must be bought by a parent, guardian or grandparent. Any prize money will normally be paid to parent or guardian. After age 16: the child takes over the bond.

Risk None. Full value of original investment returned on withdrawal.

How to invest Fill in a form and pay the money over the counter. You are sent the bonds by post.

Where from Any post office.

Always leave some of your money invested where you can get at it at once or within a few days without penalty. Only tie up money for as long as you are sure you will not need it.

NATIONAL SAVINGS

Yearly Plan

An agreement to save a fixed amount each month for a year. At the end of the year a certificate is issued to the value of the payment plus interest earned in that year. The certificate then earns a higher rate of interest for another 4 years. You can continue making regular payments a year at a time. Each year's payments buys a new certificate. You are notified of the fixed interest rate applying to your new agreement, and will receive a second certificate automatically after another year. If you want to vary the amount or payment date after the first year you have to start a new Yearly Plan. The interest rate for the first year's agreement is fixed on the day when your application is received at the Savings Certificate Office in Durham.

Who can invest   Anyone.

How worthwhile   Good value for taxpayers provided interest rates don't rise over 5 years, in which case might be poor value. Also consider *Building Society SAYE.* Non-taxpayers normally should not make a regular commitment to save.

Minimum   £20 a month.

Maximum   £400 a month in multiples of £5. The Yearly Plan may also be held in trust thus doubling the maximum holding.

Suitable   Regular savings.

Money back   Normally 3 weeks by cheque. Ask for a post-paid envelope and repayment form at a post office. No interest paid on payments cashed before a Certificate has been issued for them; 4% interest if cashed after 12 months; 4.5% a year interest on Certificate value for amounts cashed between month 13 and end of year 2; 5.25% a year interest on Certificate value if cashed in years 3 to 5.

Interest   Fixed. No interest until after each set of 12 payments is completed. Interest for these payments is added at a rate of 4%. Then 6% for the next 4 years. Overall return over 5 years currently 5.75%. For current rate, see Channel 4 Teletext page 543 or phone 071-605 9483 or 9484. If you don't cash after 5 years you get the variable general extension rate which applies to old issues of National Savings Certificates, see Appendix 3.

Interest paid   When Certificate is cashed.

Tax   Interest is tax-free. It need not be declared on a tax return.

Fees to pay   None.

Passbook   None. Certificates issued every 12 months for each Plan.

Children   Convenient for gifts from parents to save money in a child's name or held in trust (for a sole beneficiary only). Parents can open an account on a child's behalf if child under 7.

Risk   None. Full value of investment returned on withdrawal.

How to invest   Payments must be made by standing order from a bank, or building society account.

Where from   Application forms (buff coloured) from post offices. Trust purchases on special form (YP2, green coloured) from Yearly Plan Section, Durham DH99 1NS (091-386 4900).

OFFSHORE BANK

Foreign Currency Cheque Account

(Also called Multicurrency, Interbank, Offshore Reserve)

A bank account which holds money in foreign currencies eg US\$, Yen, DM. You choose one currency as your 'settlement' currency eg US\$ which debit card cash advances and payments are debited from, although cheques are normally first debited to the currency deposit they are drawn in; then the settlement account. Cheques can be written in any convertible currency, not just the ones you hold deposits in. At Charterhouse you have a different cheque book for each currency.

Who can invest   Anyone.

How worthwhile   Useful if you travel abroad a lot or receive payments in foreign currency. Poor to fair value for taxpayers. Unless you need a cheque book, compare with *Offshore Single Currency Fund*.

Minimum   Charterhouse, Guinness Mahon, Robert Fleming: US\$5,000, DM 7,500, Yen 1 million, £2,500 and currency equivalent of £2,500 for 21 other currencies at Charterhouse; most major currencies (including FF and SwF) at Guinness Mahon. Jardine Fleming: \$10,000.

Maximum   None.

Suitable   Lump sums.

Money back   A few days. Jardine Fleming offers a US\$ Visa card, Guinness Mahon an Amex Gold card.

Interest   Variable. No interest while balance below minimum (or sometimes a lower limit).

Interest paid   Added quarterly (monthly at Jardine Fleming).

Tax   *If account abroad, Isle of Man or Channel Islands:* No tax deducted but interest liable to income tax and should be declared on a tax return. *If account at UK bank:* Basic rate income tax deducted from interest for UK residents. Non-taxpayers can reclaim the tax from the Inland Revenue (or have interest paid with no deduction). Higher rate taxpayers pay extra. Gains on exchange rate changes on withdrawal liable to capital gains tax unless you spend the withdrawal (eg by paying a credit card bill).

Fees to pay   Jardine Fleming, Robert Fleming: none. Charterhouse: first 15 cheques free per quarter, then 50p (or equivalent) per cheque. Guinness Mahon US\$200 a year per Amex card.

Passbook   None. You get a separate statement for each currency quarterly (monthly at Jardine Fleming).

Children   Over 18 only except Charterhouse.

Risk   Full value of original investment in the foreign currency returned on withdrawal but if the currency has fallen against the £ sterling there will be a loss. Isle of Man banks only are covered by a compensation scheme 75% on the foreign currency equivalent of the first £20,000 for each investor.

How to invest   Phone for details.

Where from   *Isle of Man*: Jardine Fleming (Interbank; US\$, £; other currencies: DM, Yen, A\$, C\$ under review); Robert Fleming (Offshore Reserve; US\$, DM, Yen, £). *Guernsey*: Guinness Mahon (Private Interest Cheque Account; US\$, DM, Yen, FF, SwF and any major currency). *UK*: Charterhouse Bank (World Currency Account; choice of 25 currencies).

If you need to write occasional cheques in foreign currencies ask your bank for Eurocheques (unsuitable for US\$, C\$, A\$) or a foreign currency bank draft (over the counter at Barclays for US\$).

OFFSHORE BANK

Instant Access Account

(Also called Gold, Independent Reserve)

An account where you pay in by post and withdraw by post (or by immediate credit to a bank account for a charge). The account is held at a bank in the Isle of Man, Guernsey or Jersey. Higher rates of interest for larger sums. Some accounts not listed here, are exclusively for expatriates and may pay higher interest.

Who can invest Anyone.

How worthwhile Good value for non-taxpayers not eligible to have interest in a UK bank or building society paid with no tax deducted. Taxpayers consider instead *Building Society Postal Account*.

Minimum £1,000–£15,000. Minimum balance £5,000 at Yorkshire Guernsey.

Maximum £250,000–£3m.

Suitable Lump sums.

Money back By post or for large amounts directly credited to a bank account for a charge.

Interest Variable. More interest paid over £10,000, £25,000, £50,000, £100,000, £250,000.

Interest paid Usually yearly. Halifax (Jersey) half-yearly. By cheque; direct to a bank account; or left to accumulate.

Tax Not deducted. Taxpayers are liable to pay income tax on the interest which should be declared on a tax return.

Fees to pay None.

Passbook Or statements sent.

Children Suitable for gifts from grandparents or ones which are expected to be accumulated.

Risk Full value of original investment returned on withdrawal. Subsidiaries of building societies are guaranteed by the parent. *Isle of Man*: 75% compensation scheme on the first £20,000 for each investor.

How to invest Phone or write to a company listed below which are all subsidiaries of building societies or subscribe to *Moneyfacts*, monthly.

Where from *Your minimum £500*: Woolwich Guernsey (International Account), Portman (Channel Islands). *£2,500*: Woolwich Guernsey (International Account), Derbyshire (IoM), Portman (Channel Islands). *£25,000*: Derbyshire (IoM), Woolwich Guernsey (International Account), N & P (Overseas). *£50,000*: Derbyshire (IoM), Yorkshire Guernsey. *£100,000*: Derbyshire (IoM), Britannia IoM (Taxwise).

If you have over £25,000 you may do better by investing in an Offshore Bank Notice Account which requires no notice so long as the balance does not fall below £10,000: Britannia IoM (Special Deposit), Leeds Permanent IoM (Solid Gold).

OFFSHORE BANK

Notice Account

(*Also called Investment Account, Extra Interest, Monthly Income*)

An account with a bank, or a branch of a UK bank, or a subsidiary of a UK building society based in the Isle of Man, Guernsey or Jersey. It has a minimum investment which can be added to but notice of 60, 90 or 180 days must be given to withdraw.

Who can invest   Anyone.

How worthwhile   Good value for non-taxpayers not eligible to have interest in a UK bank or building society paid with no tax deducted. Taxpayers consider instead *Building Society 30, 60 or 90 Day Notice Accounts*. 180 days notice not recommended.

Minimum   £5,000. £500 Leeds Permanent Overseas. £2,500 Derbyshire IoM. £10,000 Portman Channel Islands.

Maximum   £500,000 to £5m.

Suitable   Lump sums.

Money back   All or part after 60 or 90 days notice. Some allow early withdrawal with a loss of interest on the notice period. Britannia (IoM) and Leeds Permanent (IoM) allow balance over £10,000 as no notice, no penalty as in UK.

Interest   Variable. More interest paid over £10,000, £25,000, £50,000 and £100,000.

Interest paid   Usually yearly. Added to account or paid by cheque or direct to a bank account or UK account. Monthly income option at slightly lower nominal interest rate.

Tax   Not deducted. Taxpayers are liable to pay income tax on the interest which should be declared on a tax return.

Fees to pay   None.

Passbook   Or statements sent.

Children   Suitable for gifts from grandparents or ones which are expected to be accumulated.

Risk   Full value of original investment returned on withdrawal. Subsidiaries of building societies are guaranteed by the parent. *Isle of Man*: 75% compensation scheme on the first £20,000 for each investor.

How to invest   Phone or write to one of the companies listed below in the Isle of Man, Guernsey, Jersey and Alderney which are all subsidiaries of building societies.

Where from   *Your minimum £2,500*: Derbyshire IoM (90 day), Yorkshire Guernsey (90 day), *£10,000*: As for £2,500 plus Portman Channel Island (Plus 60 day), Leeds Permanent Overseas (Solid Gold 90 day), Britannia IoM (High Interest 60 day). *£25,000*: Derbyshire IoM (90 day), Portman Channel Island (Plus 60 day). *£50,000 and over*: Derbyshire IoM, Yorkshire Guernsey, Portman Channel Island.

Don't tie your money up for too long.

OFFSHORE

Investment Fund

You invest in units or shares which closely reflect the value of the shares or other assets held within the fund. Offshore funds are managed by professionals and although with many you are buying shares in a company, they work in a similar way to unit trusts but are outside the control of the UK authorities. They are usually based in places like Jersey, Guernsey, the Isle of Man, Luxemberg, Bermuda or the Cayman Islands, but the investment advice may be provided from London. The assets are sometimes held by a custodian who acts rather like a UK trustee.

Who can invest Anyone.

How worthwhile Suitable for people living abroad or thinking of doing so. For fixed interest funds see *Offshore Stock and Bond Fund*.

Minimum £100 to £4,000 or more.

Maximum None.

Suitable Lump sums.

Money back Usually immediately at the market price.

Interest Variable. Called *dividend* or *distribution*. Some funds do not pay interest. You hope to make a capital gain by selling for more than you buy; you may lose money.

Interest paid Often half-yearly by cheque or accumulated.

Tax Not deducted. If you are a UK resident and a taxpayer you are liable to pay tax on the income. If the fund accumulates more than 15% of its income UK residents are liable to income tax instead of capital gains tax on any gain you make when you dispose of your units or shares or since 15 March 1989 make a switch in an 'umbrella fund'. Disposals and switches may be liable to capital gains tax for UK residents, but see Chapter 5.

Fees to pay Initial charge: up to 6%. Yearly charge around 1% to 1½% deducted from your income.

Passbook None. Share certificate issued.

Children Unsuitable.

Risk High. The price of units fluctuates down as well as up. There is a chance that the managers will run off with your money but not if the fund is 'recognised' in a territory with a compensation scheme – see page 44.

How to invest Write to or phone the manager of the fund you are interested in, ask for a prospectus and read it carefully. You should be able to place your order by phone. Sales are also best made by phone so you know what price you get.

Where from The magazine *Money Management* lists funds and performance. See the *Financial Times* 'Offshore Funds' page for prices, yields and 'recognised' funds.

There are also offshore unit-linked life insurance policies, which are not recommended for reasons of safety and tax complications.

OFFSHORE

Managed Currency Fund

(*Also called Multicurrency, International Reserves*)

You buy shares in a fund of an investment company which invests in bank deposits in foreign currencies (including £ sterling). The choice of currencies is made by professionals and you hope to gain by their skill in investing in currencies which appreciate against the £, or staying in £ sterling if it appreciates against other currencies. These funds are generally one of a number of sub-funds of an investment company based in Guernsey or Jersey. There is usually a choice of a US$ or £ denominated fund.

Who can invest   Anyone except US permanent residents.

How worthwhile   Suitable for taxpayers. Some managers are more skilful than others. Potential gains, and losses, are less than a *Unit Trust Invested in Shares*. If you want to choose the currencies and decide yourself when to move in and out, consider *Offshore Single Foreign Currency Fund* instead.

Minimum   Old Court none; Hambros £2,000; Guinness Flight £5,000; Lloyds Bank US$10,000.

Maximum   None.

Suitable   Lump sums. Old Court has a regular savings plan.

Money back   Up to 4–7 days. Shares in joint names avoids probate in Jersey or Guernsey.

Interest   Variable.

Interest paid   Paid yearly or half-yearly or accumulated in the fund.

Tax   Not deducted. *If interest is distributed*: (eg Guinness Flight Global Strategy) taxpayers are liable to income tax on it and it should be declared on a tax return; gains on shares sold are liable to capital gains tax (see Chapter 5). *If income is accumulated*: (eg Lloyds Bank, Old Court International Reserves), it need not be declared until you sell your shares (or switch to another fund) when capital gains as well as income are liable to income tax.

Fees to pay   Initially none at Lloyds Bank, Old Court; 4% Hambros; 5% Guinness Flight. Yearly (including custodian fees): Guinness Flight ¾%; Old Court 1½%; Hambros 1⅛%; Lloyds Bank 1.7%.

Passbook   None. Share certificate or statement issued.

Children   Under 18, shares must be held in an adult's name.

Risk   Moderate. The value of the fund can go down as well as up if the managers get the timing or choice of currencies wrong. There are compensation schemes for 'recognised' funds – see page 44.

How to invest   Get details from the 'recognised' funds listed below and compare what they have to offer. Past performance of most funds is monitored in magazines like *Money Management*. Prices, yields and 'recognised' funds are listed in the *Financial Times* Offshore Funds page.

Where from   *Distributor*: Guinness Flight (Global Strategy), Hambros (EMMA). *Accumulation*: Guinness Flight (International Managed Currency), Lloyds Bank (International Money Market), Old Court International Reserves (Managed, Rothschild).

A managed currency fund is an alternative to a unit trust and not to a bank or building society type investment.

OFFSHORE

Single Foreign Currency Fund

(Also called International Reserves, Money Funds)

A sub-fund of an investment company where you pay in and withdraw like a bank account but technically you buy and sell its shares. Each sub-fund invests in one currency and the combined deposits from small investors are reinvested in bank and other deposits of less than 12 months. Currencies available are: US $, German DM, Japanese Yen, Swiss Franc, Canadian $, French Franc, Belgian Franc, Dutch Guilders, Italian Lira, Spanish Peseta, Portuguese Escudo, Danish Kroner, Swedish Kroner, Austrian Schilling, Irish Punt, Singapore $, Hong Kong $, Australian $, New Zealand $, the ECU (European Currency Unit) and £ sterling. Shares can be switched between sub-funds on demand and withdrawn at up to 7 days notice. Money can be deposited and withdrawn in any currency.

Who can invest Anyone except US permanent residents.

How worthwhile A convenient way to invest in foreign currency deposits. Higher rate taxpayers may find an 'Accumulation' fund can defer tax. For £ sterling see *Offshore Sterling Currency Fund*. See also *Offshore Bank Foreign Currency Cheque Account*.

Minimum None at Fidelity, Old Court.

Maximum None.

Suitable Lump sums. Old Court has a regular savings plan.

Money back Up to 4–7 days. Switching on demand. Shares in joint names avoid probate in Guernsey and Jersey. You cannot draw cash.

Interest Variable. Calculated daily.

Interest paid Interest is either *accumulated* to increase the value of the shares or *distributed*. If distributed it can be paid in the foreign currency, paid in £, or reinvested in extra shares.

Tax Not deducted. *If interest distributed*: Taxpayers liable to income tax on it; gains on shares sold, or switched to another currency, liable to capital gains tax (see Chapter 5). *If interest accumulated*: It need not be declared until you sell shares, or switch to another currency, when gains (on exchange rate changes) as well as interest are liable to income tax.

Fees to pay None initially. Yearly (including custodian fees): Old Court 1%; Fidelity 1.03%.

Passbook None. No share certificates. Statement issued with each transaction.

Children Under 18 shares should be held in an adult's name and may be *designated* with the child's name or initials.

Risk Full value of original investment plus interest on withdrawal in currency chosen. If you convert to £ the value may have risen or fallen depending on the exchange rate. There are compensation schemes for 'recognised' funds – see page 44.

How to invest Phone or write for details from the 'recognised' funds listed below. Prices and yields are published in the *Financial Times* 'Offshore Funds' page.

Where from *Distributor*: Fidelity (Money Funds), Old Court Currency Fund (Rothschild); *Accumulation*: Fidelity (Money Funds), Old Court International Reserves. Both Old Court funds offer all currencies listed above except Portugal, Austria, Ireland. Both Fidelity funds offer all except Belgium, Denmark, Sweden, Singapore.

OFFSHORE

Sterling Currency Fund

(*Also called International Reserves, Multicurrency Reserves*)

A fund where you pay in and withdraw like a bank account but technically you buy and sell its shares. There are two main types which have different tax treatment. *Distributor* **funds pay out interest half-yearly; no tax is deducted from the interest but it counts as your income in the tax year it is paid.** *Accumulation* **funds accumulate interest without deduction of tax. No tax is payable until you dispose of the shares (or switch to another fund). Then the 'gain' on the shares is liable to UK income tax in the tax year of the disposal or switch.**

Who can invest   Anyone except US permanent residents.

How worthwhile   Higher rate taxpayers may find an *Accumulation* fund can defer tax. Non-taxpayers compare *Distributor* funds with *National Savings Investment Account*, *Offshore Bank Notice Account* or *Offshore Bank Instant Access Account*.

Minimum   None at Fidelity, Old Court. £5,000 Lloyds Bank.

Maximum   None.

Suitable   Lump sums. Old Court has a regular savings plan.

Money back   Up to 4–7 days. Switching to foreign currencies (see *Offshore Single Currency Fund*) on demand. If you leave the shares in your will your executors will have to obtain probate in Jersey or Guernsey unless the shares are in joint names.

Interest   Variable. Calculated daily.

Interest paid   Interest is either accumulated to increase the value of the shares or distributed. If distributed it can be paid by cheque, to a bank account, or reinvested in extra shares.

Tax   Not deducted. See main description.

Fees to pay   None initially. Yearly (including custodian fees): Old Court 1%; Fidelity 1.03%; Lloyds 0.95%.

Passbook   None. Share certificate or statement issued.

Children   Under 18 shares should be held in an adult's name and may be *designated* with the child's name or initials.

Risk   Full value of original investment plus interest returned on withdrawal. There are compensation schemes for 'recognised' funds – see page 44.

How to invest   Phone or write for details from the 'recognised' funds listed below. Fund prices and yields are published in the *Financial Times* Offshore Funds page.

Where from   *Distributor*: Fidelity (Money Funds), Old Court Currency Fund (Rothschild). *Accumulation*: Fidelity (Money Funds), Lloyds Bank (International Money Market), Old Court International Reserves.

If you want to invest in foreign currencies, read Offshore Single Foreign Currency Fund.

OFFSHORE

Stock and Bond Fund

(*Also called International Bond Fund*)

You invest in a sub-fund of an investment company in shares which reflect the value of foreign currency fixed interest stocks held by the fund. Some specialise in stocks in one area eg North America, Europe, Australasia. Or alternatively the fund may invest world-wide.

Who can invest Anyone.

How worthwhile Suitable for people who expect interest rates to fall in the country or area they choose to invest in thus boosting the capital value of the fund. Taxpayers should probably use 'distributor' funds – see Tax. Compare with *Unit Trust Stock and Bond Fund*.

Minimum £2,000 Hambros. £5,000 Guinness Flight.

Maximum None.

Suitable Lump sums.

Money back Usually immediately at the market price.

Interest Variable. Called *dividend* or *distribution*. Some funds accumulate interest. You hope to make a capital gain by selling for more than you buy; you may lose money.

Interest paid Half-yearly by cheque or accumulated within the fund.

Tax Not deducted. If you are a UK resident and a taxpayer you are liable to pay tax on the income. *Accumulation funds*: If the fund accumulates more than 15% of its income UK residents are liable to income tax instead of capital gains tax on any gain you make when you dispose of your shares or switch to another sub-fund. *Distributor funds*: Capital gains on disposals or switches are liable to capital gains tax but see Chapter 5.

Fees to pay Initial Emma 4%; Global Strategy. 5%. Yearly (including custodian fees): Emma $13/16$%; Global Strategy $7/8$%.

Passbook None. Share certificate issued.

Children Under 18 shares must be held in an adult's name and may be 'designated' with the child's initials.

Risk High. The price of units fluctuates down as well as up. There is a chance that the managers will run off with your money but not if the fund is 'recognised' – see page 44.

How to invest Phone or write for details; ask for a prospectus and read it carefully. If you are investing a large amount, say, £30,000 or more, ask for a reduced initial charge. You can buy and sell by phone. Magazines like *Money Management* list funds and performance. Also see the *Financial Times* 'Offshore Funds' page for prices, yields and 'recognised' funds.

Where from *Distributor*: Guinness Flight (Global Strategy: Global Bond, Global High Income Bond, European Bond, European High Income Bond, US$ Bond, Yen Bond). Hambros (Emma: Continental European, North American, Japanese, Australasian).

Offshore Stock and Bond Fund is a risky investment because you can make or lose money from changes in exchange rates as well as changes in interest rates.

PENSION

Additional Voluntary Contributions

(Also called AVC)

A commitment to making extra contributions to increase the pension you get from your job when you retire. Whilst your main job pension usually depends on how many years you have been in the scheme and your salary at or near retirement, the extra pension you get for *Additional Voluntary Contributions* is usually based on how much you have paid and the interest or capital gains on the investments in which your contributions are placed. *Additional Voluntary Contributions* can be invested in a special building society account or with a life or unit trust company.

Who can invest   Anyone in a job pension scheme.

How worthwhile   Good value for taxpayers who want a larger pension than the one they have earned under their job scheme. Mainly of interest to people with 10–15 years or less to retirement age. Compare your company's AVC scheme with *Pension Free Standing Additional Voluntary Contributions*.

Minimum   Around £10 a month.

Maximum   The total of your normal and additional voluntary contributions to a company pension scheme must not normally be more than 15% of your pay from that job up to £75,000 for the 1993–94 tax year. The voluntary contributions can either be a fixed amount (eg £20 a month) or a % of your salary (so when your salary rises, so do your contributions). Your pension on retirement from your company and from your voluntary contributions can normally be up to two-thirds of your salary just before you retire.

Suitable   Regular savings.

Money back   As a pension (*no* lump sum) starting at the retirement age for your company's pension scheme and continuing until you die (or for a guaranteed period of say, 5–10 years) or until your surviving spouse dies. If you die before you start the pension, contributions, usually with interest, are returned. If you lose your job or move to another, you stop contributions and extra pension is based on what is saved so far plus interest; or you can transfer to a new employer or to a *Pension Personal Pension* or a *Pension Buy Out Bond*. With a life insurance scheme there may be a penalty for job changers.

Interest   Variable or fixed.

Interest paid   When you reach your company's pension age as a pension, or on death.

Tax   None on the interest or capital gain accumulated. The pension is taxed as earned income. Contributions get full tax relief.

Fees to pay   Building societies make no charges. Life insurance companies and unit trusts deduct charges in different ways.

Passbook   None. Statements sent.

Children   Not eligible.

Risk   Depends on the investment in which the contributions are placed.

How to invest   Your employer invests for you in a building society, life insurance company or unit trust.

Where from   Ask your employer. You have to use the scheme, or one of the schemes, offered by him. If your employer wants to set up a scheme he should consult the Pensions Report 'Additional Voluntary Contributions' published by the *Financial Times*.

PENSION

Buy Out Bond

(Also called Transfer Plan 32, Job Changers Pension Fund, Early Leaver Bond)

If you leave your job for a new one or are made redundant, you can transfer the value of your pension rights from your firm's scheme to an individual fund where the money accumulates tax free until retirement normally to the age when you would have retired at your former firm when you start to receive a pension. You can take part as a lump sum when you start the pension. Schemes work like *Pension Personal Pension*; they either give a fixed pension, are 'with-profits' and have bonuses or interest added or are linked to a unit fund.

Who can invest An employee who has left a firm's pension scheme. You can only put in money transferred from a previous firm's pension fund.

How worthwhile This depends on what terms you are offered as an alternative, either by the pension scheme you are leaving, or if you are joining a new scheme with a new job, what terms your new employer offers. You can also usually transfer instead to *Pension Personal Pension* which may be less trouble and gives you a choice of retirement date between 60 and 75.

Minimum Normally £1,000–£4,000.

Maximum None.

Suitable Lump sums.

Money back As pension and lump sum starting on retirement until you die. Widows' or dependants' pensions are available and you can choose between a level pension or a (lower) rising pension. If you die before you start the pension, the value of your money then plus any interest may be returned.

Interest Variable (except non-profit schemes which say at the outset what you will get). Income is accumulated.

Interest paid When the scheme matures at retirement age, mostly as a pension, or on death.

Tax There is no tax on the lump sum you receive nor on the interest or capital gains accumulated. The pension is taxed as earned income.

Fees to pay Charges are deducted from your investment. With schemes which add bonuses, the charges are hidden; with unit linked policies the charges may be disclosed, say ½% to 9% initially, usually ¾% to 1% yearly. You may be able to negotiate a reduction for a large investment.

Passbook None. Policy issued.

Children Not eligible.

Risk Depends on the investment to which the scheme is linked. Run by insurance companies which are UK authorised and covered by a 90% compensation scheme.

How to invest Ask an independent financial adviser specialising in pensions to help you choose.

Where from Life insurance companies.

Instead of transferring to a Buy Out Bond, you can often transfer the money from a job pension to a Personal Pension. A Personal Pension will normally give better results than a Buy Out Bond for younger employees and is more flexible. Get advice before you decide.

PENSION

Director's Pension

(Also called Executive Pension, Top Hat Pension)

A means of saving towards a pension starting between ages 50 and 75 of up to ⅔rds of final salary after 20 years if you own and work for your own company. Also available to senior executives to give them a special pension when they retire. You can take part of it as a lump sum on the chosen retirement date. Schemes have bonuses added (like *Life Insurance With-Profits Endowment Policy*), are linked to a unit fund (like *Life Insurance Mixed, Property,* or *Fixed Interest Bonds*), or give a fixed return.

Who can invest   Company directors and senior executives. It is most tax efficient if the scheme is 'non-contributory' ie the employer (or company) makes the contributions, not the director.

How worthwhile   Very good value for taxpayers who want a pension starting at age 50 to 75. Consider schemes as follows: 5 years or less to pension date, 'non-profit'; 6–15 years, 'with-profits' or 'cash fund'; 15–25 years as for 6–15 years plus mixed, equity linked or property.

Minimum   Single: £250 to £5,000; additional single none to £1,000. Regular £20–£75 a month.

Maximum   15% of earnings up to £75,000 for 1993–94 tax year for director or employee. The maximum pension is based on a salary of £75,000 (1993–94); applies to new members of existing schemes or new schemes from 14 March 1989. There were formerly few contribution restrictions for companies but new limits are currently being sought by the Inland Revenue.

Suitable   Lump sums. Regular.

Money back   As a lump sum and pension between 50 and 75 until you die (or for a fixed period of, say, 5–10 years). Widows pensions also available. If you die before you start the pension, the value of fund or premiums with interest, depending on the company, is returned subject to certain restrictions.

Interest   Variable (except non-profit schemes which say at the outset what you will get). Income is accumulated.

Interest paid   When policy matures mostly as a pension or on death.

Tax   There is no tax on the lump sum you receive nor on the interest or capital gain accumulated; the pension is taxed as earned income. Contributions get full tax relief.

Fees to pay   Charges are deducted in different ways. Reductions for large contributions.

Passbook   None. Pension document issued. Statements sent.

Children   Not eligible.

Risk   Depends on the investment to which the policy is linked. UK life companies are covered by a 90% compensation scheme.

How to invest   Ask an independent financial adviser specialising in pensions for help. See also the Pensions Report 'Executives & Directors' Pensions published by the *Financial Times.*

Where from   *Regular premium 'with profits'*: GA Life, Legal & General, Norwich Union, Scottish Life. *Regular premium 'unit-linked'*: Equitable Life, Professional Life, Provident Life.

PENSION

Free Standing Additional Voluntary Contributions

A commitment to making extra contributions to increase the pension you get when you retire. You are only eligible if you already belong to a job pension scheme. The extra pension you get from *Free Standing Additional Voluntary Contributions* is based on how much you have paid and the interest or capital gains on the investments in which your contributions are placed. The contributions can be invested in a special building society account or with a life or unit trust company.

Who can invest   Anyone in a job pension scheme.

How worthwhile   Good value for taxpayers who want a larger pension than the one they will earn under their job scheme. Mainly of interest to people with 10–15 years or less to retirement age.

Minimum   £25 a month, £250 a year, £250 single. None at Rothschild. £5,000 initial single at Professional Life then £500.

Maximum   The total amount of your normal and additional voluntary contributions to your company's pension scheme must not be more than 15% of your pay from that job in the tax year. The voluntary contributions can either be a fixed amount (eg £50 a month) or a % of your salary (so when your salary rises, so do your contributions). Your pension on retirement from your company and from your voluntary contributions can normally be up to two-thirds of your salary just before you retire.

Suitable   Regular savings.

Money back   As a pension (*no* lump sum) starting at the retirement age for your job pension scheme and continuing until you die (or for a guaranteed period of say, 5–10 years). Widows pensions also available. If you die before you start the pension, the value of the fund or your contributions, usually with interest, is returned. If you move to another job you can continue making contributions to the same Free Standing Additional Voluntary Contributions scheme.

Interest paid   When you reach pension age as a pension or on death.

Tax   None on the interest or capital gain accumulated. The pension is taxed as earned income. Contributions get full tax relief.

Fees to pay   Charges deducted in different ways.

Passbook   None. Statements sent.

Children   Not eligible.

Risk   Depends on the investment in which the contributions are placed.

How to invest   This is a new type of product without a track record. Ask an independent financial adviser specialising in pensions for help or consider the companies which are listed under *Pension Personal Pension*. The companies listed below have the lowest charges. See also the Pensions Report 'Additional Voluntary Contributions' published by the *Financial Times*.

Where from   *Banks and building societies*: None available at present. *Unit trust*: Rothschild Asset Management. *Life companies unit-linked*: Equitable Life, Professional Life. 'With-profits': Seek advice from an independent financial adviser.

For more advice on pension planning turn to Chapter 9.

PENSION

Personal Pension
(*Also called Self-Employed Pension*)

A means of saving towards a pension starting between ages 50 and 75 if you are not in a job pension scheme run by your employer or you are self-employed. You can take 25% of the accumulated pension fund as a lump sum on the chosen retirement date. Schemes have bonuses added (like *Life Insurance With-Profits Endowment Policy*), are linked to a unit fund (like *Life Insurance Mixed, Property,* or *Fixed Interest Bonds*), or give a fixed return.

Who can invest The self-employed or employees not in a job pension scheme or who wish to leave a job pension scheme.

How worthwhile Good value for taxpayers who want a pension and lump sum starting at age 50 or later. A series of single contributions can be better value. Consider schemes as follows: 5 years or less to pension date, 'non-profit' or 'cash fund' of a unit trust or life company; 6–15 years, 'with-profits', or 'cash fund'; 15–25 years as for 6–15 years plus mixed fund, equity linked or property linked.

Minimum None at Rothschild. Single: £250 to £2,000; single additions £100–£250. Regular usually £20 a month upwards.

Maximum Depends on your earnings – see Chapter 9.

Suitable Lump sums. Regular savings.

Money back As a lump sum and pension starting between ages 50 and 75 until you die (or for a guaranteed period of, say, 5–10 years). Widows pensions also available. If you die before you start the pension, the value of the fund or your contributions with interest, depending on the company, is returned.

Interest Variable except non-profit schemes where return fixed at the outset. Income is accumulated.

Interest paid When policy matures mostly as a pension or on death.

Tax There is no tax on the lump sum you receive nor on the interest or capital gain accumulated; the pension is taxed as earned income. Contributions get full tax relief (see Chapter 9).

Fees to pay Charges are deducted in different ways. Reductions for large contributions.

Passbook None. Pension contract issued. Statements sent.

Children Not usually eligible.

Risk Depends on the investment to which the policy is linked. UK life companies are covered by a 90% compensation scheme.

How to invest Ask an independent financial adviser, or the companies listed below for quotes for the type of scheme you want. See also the Pensions Report 'Personal Pensions' published by the *Financial Times*.

Where from *Unit trusts*: Fidelity, Gartmore, Rothschild Asset Management. *Life companies*: 'Non-profit': Equitable Life, Provident Life. *With-profits*: Ask an independent financial adviser. *Unit-linked*: Equitable Life, London Life, Mercury Life, Norwich Union, Professional Life, Provident Life, Scottish Widows.

PENSION

Retirement Annuity

(Also called Self-Employed Pension, Personal Pension)

A means of saving towards a pension starting between ages 60 and 75. You can now only add to an existing policy, you cannot take out a new one. You can take part of it (about 23% to 37½%) as a lump sum on the chosen retirement date. Schemes have bonuses added (like *Life Insurance With-Profits Endowment Policy*), are linked to a unit fund (like *Life Insurance Mixed, Property,* or *Fixed Interest Bonds*), or give a fixed return.

Who can invest   The self-employed or employees not in a company pension scheme who already have a policy.

How worthwhile   Good value for taxpayers who want a pension and lump sum starting no earlier than age 60. A series of single premiums (lump sums) can be better value. Consider schemes as follows: 5 years or less to pension date, 'non-profit'; 6–15 years, 'with-profits' or 'cash fund'; 15–25 years as for 6–15 years plus mixed, equity linked or property linked.

Minimum   Single additional £150–£250. Regular £10 a month upwards.

Maximum   Depends on your earnings but normally lower than for a Pension Personal Pension if you are over age 35 – see Chapter 9.

Suitable   Lump sums. Regular savings.

Money back   As a lump sum and pension starting between ages 60 and 75 until you die (or for a guaranteed period of, say, 5–10 years). Widows pensions also available. If you die before you start the pension, the value of the fund or your premiums with interest, depending on the company, is returned.

Interest   Variable (except non-profit schemes which say at the outset what you will get). Income is accumulated.

Interest paid   When policy matures mostly as a pension or on death.

Tax   There is no tax on the lump sum you receive nor on the interest or capital gain accumulated; the pension is taxed as earned income. Premiums get full tax relief (see Chapter 9).

Fees to pay   Charges are deducted from your investment in different ways.

Passbook   None. Pension policy issued. Statements sent.

Children   Not usually eligible.

Risk   Depends on the investment to which the policy is linked. UK authorised insurance companies are covered by a 90% compensation scheme.

How to invest   You can only add to an existing policy (including a single premium policy) if it allows additions or increases.

Where from   The company or companies you already invest with.

PROPERTY

Business Expansion Shares

A means of investing in the shares of businesses which invest in residential property for letting. The shares are not listed by the Stock Exchange but you get full tax relief on the money you invest provided you do so before 31 December 1993. You pool your money with other investors in the company which builds, converts or buys property to let to 'assured' tenants. Your money buys new shares in the business. Your money is tied up for about 6 years. Many schemes now offer a 'guaranteed' return which is rather poor considering the tax relief given.

Who can invest   Anyone.

How worthwhile   Potentially good value for higher rate taxpayers. Unsuitable for non-taxpayers and basic rate taxpayers who get no or less tax relief. Compare with *Property Enterprise Zone Trust*.

Minimum   £1,000, £2,000, £3,000.

Maximum   £40,000 for all investments in all schemes in each tax year including investment in *Shares Business Expansion Fund*.

Suitable   Lump sums.

Money back   You should be able to sell the shares after you have held them for 5 years.

Interest   The company rarely pays dividends. You hope to make a capital gain by selling for more than you paid and this is often 'guaranteed'.

Tax   You get full income tax relief on your investment in the tax year in which the shares are bought. You can carry back half the relief on shares bought between 6 April to 5 October to the previous tax year (maximum £5,000). The actual tax rebate may be delayed if the company whose shares the fund has bought does not start to trade at once. The tax certificate may take a year or longer to reach you so delaying your rebate. When you sell the shares after 5 years you are exempt from capital gains tax provided tax relief is not withdrawn. Losses cannot be set against other gains unless tax relief is withdrawn.

Fees to pay   There are likely to be charges which could amount to 7%–10% of your money plus about 1½% a year. These are paid by the company. 'Guaranteed' returns leave scope for hidden charges.

Passbook   None. Share certificate issued.

Children   Unsuitable.

Risk   Moderate. The investment is backed by property assets which should make it less risky than *Shares Business Expansion Fund*. Only invest in a scheme sponsored by an established financial body. If the scheme turns out to be a fraud, you do not get tax relief. You may be unable to sell shares when you want.

How to invest   Get advice from a magazine or newspaper on which issue to choose.

Where from   Look out for advertised offers and surveys in the press. The offers tend to be available for limited periods. Expect a rush in the period September to November 1993.

PROPERTY

Commercial Direct Investment

You buy commercial property (ie a shop, offices, warehouse, factory) which is already let on a *lease* to a tenant or tenants and you receive rent as an income. A commercial lease usually provides for *rent reviews* every 3, 4, 5 or 7 years depending on the lease, at which time you may be able to negotiate an increase. You can borrow all or part of the money you wish to invest – and interest on the money borrowed is eligible for tax relief though only against rents from the property you are buying and other property you own.

Who can invest Anyone 18 or over.

How worthwhile Potentially good value for taxpayers who do not want to sacrifice current income but want protection against inflation. In the past commercial rents have usually kept up with inflation and in some areas exceeded it. Commercial property within the means of most investors is called *secondary property*; it is located in less good locations, is often let to small businesses who may not always pay the rent on time and where there may be difficulty finding a new tenant if premises are vacated. To compensate *secondary property* shows a better return than *primary property*. Before tax rental returns of 10%–15% on the initial investment can be found. When you sell, if the rents have gone up, you can also expect to make a capital gain. Compare with *Property Enterprise Zone Trust* and *Property Business Expansion Shares*. Too expensive for non-taxpayers.

Minimum £30,000 upwards. Less if you borrow to buy.

Maximum None.

Suitable Lump sums.

Money back You can sell your property when you wish but finding a buyer may not be easy. Sometimes a tenant or adjoining landlord will be interested or someone will approach you.

Interest You get an income from the rent. This can be paid by standing order or you can employ *managing agents* to collect it for 7%–15% of the rent; they will also act as a buffer between you and the tenants. Rent reviews usually provide increases.

Interest paid Usually quarterly in advance. You can ask the tenant to pay monthly by standing order if you prefer.

Tax The rent after deduction of expenses (eg agent's fees and repairs not paid for by tenants) is liable to income tax but no tax is deducted unless you live abroad. You get full income tax relief on any interest paid on a loan to buy a property provided it is less than all your rents. See also Chapter 4. When you sell or give the property away the gain is liable to capital gains tax, see Chapter 5.

Fees to pay Legal costs when you buy or sell of £250–£600; 1% stamp duty when you buy. Estate agent's costs for negotiating rent review or new lease, 10% of rent. Agent's costs when you sell 1%–2%.

Children Normally unsuitable; property may be held by a trust.

Risk Moderate. The investment is not easily sold so you should only put in money you are saving towards retirement. If tenants stop paying rent, you may have extra legal expenses.

How to invest Get advice from a firm of commercial estate agents in the locality where you want to invest. Look in the newspapers and the magazine *Estates Gazette*.

PROPERTY

Enterprise Zone Trust

A means of investing in new commercial property (ie shops, offices, warehouses, factories) which are situated in designated areas called Enterprise Zones. You get a 100% Capital Allowance on your investment excluding land costs which means you get tax relief on 90%–98% of the money you invest. The trust has a maximum 25 year life after which the assets will be sold. You can borrow money to invest in the trust – and interest on money borrowed is also eligible for tax relief though only against rents from the trust or other rents.

Who can invest   Anyone 18 or over.

How worthwhile   Potentially good value for higher rate taxpayers. Compare with *Property Business Expansion Shares* and *Property Commercial Direct Investment*.

Minimum   £5,000.

Maximum   None.

Suitable   Lump sums.

Money back   After 25 years or sooner. You can sell your investment before then but there may be a tax 'balancing charge' to pay. If you give away the investment or die the 'balancing charge' can be 'rolled over' to the person who receives the investment. If majority of investors agree, the property can be sold early without a tax clawback.

Interest   The trust pays an income from the rents it receives on the properties. The rent should rise but may slow down later when the Enterprise Zones in which the property is situated cease to be Enterprise Zones and have their special concessions – like no rates for 10 years – withdrawn.

Interest paid   Usually quarterly.

Tax   You get full income tax relief on your investment but land costs are not tax allowable, so you normally get around 95% income tax relief. The rent you receive is liable to income tax but none is deducted unless you live abroad – see Chapter 4. When you sell, any gain is liable to capital gains tax; see also Chapter 5.

Fees to pay   Charges are around 5%–7% of the money you invest paid by the developer, plus up to around ¼% a year, paid by the trust.

Passbook   None. Share certificate issued.

Children   Normally unsuitable.

Risk   Moderate. The investment is not easily sold so you should only put in money you are investing for retirement. A pre-let property to a good tenant like a Government department makes it much less risky.

How to invest   Shares are offered for a limited period often in the period January to March. Notify a financial adviser that you are interested to ensure you hear of launches as advertising is restricted.

Where from   Ask a financial adviser, solicitor or accountant to get details from the following: Capital Ventures, Close Brothers, Collective Investments, Johnson Fry (Laser Richmount), Greig Middleton, Property Enterprise Managers (PET).

A higher rate taxpayer can make this investment with no cash outlay. You invest £10,000, get tax relief of £4,000 and borrow £6,000. You have an investment worth £9,000 (after charges) but you have a £6,000 loan so your net investment is £3,000 for which you have paid nothing. The interest, say £700 a year, should be largely covered by the income from the trust of £650 a year.

PROPERTY

Ground Rents

You buy the *freehold* of residential property (ie houses and blocks of flats) or commercial property (ie shops, offices, warehouses, factories) which are already let on a *long lease* with many years still to run (usually 30 to 125 years). You usually receive a fixed low rent in relation to the value of the building. When the lease expires after, say, 50 years, you have the right to receive the market rent (commercial property) or a *regulated* rent (residential property). Tenants either occupy the property or let it to other tenants. You can either hold the ground rents for income — or hope to sell to individual tenants at a profit. Sometimes you have the duty to organise the insurance and maintenance of the property.

Who can invest Anyone 18 or over.

How worthwhile Potentially good value for non-taxpayers and basic taxpayers because the income is usually high in relation to the investment and does not fall when interest rates fall. No protection against inflation except for commercial property when your children or grand-children inherit the *reversion*, the right to demand the market rent, when the lease expires. Residential owner occupiers of houses with long leases usually have the right to force a freeholder to sell them the freehold; this right is to be extended to flat owners. Compare with *Life Insurance Annuity*. Unsuitable for higher rate taxpayers; consider *Property Commercial Direct* instead.

Minimum £250 for a £50 year ground rent; £1,000 to £1,500 for a small block of 5 flats with ground rents of £50 a flat; £10,000 for a commercial property with a ground rent of £1,500 a year.

Maximum None.

Suitable Lump sums.

Money back Finding a buyer may not be easy. Often sold at auctions.

Interest You usually get a fixed income from the rent. This can be paid by standing order or you can employ *managing agents* to collect it and organise the insurance and maintenance if applicable; they will charge around 10% of the rent and act as a buffer between you and the tenants.

Interest paid Usually yearly, half-yearly or quarterly in advance.

Tax Rent after deduction of expenses (eg agent's fees and repairs not paid for by tenants) is liable to income tax but no tax is deducted unless you live abroad. You get full income tax relief on any interest paid on a loan to buy a property provided it is less than all your rents. See also Chapter 4. When you sell or give the property away the gain may be liable to capital gains tax but see Chapter 5.

Fees to pay Legal costs when you buy would make most purchases not worthwhile: you would therefore have to do it yourself. Estate agent's costs of management about 10% of rent. Possible auctioneer's costs when you sell of up to 5%.

Children Children can eventually benefit from the *reversion*, see Chapter 11 for the different types of trust you can set up.

Risk Moderate. The investment is not easily sold so you should only put in money you will never need in a hurry. If tenants stop paying rent, you may have extra legal expense.

How to invest Look for auctions in the newspapers and the magazine *Estates Gazette*.

PROPERTY

Residential Direct Investment

You buy residential property (eg a house, flat or small block of flats) which you let out to a tenant or tenants and you receive rent as an income. A residential lease can last from 1 to 5 years and can have *rent reviews* depending on what is agreed in the lease. Rents on new lettings are not regulated by the government; rents on some tenancies which started before are. However, if you don't follow the proper procedures you can find yourself with a tenant whom you are unable to get rid of which will lower the resale value of the property.

Who can invest   Anyone 18 or over.

How worthwhile   Good value if you do not mind the problems of being a residential landlord. The value of residential property is related to residential property in general, not the rent which you can command. The return is generally lower than with *Property Commercial Direct Investment*. Compare with *Life Insurance Property Bond* where some funds invest in residential property.

Minimum   £30,000 upwards. Less if you borrow to buy.

Maximum   None.

Suitable   Lump sums.

Money back   You can sell your property when you wish but finding a buyer may not be easy.

Interest   You get an income from the rent. This can be paid by standing order or you can employ *managing agents* to collect it at around 10% of the rent; they will also at as a buffer between you and the tenants.

Interest paid   Usually monthly.

Tax   The rent after deduction of expenses (eg agent's fees, repairs, utilities not paid for by tenants) is liable to income tax but no tax is deducted unless you live abroad. You get full income tax relief on any interest paid on a loan to buy a property provided it is less than all your rents. There are special rules for *holiday lettings* and *furnished lettings* – see also Chapter 4. When you sell or give the property away the gain is liable to capital gains tax – see Chapter 5.

Fees to pay   Legal costs when you buy or sell of £250–£600; 1% stamp duty when you buy. Estate agent's costs of management about 10% of rent. Estate agent's costs for finding new tenants 10% of rent. Estate agents will provide a standard lease or you can buy one from a legal stationers. Estate agents costs when you sell around 2%.

Children   Unsuitable directly but property may be held by a trust.

Risk   Moderate. The investment is not easily sold. If tenants stop paying rent, you may have extra legal expense.

How to invest   Get advice from more than one firm of residential rental estate agents in the locality in which you want to invest. Certain types of properties which are less attractive to owner occupiers (eg on main roads) cost much less to buy but can still be rented. However such properties may be more difficult to sell and appreciate by less if house prices start to rise again.

Where from   Estate agents.

SHARES

Business Expansion Fund

A means of investing in the shares of businesses not listed by the Stock Exchange and obtaining full tax relief on the money you invest provided you do so before 31 December 1993. Your money buys new shares in the businesses. You can either choose individual shares or go for a fund which invests in 6 to 13 companies. Your money is tied up for about 6 years. Many investors have been disappointed in these schemes.

Who can invest   Anyone 18 or over not connected with the businesses invested in by the fund.

How worthwhile   Potentially good value for higher rate taxpayers. People who invested in some of the early funds have lost most of their money. Compare with *Property Business Expansion Shares* which is less risky. Unsuitable for non-taxpayers and basic rate taxpayers who get no or less tax relief.

Minimum   £1,000–£5,000.

Maximum   £40,000 for all investments in all schemes in each tax year including investment in *Property Business Expansion Shares*.

Suitable   Lump sums.

Money back   You should be able to sell the shares after you have held them for 5 years; if you invest in a fund there is likely to be a delay after you have invested but before the shares are bought of about 6 months.

Interest   None. By the time the shares start to pay dividends you will normally want to sell. You hope to make a capital gain by selling for more than you paid.

Tax   You get full income tax relief on your investment in the tax year in which you subscribe to the fund (provided the fund invests in the shares within 6 months). The tax certificates often take a year to reach you so delaying your rebate. You can carry back half the relief on shares bought between 6 April to 5 October to the previous tax year (maximum £5,000). When you sell the shares after 5 years you are exempt from capital gains tax if the shares were issued after 18 March 1986. Losses cannot be set against other gains unless BES relief is withdrawn.

Fees to pay   Most funds charge an initial fee of 2% to 7%, not eligible for tax relief. They also keep interest on money waiting to be invested and often delay investment for up to 6 months. Some also reserve right to charge 1% a year.

Passbook   None. Certificate of participation in fund or share certificate. After 5 years the shares are transferred to your own name if you invested through a fund.

Children   Unsuitable.

Risk   High. Some shares usually go bust. It is hoped that the rest more than make up for this. As there is no trustee to look after your money, only invest in a scheme sponsored by an established financial body. If the scheme turns out to be a fraud, you do not get tax relief. You may be unable to sell shares when you want.

How to invest   Get advice from a magazine or newspaper on which fund or shares to choose.

Where from   Shares tend to be limited issue. Expect a rush in the period September to November 1993.

SHARES

Ordinary Quoted

Lump sum invested directly in the shares of a company which are *quoted*, that is bought and sold in the Stock Exchange. You usually receive an income (which you hope will rise) and hope to make a capital gain by selling for more than you paid but you may end up with a loss by selling for less. If the company you invest in goes bust you will lose all your money which is why it is best to *diversify* or spread your money in a portfolio of between 7 and 16 different shares. For more advice on investing in shares, read Chapter 8.

Who can invest   Anyone.

How worthwhile   Potentially good value as a long-term investment for taxpayers if you choose the right shares and buy and sell at the right time; poor value if you do not. Alternatively you can invest through a *Unit Trust* or *Investment Trust* or *Shares Self Select Personal Equity* Plan (maximum £6,000 a year; plus £3,000 in a single share).

Minimum   £14,000–£20,000 for a portfolio of shares bought for, say, £2,000 each, in 7–10 companies. Lower amounts not worthwhile because of minimum commission and lack of a diversified portfolio.

Maximum   None.

Suitable   Lump sums.

Money back   1–3 weeks. You get the market price at the time you sell.

Interest   Variable. Called *dividend*. The before-tax interest is called the *yield* which varies between different companies and different types of companies.

Interest paid   Usually half-yearly by cheque or direct to a bank account.

About 5 weeks before the dividend date the shares go *ex-dividend*; this means the seller gets the next dividend, not the buyer.

Tax   20% tax is deducted from the dividend (called a *tax credit*). Non-taxpayers can reclaim the tax credit from the Inland Revenue. Higher rate taxpayers have to pay extra; basic taxpayers don't. Gains on shares are liable to capital gains tax, but see Chapter 5.

Fees to pay   When you buy stockbrokers commission: 1% to 1.9% on first £5,000; then usually ½%; minimum £15 to £25; stamp duty ½%. No commission or stamp duty on new issue. When you sell commission only.

Passbook   Share certificate issued.

Children   Under 18 shares must be held in an adult's name but can be *designated* with a child's initials.

Risk   High. The value of shares goes down as well as up.

How to invest   You can choose shares by doing your own research or get advice from a stockbroker or the press. Stockbrokers or professional managers will make the choice for you. Buy and sell by phone to a stockbroker or bank if they know you.

Where from   A stockbroker or bank. Stockbrokers with low cost dealing services are: Charles Stanley & Co, Norwich & Peterborough, Pilling & Co, Walker Crips Weddle & Beck. For other brokers phone or write to the Pro-Share Department, Stock Exchange for a copy of the *Private Investors' Directory*.

SHARES

Self Select Personal Equity Plan

(Also called PEP, Share Purchase Plan, Blue Chip Portfolio, Equi-Plan)

A means of investing up to £6,000 a year in UK shares free of tax plus £3,000 each year in one single share. You choose which shares to buy and sell and when (any share with most Managers). Minimum in one share £1,500 to £3,000.

Who can invest Anyone 18 or over. Joint plans are not allowed but husband and wife can have one each. In any one tax year you can only invest in one Personal Equity Plan from one manager plus a separate plan for one single share.

How worthwhile Good value for taxpayers especially higher rate taxpayers. Best suited to a few shares. If you want someone else to choose the shares or you wish to invest less than the maximum, consider instead *Investment Trust Personal Equity Plan*. Poor value for non-taxpayers.

Minimum Usually £1,000 to £6,000 a year. None at Killik. £400 a year (Yorkshire Bank).

Maximum £6,000 plus £3,000 in a single share for 1993–94. Plus managers' charges.

Suitable Lump sums. Regular savings for Discretionary Plans only.

Money back Any time. If you die the plan ends.

Interest Variable. Called *dividend*. The before tax interest is called the *yield* and shares which show the highest yield are most attractive as they make the most use of the tax exemption. Money on deposit awaiting investment is tax free. The single share PEP must be invested within a few weeks but otherwise you can leave money on deposit indefinitely (you have to invest in shares before you cash, however).

Interest paid Your choice to accumulate within the plan or paid out by cheque or to a bank account. The 'tax credit' is usually repaid later.

Tax Dividend income and capital gains are completely tax free and need not be entered on a tax return. Any tax deducted from dividends is reclaimed by the PEP manager on your behalf.

Fees to pay Initially none to 5% or £25–£75; yearly ¾% to 1½%. Commission on shares bought and sold 1%–1.85% (minimum nil to £40). Killik & Co, Pilling & Co, and Pointon-York charge commission at normal rates on deals only.

Passbook None. Statements sent.

Children Not allowed.

Risk High. Just like buying individual shares so if you only have 1 to 3 shares in your plan you should have others outside the plan to balance your portfolio. There is no trustee.

How to invest Contact a plan manager below.

Where from *Self Select Plans*: Barclays Stockbrokers, Killik & Co, Pilling & Co, Pointon-York, Yorkshire Bank.

If you don't want to choose your own shares, consider Investment Trust Personal Equity Plan instead.

SHARES

Preference

Lump sum invested in a special type of share in a company *quoted* on the stock market at a fixed rate of interest. There is no fixed life for the shares which may be bought and sold at any time for the market price through a stockbroker. You may make or lose money when you sell. If the company you invest in goes bust you will probably lose all your money. They are more like a Stock than a Share.

Who can invest Anyone.

How worthwhile Good value for non-taxpayers and basic rate tax-payers either direct or through a Unit Trust specialising in Preference Shares provided interest rates don't rise after you buy in which case they may become poor value. Compare with *Stock Debenture and Loan* or *Stock Government Fixed-Interest*. Unsuitable for higher rate taxpayers.

Minimum £2,000. £500–£1,000 if you invest via a Unit Trust.

Maximum None but some shares are in short supply and a £10,000 maximum in any one share would be sensible.

Suitable Lump sums.

Money back 1–3 weeks. You get the market price at the time you sell.

Interest Fixed and high. Called *dividend*. If a company runs short of money, interest can be reduced or even stopped. *Cumulative* preference shares must have their arrears (interest not paid) paid later; non-cumulative ones need not. The *yield* of the shares varies according to the market price of the shares.

Interest paid Half-yearly by cheque or direct to a bank account. About 5 weeks before the dividend is paid, the shares go *ex-dividend*; this means the seller gets the next dividend, not the buyer.

Tax 20% rate tax is deducted from the dividend (called a *tax credit*). Non-taxpayers can reclaim the tax credit from the Inland Revenue. Higher rate taxpayers have to pay extra; basic taxpayers don't. Gains on shares are liable to capital gains tax, but see Chapter 5.

Fees to pay *Through a unit trust* 5% to 5¼% initial, 1% yearly. *If you buy the shares direct*: stockbrokers commission: On first £5,000 1% to 1.9%; then usually ½%; minimum £15 to £30; stamp duty ½%. When you sell only commission.

Passbook Share certificate issued.

Children Under 18 shares or unit trusts must be registered in an adult's name but can be *designated* with a child's initials.

Risk The company whose preference shares you own can stop paying interest or go bust so it is safer to invest in a Unit Trust which specialises in them. Posible capital loss if interest rates rise and the price of your shares or units falls.

How to invest Get advice from a stockbroker or a bank's stockbroker.

Where from *Through a unit trust*: Aetna, Gartmore, Henderson, INVESCO, Prolific. *Direct*: A bank or stockbroker.

The nominal interest on preference shares is quoted net of a 20% tax credit. This means that if the tax rate falls, non-taxpayers who can reclaim the tax credit, see their income fall as there is less tax to reclaim.

SHARES

SAYE Share Option

(Also called Share Save, SAYE Series F)

A commitment to save a fixed monthly amount, deducted from your pay by your employer, for 5 years when you are paid a bonus. If you keep the money in a further 2 years, another bonus is added. When you join the scheme you are given the option to buy a fixed number of shares in your company at the end of the 5 or 7 years. The number of shares is the amount your total savings, with or without the bonus depending on the rules of the company, could buy at the price (or 80% of it) when you *started* the scheme (ie 5 or 7 years earlier). Up to 6 payments may be delayed: your contract is then extended by the same number of months. If you change employers, you lose the right to buy the shares but may continue saving.

Who can invest Anyone age 16 or over whose company runs a scheme and who has been an employee for long enough, eg 2 to 5 years.

How worthwhile Good value. Possibly, excellent value if your company's shares go up over the 5 or 7 years you are saving.

Minimum £10 a month.

Maximum £250 a month.

Suitable Regular savings.

Money back In 2 to 3 weeks. No partial withdrawals. During the first year money back with no interest. During years 1–5: 3% interest. Completed savings withdrawn between years 5 to 7 receive the 5 year bonus plus 3% interest. If you retire, are made redundant, or become permanently disabled and leave you can normally cash in and buy some shares.

Interest Fixed. Equivalent to 5.53% a year over 5 years. If left another 2 years a further bonus is paid. The average return over 7 years is 5.87% a year. At the outset you choose to save for 5 or 7 years when you can take the proceeds; buy the shares and immediately resell them at a profit if they have risen in value; or you can hold and sell later.

Interest paid When you withdraw. Profit on shares when you sell. Dividends on shares if you keep them.

Tax Interest is tax free. Profit on the difference between the option and the current price of the shares is free of income tax (with old schemes coming to maturity, it may not be). If you hold the shares and sell later, there may be capital gains tax on the gain over the market price at the time you bought, see Chapter 5.

Fees to pay None.

Passbook SAYE certificate and share option document issued. Share certificate if you buy the shares.

Children Not eligible.

Risk None. Full value of original savings returned on withdrawal. Once you buy the shares, unless you sell at once, the risk is greater than with *Shares Ordinary Quoted* if you only hold shares in one company.

How to invest Your employer must agree to run a scheme and have it approved by the Inland Revenue.

Where from Your employer. Most large building societies and some banks (eg Halifax, Abbey National, Nationwide, Woolwich, Leeds Permanent, Bradford & Bingley) and the Department for National Savings offer the SAYE contract.

SHARES

Traded Options

You invest in a contract which gives you the right to buy or sell a certain number of shares at a fixed price before the option *expires* in up to 3, 6 or 9 months time for options in shares and 1 year for 'index' options. A contract to buy shares is called a *call* option; a contract to sell shares is called a *put* option. With a call option you make money when the share price *rises*; with a put option you make money when the price *falls*. If you take a put and a call option at the same time it is called a *straddle*. You can buy options in 64 popular individual shares – like Allied Lyons, British Gas, Marks & Spencer – and also in the FTSE 100 share index, and the Euro FTSE share index. You rarely *exercise* the option (ie buy or sell the shares); to make money you sell the option at a higher price than you bought it for.

Who can invest Anyone 18 or over.

How worthwhile Potentially good value if you like to speculate. You can lose all of your investment very quickly if you predict share prices wrongly. If you are right you can double or treble your money in a short time too. Dealing in traded options needs regular attention and to deal effectively you probably need access to share and option prices on a screen. These are available on Ceefax and Teletext but may not be completely up to date.

Minimum One contract which is normally 1,000 shares at the option price: £35 to £1,350 depending on the share chosen. Before you start trading in options your stockbroker will usually expect you to send him a deposit or *margin* to cover some or all of your options.

Maximum None.

Suitable Lump sums.

Money back When you sell the option before its expiry date in up to 3, 6 or 9 months (or 12 months for an index option). You get the current option price which may be more or less than you paid.

Interest None.

Interest paid Not applicable.

Tax Any profits you make count as capital gains and are taxable – see Chapter 5. Any losses can be set against other capital gains.

Fees to pay Stockbrokers' commission 1% to 1.9% of what you pay; minimum £20 to £30; same when you sell.

Passbook No. You receive a contract note from your stockbroker giving details of each transaction.

Children Unsuitable.

Risk High.

How to invest For a free booklet and a list of stockbrokers which specialise in traded options phone or write to Publications Department, LIFFE.

Where from A stockbroker which specialises in options.

You have to be an active investor with traded options and follow the prices every day – more than once a day when share prices are moving quickly. If you do not have the time or are not prepared to do this, forget them. You can also invest in traded options in the $/£, $/DM exchange rates and in government stocks.

SHARES

Unquoted Shares

(Also called Over The Counter, OTC)

You invest a lump sum in the shares of an *unquoted* company. The shares are bought and sold by stockbrokers who make a market in the shares of their clients. Companies may be recently formed and do not have to meet the conditions for those traded in the Stock Exchange proper. Only a few shares may be available to the public; the rest are kept by the people who run the company. You don't usually receive an income and hope to make a capital gain by selling for more than you paid but you may end up with a loss by selling for less. It is best to invest in a portfolio consisting of shares from between 7 to 16 different companies to spread the risk.

Who can invest   Anyone.

How worthwhile   Many such companies went bust during the 1990–1993 recession. Taxpayers consider *Shares Business Expansion Fund* and *Shares Ordinary Quoted* instead. Some investment trusts invest part of their portfolios in unquoted shares. Unsuitable for non-taxpayers.

Minimum   £14,000–£20,000 for a portfolio of unlisted and quoted shares: say £2,000 worth of shares in 7–10 companies. Lower amounts not worthwhile because of minimum commission and lack of diversified portfolio.

Maximum   There are limited numbers of shares available to the public in some *unquoted* companies.

Suitable   Lump sums.

Money back   1–3 weeks. You get the market price when you sell. Some shares turn out to be unsaleable.

Interest   Variable. Called *dividend*. The before tax interest is called the *yield* which is generally quite low or nil.

Interest paid   If there is any, usually half-yearly by cheque. About 5 weeks before the dividend date, the shares go *ex-dividend*; this means the seller gets the dividend not the buyer.

Tax   20% tax deducted from the dividend (called a *tax credit*). Higher rate taxpayers have to pay extra; basic taxpayers don't. Gains on shares are liable to capital gains tax. If you buy *new* shares direct from an unquoted trading company and it later goes bust, or the shares are sold realising a loss, you can normally set the loss against your income either in the tax year in which the loss occurred or the next tax year. Alternatively the loss can be set against your capital gains.

Fees to pay   Commission when you buy 1%–1.9%; minimum £17 to £30; stamp duty ½%. Commission only when you sell.

Children   Unsuitable.

Risk   High. The value of shares goes down as well as up. Safer to buy a new issue because of tax relief on losses – see *Tax* above.

How to invest   Follow the newspapers for comments on issues. Get a second opinion from a stockbroker. Sales best done by phone to a stockbroker if they know you.

Where from   A stockbroker.

STOCK

Convertible Loan

Lump sum invested in an unsecured loan stock issued by a company for a fixed term at a fixed rate of interest where you have the right to convert the stock into Ordinary Shares of the company at a fixed price before or between fixed dates in the future. If the stock is not converted, it can continue to pay interest until it is repaid in full at the end of the term just like *Stock Debenture and Loan*. The stock value therefore tends to fluctuate in line with the value of ordinary shares of the company in which there are conversion rights, but pays a higher yield. If the shares perform poorly, the value of the stock will drop to what it would be if there were no conversion rights.

Who can invest   Anyone 18 or over.

How worthwhile   Similar to *Shares Ordinary Quoted* but with a higher income which does not rise (or fall). Worth considering for basic taxpayers who think shares have too low an income. Higher rate taxpayers consider instead *Shares Ordinary Quoted*. Unsuitable for non-taxpayers.

Minimum   *Investing direct*: £7,000 to £10,000 for a portfolio of stocks (and ordinary shares) bought for, say, £1,000 each in 7–10 companies. Lower amounts not worthwhile because of minimum commission and lack of a diversified portfolio. *Through a unit trust*: £500 to £1,000 with £100 to £250 additions.

Maximum   None.

Suitable   Lump sums.

Money back   At end of term. 1–3 weeks if you sell earlier when you get the market price; same if you have converted to ordinary shares except

you sell the shares. Once converted, there is no longer any fixed term.

Interest   Fixed. The before tax income is called the *yield* which varies between different companies. It is normally quite a lot higher than the yield on the shares which you have the right to convert to. Once converted the yield is variable.

Interest paid   Usually half-yearly by cheque or direct to a bank account.

Tax   Basic rate tax is deducted from the interest. Non-taxpayers can reclaim the tax from the Inland Revenue. Higher rate taxpayers pay extra. Gains on stocks are liable to capital gains tax but see Chapter 5.

Fees to pay   *Investing direct*: when you buy: Stockbrokers commission up to around 1.9%; minimum £15 to £30); then usually ½%; plus stamp duty ½%. Commission only when you sell. *Through a unit trust*: 5% to 5.25% initial for trusts listed here. 1% yearly.

Passbook   None. Stock certificate issued. If you convert, it is replaced by a share certificate.

Children   Unsuitable.

Risk   Not as high as Ordinary Shares but the value of convertible loan stocks go down as well as up.

How to invest   You can invest through a unit trust which specialises in these types of stock or do your own research or get advice from a stockbroker. Buy and sell by phone to a bank or stockbroker if they know you.

Where from   *Investing direct*: A stockbroker. *Through a unit trust*: Baillie Gifford, Barings, Edinburgh, Framlington, Prolific.

STOCK

Debenture and Loan

Lump sum invested in a stock issued by a company for a fixed term at a fixed interest rate. At the end of the term (the redemption date), the original value is repaid in full; meanwhile the stock can be bought and sold at any time at the market price. The return you get (called the *net redemption yield*) consists of two parts: the after-tax interest, and the difference between the price you paid and the value of the stock at redemption. Sometimes a company reorganisation can result in the interest rate being raised, the stock being repaid early or a loan stock being converted into a debenture (see *Risk* below).

Who can invest   Anyone.

How worthwhile   Different stocks are good for different rate taxpayers. Compare with *Stock Government Fixed Interest*. Stock maturing in over 10 years is not recommended. See also *Stock Convertible Loan*.

Minimum   £2,000. Lower amount not worthwhile because of minimum commission rate.

Maximum   None but some stocks are in short supply.

Suitable   Lump sums.

Money back   At end of term. Or 1–3 weeks, if you sell before then when you get the market price (it may be more or less than you paid).

Interest   Fixed. About 5 weeks before the interest is paid, the stocks go *ex-dividend*. The seller gets the next interest payment. When you buy a stock (or if you sell before it matures) your *contract note*, giving details of the transaction, shows *accrued interest* as an addition or deduction from what you pay or receive.

Interest paid   Half-yearly by cheque or direct to a bank account.

Tax   Basic rate tax is deducted from the interest. Non-taxpayers can reclaim the tax from the Inland Revenue. Higher rate taxpayers pay extra. Any *accrued interest* added to your *contract note* (see *Interest* above) is liable to income tax; if accrued interest is deducted, you can deduct it from other interest from the stock and claim a tax rebate if applicable. These accrued interest rules don't apply if the nominal value of all your stocks is £5,000 or less; see Inland Revenue leaflet *IR68 Accrued Income Scheme*. Gains are exempt from capital gains tax.

Fees to pay   Stockbrokers commission when you buy and sell: On first £10,000 around ¾%; around ¼% on larger amounts; min. £17. Some may charge more e.g. 1½% on the first £7,000. Banks often charge more. Same when you sell. None if you buy a new issue direct or hold to redemption.

Passbook   Stock certificate issued.

Children   Under 18 stock must be held in an adult's name but can be *designated* with the child's initials.

Risk   If a company goes bust, debenture holders have the right to be paid in full before other creditors get anything; loan stock holders don't but are paid before ordinary shareholders. Possible capital loss if you sell early.

How to invest   Ask a stockbroker or bank which stock has the best *net redemption yield* for your tax rate and the time you want to invest for. With loan stocks check whether they think the company is likely to stay in business until your stock matures.

Where from   A stockbroker.

STOCK

Government Fixed Interest

(*Also called Gilts, British Funds*)

Lump sum invested in a stock issued by the Government at a fixed interest rate. The stock usually has a fixed life at the end of which (the redemption date) the *nominal value* is repaid in full; it can be bought and sold at any time at the market price. The yearly return you get (called the *net redemption yield*) consists of two parts: the after-tax interest, and the averaged out difference between what you pay and the value at redemption.

Who can invest Anyone.

How worthwhile Different stocks are good for different rate taxpayers. Often good value for higher rate taxpayers. Fair to good value for non-taxpayers and basic rate taxpayers. Stocks maturing in over 10 years or without redemption dates (eg War Loan) are not recommended. If you want to invest for longer consider *Stock Government Index Linked*.

Minimum None through National Savings Stock Register; £5,000 through a stockbroker because of minimum commission.

Maximum None. But each purchase bought through National Savings Stock Register must not exceed £25,000.

Suitable Lump sums.

Money back At redemption date. Or within a few days if you sell before then; you get the market price at the time you sell (which may be more or less than you paid).

Interest Fixed. About 5 weeks before the interest (dividend) date, the stocks go *ex-dividend*; the seller gets the next interest payment. When you buy a stock (or if you sell before it matures) your *contract note*, giving details of the transaction, shows *accrued interest* as an addition or deduction from what you pay or receive. Whether it is an addition or deduction depends on when you buy or sell in relation to the next or last interest payment date and whether the stock is *ex-dividend* or not. There are special rules for taxing this, see *Tax* below.

Interest paid Usually half-yearly by cheque; or direct to a bank or building society account.

Tax Interest is liable to income tax. If the stock is bought through the National Savings Stock Register, no tax is deducted but taxpayers should declare it on a tax return. If stock is bought through a stockbroker (or a bank's stockbroker), tax is deducted at the basic rate. Non-taxpayers can reclaim the tax from the Inland Revenue. Higher rate taxpayers have to pay extra. War Loan does not have tax deducted. Any *accrued interest* added to your *contract note* (see *Interest* above) is liable to income tax; if accrued interest is deducted, you can deduct it from other interest from the stock and claim a tax rebate if applicable. These rules don't apply if the 'nominal' value of all your stocks is £5,000 or less; see Inland Revenue leaflet *IR68 Accrued Income Scheme*. Gains on stock are exempt from capital gains tax.

Fees to pay If bought through the National Savings Stock Register commission is usually £1 plus 0.4% on the excess over £250. Through a stockbroker: on first £7,000 around ¾%; on next £8,000 around ¼%; less on higher amounts; minimum £10 to £30. Same when you sell. None if you buy a new issue direct or hold to redemption. Some brokers charge more e.g. 1.5% on first £7,000; minimum £10 to £30. Banks often charge more.

Passbook Stock certificate issued.

Children Under 18 stock must be held in an adult's name unless bought through the National Savings Stock Register.

Risk None if you hold until redemption. Possible capital loss if you want your money back early.

How to invest Phone your bank or stockbroker. Ask which stock has the best *net redemption yield* for your tax rate and the period over which you want to invest. See list in next column for stocks available. Prices and before tax yields are published in the *Financial Times* under British Funds on the FT London Share Service page and at the beginning of the share prices page in other daily newspapers every day.

Where from Forms and post-paid envelopes for National Savings Stock Register from most post offices and banks. Stockbrokers for very large amounts.

If you want to invest in Government Fixed Interest Stocks, divide your money between stocks maturing at yearly or two yearly intervals.

---

* Available through National Savings Stock Register.
† Exempt from UK tax if held by non-residents.
NB Some stocks have two dates, eg 1995/98; this means the Government can repay the stock at any time between 1995 and 1998; usually stocks are repaid on the later date.

Government Fixed Interest Stocks

Stocks with up to 15 years to maturity	Interest dates (redemption month in **black**)	Life of stock from 1 June '93 Yrs Mths
*6% Funding 1993†	15 Mar **Sep**	3½
*13¾% Treasury 1993†	23 May **Nov**	6
*8½% Treasury 1994†	3 Feb Aug	8
*14½% Treasury 1994†	1 **Mar** Sep	9
13½% Exchequer 1994	27 **Apr** Oct	11
10% Treasury 1994	9 **Jun** Dec	1 0
12½% Exchequer 1994	22 Feb **Aug**	1 3
*9% Treasury 1994†	17 May **Nov**	1 4½
*12% Treasury 1995	25 **Jan** July	1 8
3% British Gas 1990/95	1 **May** Nov	1 11
*10¼% Exchequer 1995	21 Jan **July**	2 2
*12¾% Treasury 1995†	15 May **Nov**	2 5½
14% Treasury 1996	22 **Jan** July	2 8
*15¼% Treasury 1996†	3 **May** Nov	2 11
*13¼% Exchequer 1996†	15 **May** Nov	2 11½
10% Conversion 1996	15 May **Nov**	3 5½
*13¼% Treasury 1997†	22 **Jan** July	3 8
*10½% Exchequer 1997	21 Feb **Aug**	3 9
*8¾% Treasury 1997†	1 Mar **Sept**	4 3
*15% Exchequer 1997	27 Apr **Oct**	4 5
*9¾% Exchequer 1998	19 **Jan** July	4 8
7¼% Treasury 1998†	30 **Mar** Sep	4 10
*6¾% Exchequer 1995/98†	1 **May** Nov	4 11
*15½% Treasury 1998†	3 Mar **Sept**	5 3
12% Exchequer 1998	20 May **Nov**	5 6
*9½% Treasury 1999†	15 **Jan** July	5 7½
*12¼% Exchequer 1999	26 **Mar** Sept	5 10
10½% Treasury 1999	19 **May** Nov	5 11½
10¼% Conversion 1999	22 May **Nov**	6 5
*9% Conversion 2000†	3 **Mar** Sep	6 9
*13% Treasury 2000	14 Jan **Jul**	7 1½
*10% Treasury 2001	26 **Feb** Aug	7 9
*14% Treasury 1998/2001	22 **May** Nov	7 11
*9¾% Treasury 2002	27 Feb **Aug**	8 9
*8% Treasury 2003†	10 **Jun** Dec	10 0
*13¾% Treasury 2000/2003	25 Jan **Jul**	10 1
*10% Treasury 2003	8 Mar **Sep**	10 3
*11½% Treasury 2001/2004	19 **Mar** Sep	11 9½
*3½% Funding 1999/2004	14 Jan **Jul**	12 2½
9½% Conversion 2004	25 Apr **Oct**	12 5
*9½% Conversion 2005	18 **Apr** Oct	12 10½
10½% Exchequer 2005	20 Mar **Sep**	13 3
*12½% Treasury 2003/2005	21 May **Nov**	13 6
*8% Treasury 2002/2006†	5 Apr **Oct**	14 5

STOCK

Government Index-Linked

Lump sum invested with the Government in return for an interest payment which increases in line with the Retail Prices Index. The stock has a fixed life at the end of which the Government guarantees to repay the *nominal value* in full plus the increase in the Retail Prices Index since the stock was issued. Both interest and capital are index-linked and the capital gain is tax exempt.

Who can invest   Anyone.

How worthwhile   Good value for taxpayers who do not need a high income but wish to protect it and their capital against inflation especially over periods of 10 years or more. Unsuitable for non-taxpayers.

Minimum   For amounts up to £10,000 consider instead *National Savings Index Linked Certificates*. No minimum through National Savings Stock Register.

Maximum   None. But each purchase bought through the National Savings Stock Register must not exceed £25,000 in any one stock in any one day.

Suitable   Lump sums.

Money back   A few days. You can sell the stock at any time at the current market price. The interest and repayment value depends on the current and expected rate of inflation. The price does not match changes in the Retail Prices Index.

Interest   Variable. Changes at each interest payment to reflect changes in the Retail Prices Index over a previous 6 month period with a lag of 8 months. About 5 weeks before the interest (dividend) date, the stocks go *ex-dividend*; the seller gets the next interest payment, not the buyer. When you buy a stock (or if you sell before it matures) your *contract note*, giving details of the transaction, shows *accrued interest* as an addition or deduction from what you pay or receive. Whether it is an addition or deduction depends on when you buy or sell in relation to the next or last interest payment date and whether the stock is *ex-dividend* or not. There are special rules for taxing this, see *Tax* below.

Interest paid   Half-yearly by cheque or direct to bank account.

Tax   Interest is liable to income tax. If the stock is bought through the National Savings Stock Register, no tax is deducted; taxpayers should declare it on a tax return. If stock is bought through a stockbroker (or a bank's stockbroker), tax is deducted at the basic rate. Non-taxpayers can reclaim the tax from the Inland Revenue. Higher rate taxpayers have to pay extra. Any *accrued interest* added to your *contract note* (see *Interest* above) is liable to income tax; if accrued interest is deducted, you can deduct it from other interest you receive from the stock and claim a tax rebate if applicable. These rules don't apply if the 'nominal' value of all your stocks is £5,000 or less. Gains on stock are exempt from capital gains tax.

Fees to pay   If bought through National Savings Stock Register commission is usually £1 plus 0.4% on the excess over £250. Through a stockbroker: on first £7,000 around ¾%; next £8,000 around ¼%; less on higher amounts; minimum £17. Same when you sell. Some may charge more e.g. 1½% on first £7,000. None if you buy a new issue direct or on redemption.

Passbook   Stock certificate issued.

Children Under 18 stock must be held in an adult's name unless bought through the National Savings Stock Register.

Risk None if you hold until redemption. Some if sold before, but interest rate rises will not cause the price to fall as much as it does with stocks which have a fixed rate.

How to invest Choose a stock from the list in the next column which matures close to the date you want your money back (eg expected retirement date) or invest in a number of different stocks so you have money maturing over a number of years.

Where from Banks or stockbrokers. Forms and post paid envelopes for National Savings Stock Register from most post offices and banks. If you want to buy 5 stocks you will need 5 forms.

Government Index-Linked Stocks

Index-Linked Treasury Stock	Notional value on 1 June 1993‡	Interest dates (redemption month in black)	Life of stock from 1 June '93 Yrs	Mths
*2% 1994	134	16 **May** Nov		10½
*2% 1996	203	16 Mar **Sep**	3	3½
4⅝% 1998†	102	27 **Apr** Oct	4	10
*2½% 2001	176	24 Mar **Sep**	8	4
*2½% 2003	175	20 **May** Nov	9	11
4⅜% 2004†	102	21 Apr **Oct**	10	10
*2% 2006	198	19 Jan **July**	13	2
*2½% 2009	175	20 **May** Nov	15	11½
*2½% 2011	185	23 Feb **Aug**	18	3
*2½% 2013	155	16 Feb **Aug**	20	2½
*2½% 2016	169	26 Jan **July**	23	2
*2½% 2020	166	16 **Apr** Oct	26	10½
*2½% 2024†	141	17 Jan **July**	31	1½
4⅛% 2030†	102	22 Jan **July**	37	2

* Available through National Savings Stock Register.
‡ Nominal value (the value to which index linked additions are made) plus index-linking added so far.
† Tax exempt to non-residents.

In the table above, the column 'notional value on 1 June 1993' gives you an idea as to the value for money of each stock. This figure is the amount of index-linking added so far to the initial issue price of the stock. When you compare it to the actual market price which the stock is offered at, the market price is usually less. However in the case of stocks which pay higher interest, the market price may actually be more than the 'notional value'. Your choice depends on whether you want income now, in the form of higher interest each year, or in the future, in the form of a higher redemption value. Government Index-Linked Stock is an excellent long term investment even if high rates of inflation do not return.

STOCK

Private Index-Linked

Lump sum invested with a loan stock in a building society or private company in return for an interest payment which increases in line with the Retail Prices Index. The stock has a fixed life at the end of which the company guarantees to repay the *nominal value* in full plus the increase in the Retail Prices Index since the stock was issued. Both interest and capital are index-linked.

Who can invest   Anyone.

How worthwhile   Good value for taxpayers who do not need a high income but wish to protect it and their capital against inflation. There may be more choice of stock with *Stock Government Index-Linked.*

Minimum   For amounts up to £10,000 for periods of 5 years, consider instead *National Savings Index-Linked Certificates.*

Maximum   None.

Suitable   Lump sums.

Money back   A few days. You can sell the stock at any time at the current market price. The interest and repayment value depends on the current and expected rate of inflation. The price does not match changes in the Retail Prices Index.

Interest   Variable. Changes at each interest payment to reflect changes in the Retail Prices Index over a previous 6 month period. About 5 weeks before the interest (dividend) date, the stocks go *ex-dividend.* The seller gets the next interest. When you buy a stock (or if you sell before it matures) your *contract note,* giving details of the transaction, shows *accrued interest* as an addition or deduction from what you pay or

receive. There are special rules for taxing this, see *Tax* below.

Interest paid   Half-yearly by cheque or direct to bank account.

Tax   Tax is deducted from interest at the basic rate. Non-taxpayers can reclaim the tax from the Inland Revenue. Higher rate taxpayers have to pay extra. Any *accrued interest* added to your *contract note* (see *Interest* above) is liable to income tax; if accrued interest is deducted, you can deduct it from other interest you receive from the stock and claim a tax rebate if applicable. These accrued interest rules don't apply if the nominal value of all your stocks is £5,000 or less; see Inland Revenue leaflet *IR68 Accrued Interest Scheme.* Gains on stock are exempt from capital gains tax.

Fees to pay   Through a stockbroker: on first £100,000 around ¾%; around ¼% on larger amounts; minimum £17. Same when you sell. Some may charge more e.g. 1½% on first £7,000. None if you buy a new issue direct or on redemption.

Passbook   Stock certificate issued.

Children   Under 18 stock must be held in an adult's name.

Risk   Low if you hold until redemption. Some if sold before, but interest rate rises will not cause the price to fall as much as they do with stocks which have a fixed rate.

How to invest   Ask a stockbroker about Nationwide 3⅞% Index-Linked 2021, 4¼% Index-Linked 2024 and other issues.

Where from   A stockbroker.

STOCK

Unit Trust Invested in Gilts

You invest in a fund of Government fixed-interest stocks managed by professionals. The units closely reflect the value of the stocks held within the trust. The aim of some Gilt unit trusts is to achieve capital growth; these trusts have a low yield. 'Income' trusts have a higher yield. Gilt trusts rise in value when interest rates fall (or are expected to fall); when interest rates rise (or are expected to rise) the trusts tend to fall in value but see note at the end of this page.

Who can invest   Anyone.

How worthwhile   Poor value for large amounts or higher rate taxpayers. Consider investing directly in gilts yourself – see *Stock Government Fixed Interest*. If you want this type of investment in foreign currencies, see *Unit Trust Stock and Bond Fund*. Non-taxpayers also consider *Shares Preference Shares*.

Minimum   £500 to £1,000.

Maximum   None.

Suitable   Lump sums.

Money back   Usually immediately at the market price. At most 1–3 weeks.

Interest   Variable. Called *distribution*.

Interest paid   Half-yearly or quarterly by cheque or direct to a bank account.

Tax   Tax is deducted from the interest. Non-taxpayers can reclaim the tax from the Inland Revenue. Higher rate taxpayers have to pay extra; basic taxpayers don't. Gains on units are liable to capital gains tax (see Chapter 5) even though direct investments in Government stock is exempt. The managers pay no capital gains tax when they make gains on stock held within the trust.

Fees to pay   Initial charge 1%–5% included in difference between buying and selling price of 1½%–5%. Yearly charge ¾%–1% deducted from your income.

Passbook   None. Unit trust certificate issued. Report and distribution voucher usually half-yearly.

Children   Under 18 units should be held in an adult's name and are *designated* with the child's name or initials.

Risk   Some. The value of units goes down as well as up as interest rates are expected to change. The stocks in the trust are held by a Government approved trustee to ensure the managers invest in what they say they do.

How to invest   Get advice from an independent financial adviser on the best time to buy (and sell) and which trust to choose. Purchases and sales can be made by phone so you know what price you get.

Where from   Around 50 trusts from many unit trust groups.

It is better to invest in Gilts direct rather than through a unit trust – see Stock Government Fixed-Interest.

UNIT TRUST

Cash Trust

(*Also called Money Market, Reserve, Sterling Deposit, Maximum Income*)

A fund where you pay in and withdraw like a postal bank or building society account but technically you buy and sell units in a unit trust. The units only rise and fall slightly to reflect accumulating income and distributions (see *Interest paid*). Cash trusts generally only invest in bank and building society accounts but they are allowed to invest in a number of other types of short term investments including *treasury bills*, *certificates of deposit* and short dated *British Government stocks*.

Who can invest Anyone.

How worthwhile Compare with *Building Society Instant Access Account*, *Building Society Cheque Account With Interest* and *Building Society Postal Account*. Likely to be most worthwhile for smaller amounts eg £500–£20,000 as the same interest rate is paid for all sizes of investment, whereas building societies usually pay more for larger amounts.

Minimum Usually £1,000. Baring £500.

Maximum None.

Suitable Lump sums. You can only deposit by cheque, not cash.

Money back Usually a few days.

Interest Variable. Called *distribution*. The before tax interest (after deduction of the yearly charge – see *Fees to pay*) is called the *yield*. This is similar to the before tax interest rate on building society accounts.

Interest paid Half-yearly, quarterly or monthly depending on the trust; by cheque or direct to a bank account. Around half the trusts only have accumulation units which accumulate income; with most others your income can automatically buy extra units or there is a choice of units.

Tax Tax is deducted from the distribution (called *tax credit*). Non-taxpayers can reclaim the tax credit from the Inland Revenue. Higher rate taxpayers pay extra; basic taxpayers don't. The first distribution you receive after buying the units consists partly of interest and partly of an *equalisation payment*. This equalisation payment counts as a return of capital and is not taxable.

Fees to pay Initial charge nil to 2%. Yearly ½%–1% deducted from the interest. Trusts listed below all nil initial, ½% yearly.

Passbook None. Unit trust certificate issued. Report and distribution voucher usually half-yearly.

Children Under 18 units must be held in an adult's name but can be designated with a child's name or initials.

Risk None.

How to invest Phone the managers below and ask what their current yield and minimum investment are.

Where from *Income distributed monthly*: Fidelity. *Quarterly*: Abtrust, Legal & General, Prudential. *Half-yearly*: Barings, INVESCO, Save & Prosper.

Unit Trust Cash Trust is an excellent home for relatively small sums eg £500 to £20,000.

UNIT TRUST

Index Tracker

(*Also known as Index*)

**A unit trust which aims to dupli-
cate the growth of a stock exchange
index, usually an index of ordinary
shares. It also aims to duplicate
the income from the index. This
way the trust is always invested in
shares so the trust will not under-
perform the market because part is
in cash on deposit. Charges are
generally less than for other unit
trusts. There are tracker trusts for
stock markets in the UK, USA,
Europe, Japan and the Far East.**

Who can invest   Anyone.

How worthwhile   Potentially good
value as a long term investment for
taxpayers if you buy and sell at the
right time; poor value if you do not.
Compare with *Investment Trust
Shares* which generally do not have
an initial charge.

Minimum   Usually £1,000. £5,000
Gartmore UK Index.

Maximum   Phone deals of £15,000
or more per trust may be delayed
until the next valuation.

Suitable   Lump sums. Regular savings, see *Unit Trust Savings Plan.*

Money back   A few days at the
market price. You can usually buy and
sell by phone.

Interest   Variable. Called *distribution.*
The before tax interest is called *yield*;
trusts which track overseas markets
tend to have a low yield or none at all.

Interest paid   Usually yearly or half-
yearly by cheque; direct to a bank
account. Some trusts have accumulation units which accumulate income;
with others your income can automatically buy extra units (at a charge).

Tax   20% tax is deducted from the
distribution (called a *tax credit*)

whether or not you accumulate
income. Non-taxpayers can reclaim
the tax from the Inland Revenue.
Higher rate taxpayers pay extra; basic
taxpayers don't. Gains on units are
liable to capital gains tax (see Chapter
5) though the managers pay no tax on
gains on shares held by the trust.

Fees to pay   Initial charge 4%–6%
(maximum 5¼% for trusts listed
here; nil Gartmore UK Index) included
in *spread* between buy (offer) and sell
(bid) price of 5½%–7½% (1.9% Gartmore). Yearly ½%–1% (maximum
¾% for trusts listed here).

Children   Under 18 units should be
held in an adult's name and *designated*
with the child's name or initials.

Passbook   None. Statement or certificate sent with each transaction.
Report and distribution voucher
usually half-yearly.

How to invest   Phone the managers
of the trusts listed below and ask for
literature. You can buy by phone too.

Where from   Gartmore (UK Index),
Morgan Grenfel (UK Index "Tracker",
US Index "Tracker", Japan "Tracker"),
Legal & General (UK Index, US Index,
Euro Index, Japan Index).

*These funds are linked to an index of
share prices, not retail prices. So they
can go down as well as up.*

UNIT TRUST

Invested in Shares

You invest in a fund of shares managed by professionals. The units closely reflect the value of the shares held within the trust. You may receive an income and hope to make a capital gain by selling for more than you paid, but you may end up with a loss by selling for less. Some trusts specialise in particular types of shares. See lists on the next two pages.

Who can invest   Anyone.

How worthwhile   Potentially good value as a long-term investment for taxpayers if you buy and sell at the right time; poor value if you do not. High charges make most trusts unattractive. Consider instead *Investment Trust Shares, Unit Trust Index Tracker*. A couple of managers with low initial charges are listed below.

Minimum   Usually £250, £500 or £1,000. Lazard £5,000.

Maximum   None.

Suitable   Lump sums.

Money back   At the market price; at once or in a couple of weeks.

Interest   Variable. Called *distribution*. The before-tax interest is called *yield*; different types of trusts have different yields. Some allow you to take a fixed income, say 10% of the original investment or the current value; if the interest does not reach this amount, units are cashed to make it up.

Interest paid   Usually half-yearly. Some managers can arrange a monthly income. By cheque or direct to a bank account. Some trusts have accumulation units which accumulate income; with others your income automatically buys extra units (at a small charge).

Tax   20% tax is deducted from the distribution (called a *tax credit*) whether or not you accumulate it. Non-taxpayers can reclaim the tax from the Inland Revenue. Higher rate taxpayers have to pay extra; basic taxpayers don't. You can avoid this tax by investing through a *Unit Trust Personal Equity Plan*. Gains on units are liable to capital gains tax (see Chapter 5) though the managers pay no capital gains tax if they make gains on shares held by the trust.

Fees to pay   Initial charge usually 5%–6% included in difference between buying and selling price of 5½%–7%. Yearly charge 1%–1½% deducted from income or capital.

Passbook   None. Unit trust certificate. Report and distribution voucher usually sent half-yearly.

Children   Under 18 units should be held in an adult's name and are *designated* with the child's name or initials.

Risk   High but not as risky as buying individual shares. The value of units goes down as well as up. The shares owned by the trust are held by a Government approved trustee.

How to invest   Phone the managers of the trust you are interested in and ask for their literature; you can buy by phone too. They will send you a contract note and you then send your money. Sales can also be made by phone. Watch what the newspapers say or follow your own hunch.

Where from   Lazard (no initial charge); Murray Johnstone (initial charge 1%).

UNIT TRUST

Invested in UK Shares

The best performing trusts change frequently. Average performance is based on Micropal figures for 12 months to the beginning of February 1993.

UK Equity Growth Trusts which invest at least 80% of their assets in UK shares. Their main aim is capital growth. The 148 trusts rose on average by 8%. The best rose by 26%, the worst fell by 10%.

UK Equity General Trusts which invest at least 80% in UK shares. Their aim is to produce a combination of income and growth with an income yield of between 80% and 110% of the yield of the Financial Times All Share Index. The 99 trusts rose on average by 8%. The best rose by 18%, the worst fell by 10%.

UK Equity Income Trusts which invest at least 80% in UK shares. Their income yield is over 110% of the yield of the Financial Times All Share Index. The 115 trusts on average rose by 12%. The best rose by 29%, the worst fell by 5%.

UK Balanced Trusts where at least 80% is invested in UK shares, UK government stocks and other UK fixed interest stocks. The 38 trusts on average rose by 13%. The best rose by 23%.

Financial and Property Trusts which invest at least 80% in financial and property shares (usually in the UK) but some investments may be abroad. The 15 trusts on average fell by 9%. The best rose by 40%, the worst fell by 16%.

UK Smaller Companies Trusts which invest at least 80% of their assets in UK equities which form part of the Hoare Govett UK Smaller Companies Extended Index. This Hoare Govett index includes the 10% of smallest companies by market capitalisation in the main UK stockmarket plus all £ sterling denominated companies on the USM. The 66 trusts on average rose by 7%. The best rose by 24%, the worst fell by 13%.

Investment Trust Units Invest direct. See *Investment Trust Shares.*

Commodity and Energy Trusts which invest at least 80% in commodity and energy shares in the UK and abroad. The 20 trusts on average fell by 2%. The best rose by 25%, the worst fell by 19%.

Gold Shares M&G, NM Financial. Note many gold mining shares are in overseas companies or ones with assets overseas.

Convertibles Trusts where at least 60% is invested in convertible loan stocks in the UK or overseas. See *Stock Convertible Loan.*

Fund of Funds Trusts which invest in other unit trusts. Not recommended.

For pessimists If you think shares are going to crash, make money by investing in Govett MIS Bear Funds. The snag is a minimum investment of £100,000.

Trusts which avoid investments in arms companies, tobacco companies, etc are called 'ethical' unit trusts. Some also try to invest in companies which have a positive attitude to the environment. A guide 'Choosing an Ethical Investment Fund' is available from EIRIS. Ethical trusts include: Allchurches Amity, Buckmaster Fellowship, Friends Provident Stewardship and Stewardship Income, Merlin Jupiter Ecology, NM Conscience.

UNIT TRUST

Invested in Overseas Shares

(*Also called International Unit Trust, Worldwide Unit Trust*)

The best performing trusts change frequently. Where trusts are listed, there is little choice, or the trusts are the only ones available. Average performance is based on Micropal figures for 12 months to the beginning of February 1993. Most trusts invested abroad in ordinary shares have a low income yield or none at all. Trusts investing in N. America, the Far East, and Japan are more volatile and therefore have a chance of a greater loss or gain.

International Equity Growth   Trusts which invest at least 80% of their assets in overseas shares and whose main aim is capital growth. The 158 trusts rose on average by 8%. The best rose by 48%, the worst fell by 8%.

International Equity Income   At least 80% in overseas shares whose income yield is more than 110% of the FT Worldwide Index. The 16 trusts rose on average by 16%. The best rose 23%, the worst rose 10%.

International Fixed Interest   See *Unit Trust Stock & Bond Fund.*

International Balanced   At least 80% in overseas shares and overseas or foreign currency government or fixed interest stocks. The 21 trusts rose on average by 10%. The best rose by 23%, the worst was unchanged.

North America   At least 80% in North American stocks and shares and 20% to 100% in shares. The 123 trusts on average rose by 21%. The best rose by 56%, the worst lost 19%.

Canada   Hambros, New Court.

Latin American   Edinburgh.

Europe   At least 80% in European stocks and shares (including the UK) and 20% to 100% in European shares (excluding the UK). The 131 trusts rose on average by 4%. The best rose by 27%, the worst fell by 18%. For individual countries **France**: INVESCO. **Germany**: Brown Shipley, GT, Lloyds Bank. **Scandinavia**: Hambros. **Spain**: AEtna Iberian.

Japan   At least 80% in Japanese stocks and shares and 20% to 100% in Japanese shares. The 88 trusts on average fell by 9%. The best rose 31%, the worst lost 27%.

Far East including Japan   At least 80% in the Far East including Japan and Australia, where 20% to 100% is in Far Eastern shares, and 20% to 100% in countries other than Japan, and 20% to 100% in countries other than Australia and New Zealand. The 47 trusts on average rose by 9%. The best rose by 31%, the worst lost 9%.

Far East excluding Japan   At least 80% in the Far East excluding Japan, where 20% to 100% is in Far Eastern shares, and 20% to 100% is in countries other than Australia and New Zealand and none in Japan. The 54 trusts on average rose by 28%. The best rose by 66%, the worst rose by 6%. For individual countries: **Hong Kong (and China)**: Gartmore, INVESCO. **Singapore & Malaysia**: INVESCO, NM Financial. **Korea**: GT.

Australasia   At least 80% in Australia and New Zealand and 20% to 100% in shares. The 7 trusts on average rose 3%. The best rose 37%. The worst lost 9%. Barclays, Henderson, M&G, NM Financial.

UNIT TRUST

Personal Equity Plan

(Also called Unit Trust PEP, Tax Break, Stratagem, Tax Free Portfolio)

A means of investing up to £6,000 a year in unit trusts with at least 50% of their assets in UK or EC shares free of all tax. Up to £1,500 can be in 'non-qualifying' trusts where 50% of the assets must be in shares, but not necessarily in the UK or EC. It's easiest to invest monthly. You usually have a choice of trusts and should choose one with a higher income to benefit from the tax exemption.

Who can invest   Anyone 18 or over. Joint plans are not allowed but husband and wife can have one each. In any one tax year you can only invest in one Personal Equity Plan from one manager.

How worthwhile   Good value for taxpayers especially higher rate taxpayers. Compare with *Investment Trust Personal Equity Plan*. Higher rate taxpayers also consider *Shares Self Select Personal Equity Plan*.

Minimum   *£30 a month:* Barclays Unicorn. *£40 a month:* Equitable Life, Friends Provident. *£50 a month:* GT, Mercury, M & G. *£100 a month:* Murray Johnstone.

Maximum   £6,000 a year, £500 a month plus managers' charges.

Suitable   Lump sums. Regular savings.

Money back   You can normally sell the units when you like. If you die the plan ends.

Interest   Variable. Called *distribution.* The before tax interest is called the *yield* and plans which show the highest yield are most attractive as they make the most use of the tax exemptions.

Interest paid   Dividends and interest may be accumulated; or paid by cheque or to a bank account, half-yearly or quarterly; or you have a choice of whether interest is paid out (with those listed here).

Tax   Income and capital gains are completely tax free and need not be entered on a tax return. Tax deducted from the distribution is reclaimed by the manager on your behalf.

Fees to pay   Same as for unit trusts: Initial 5¼% to 6%, yearly 1% to 1½%. Some managers, not listed here, charge you twice: once for the personal equity plan and again within the unit trust.

Passbook   None. Receipt provided. Statements sent.

Children   Not allowed.

Risk   High but not as risky as buying individual shares. The value of the units can go down as well as up.

How to invest   Call, phone or write to a unit trust manager, ask for details and compare them. Choose their highest yielding unit trust. Monthly investment will normally have to be by direct debit or standing order from a bank account.

Where from   Barclays Unicorn, Equitable Life, Friends Provident, GT, M&G, Mercury, Murray Johnstone.

UNIT TRUST

Savings Plan

A commitment to save a fixed minimum amount regularly, usually monthly, which is invested in units of a unit trust (a fund of stocks and shares managed by professionals). The units closely reflect the value of the stocks and shares held within the trust. You can make additional savings in any month. The plan can be stopped at any time; you either sell the units back to the managers at the current market price or continue holding the units as an ordinary unit trust – see *Unit Trust Invested in Shares* **and** *Unit Trust Index Tracker*.

Who can invest Anyone.

How worthwhile Flexible and potentially good value for taxpayers who want to link their regular savings to the value of a fund of stocks and shares provided you avoid trusts with high charges. If you have less than £6,000 a year (£500 a month) consider instead *Unit Trust Personal Equity Plan*. Compare with *Investment Trust Savings Plan* and *Investment Trust Personal Equity Plan*. Unsuitable for non-taxpayers.

Minimum £20 to £100 a month. You can buy more when you feel like it.

Maximum None.

Money back Within a couple of weeks. Units are sold at the current market price. Some companies allow partial withdrawals.

Interest Variable. Called *distribution*.

Interest paid Accumulated within the trust or used to buy extra units (there is a small charge).

Tax 20% tax is deducted from the interest (called a *tax credit*). Non-taxpayers can reclaim the tax credit from the Inland Revenue. Higher rate taxpayers have to pay extra; basic taxpayers don't. Gains on units are liable to capital gains tax (see Chapter 5) though the managers pay no capital gains tax on gains on shares held within the trust.

Fees to pay Initial charge usually 5–6% included in difference between buying and selling price usually of between 5½% and 7%. Yearly charge of 1%–1½% deducted from your income. A few trusts make extra charges. Others give a discount if you keep saving or from the start.

Passbook None. Statements of units and distributions sent half-yearly.

Children Under 18 (sometimes 14) units should be in an adult's name and are *designated* with the child's name or initials.

Risk By buying regularly you even out fluctuations in the market price, eg you buy when prices are low as well as high. You still need to choose the right time to sell. Otherwise the same as *Unit Trust Invested in Shares*.

How to invest Choose a trust. Phone the managers and ask for their literature, whether they operate a scheme (most do), and an application form.

Where from The following managers give discounts or loyalty bonuses: Abtrust, Allchurches, Brown Shipley, Commercial Union, Crown, Framlington, Friends Provident, Lloyds Bank, Manulife, Sun Life.

UNIT TRUST

Stock and Bond Fund

(Also called: International Fixed Interest, Worldwide Bond, Currency Bond, International Bond, Global Bond, EMU)

You invest in a fund of foreign currency fixed interest stocks. Most funds invest in a mixture of stocks in different foreign currencies including £. Others invest in certain areas eg Europe, North America.

Who can invest   Anyone.

How worthwhile   Suitable for people who expect interest rates to fall in the country or areas the managers choose to invest in thus boosting the capital value of the fund. Unsuitable for non-taxpayers unless the fund has a high yield. If you want to invest in stocks in a single foreign currency see *Offshore Stock and Bond Fund*. If you want a similar investment confined to the UK, see *Shares Preference Shares* and *Stock Unit Trust Invested in Gilts*.

Minimum   Around £1,000 initially.

Maximum   None.

Suitable   Lump sums. Regular savings.

Money back   A few days.

Interest   Variable. Called *distribution*. The before-tax interest is called the *yield*; trusts specialising in different countries will have different yields. Invest in trusts which have a relatively high yield.

Interest paid   Half-yearly or quarterly by cheque or direct to a bank account.

Tax   Variable. Tax is deducted from the interest. Non-taxpayers can reclaim the tax from the Inland Revenue. Higher rate taxpayers have to pay extra; basic taxpayers don't. Gains on units are liable to capital gains tax but see Chapter 5.

Fees to pay   Initial charge: 3¼–6% included in difference between buying and selling price of 4%–7%. Yearly: 1%–1.5% deducted from your income.

Passbook   None. Unit trust certificate issued. Report and distribution voucher usually sent half-yearly.

Children   Under 18, units should be held in an adult's name and are *designated* with the child's name or initials.

Risk   Reasonably high. The value of the units goes down as well as up in line with changes in exchange rates as well as interest rates in the relevant countries. Some funds are 'hedged' to avoid the currency risk. The stocks in the trust are held by a Government approved trustee to ensure managers invest in what they say they do.

How to invest   Phone the managers for details or get advice from an independent financial adviser on the best time to buy (and sell) and which trust to choose.

Where from   Listed in order of highest 'yield' on 1 January 1993: Guinness Flight EMU, Guinness Flight Global High Income, Cannon International Currency Bond, Waverly Global Bond, Newton International Bond, Baring Global Bond, Thornton Dresdner European.

Appendix 1

Useful Addresses

Note: Calls to numbers which start with 0800 and 0500 are free and those with 0345 are at local call rates.

Abbey Life plc
100 Holdenhurst Road, Bournemouth, BH8 8AL. Tel: 0202-292 373. Unit Trust dealers: 0345-717 373.

Abbey National plc
Abbey House, Baker Street, London NW1 6XL. Tel: 071-486 5555.

Abtrust Unit Trusts
10 Queens Terrace, Aberdeen, AB9 1QJ. Tel: 0224-633 070.

Aetna Life Insurance Company
2–12 Pentonville Road, London N1 9XG. Tel: 0800 181 766 or 071-837 6494. Life company and unit trust managers.

AIB Bank
Bank Centre Britain, Belmont Road, Uxbridge UB8 1SA. Tel: 0895-272 222. Subsidiary of Allied Irish Banks, Eire.

Albany Life
Metropolitan House, 3 Darkes Lane, Potters Bar, EN6 1AJ. Tel: 0707-642 311.

ALICO
22 Addiscombe Road, Croydon, CR9 5AZ. Tel: 081-680 6000. Life company, formerly called American Life.

Allchurches
Beaufort House, Brunswick Road, Gloucester GL1 1JZ. Tel: Life: 0452-526 265. Unit trusts: 0452-305 958.

Alliance & Leicester Building Society
Administration Centre, Hove Park, Hove, East Sussex BN3 7AZ. Tel: 0273-775 454.

Alliance Trust
Meadow House, 64 Reform Street, Dundee DD1 1TJ. Tel: 0382-201 700. Investment trust managers.

Allied Dunbar Group
Allied Dunbar Centre, Swindon SN1 1EL. Tel: 0793-514 514. Life and unit trust company.

American Express
International Dollar Card, Prestamex House, 171–173 Preston Road BN2 1YX. Tel: 0273-693 555.

Anglia Regional Co-op
Park Road, Peterborough, PE1 2TA. Tel: 0733-631 51.

Association of Investment Trust Companies
Park House, (6th Floor), 16 Finsbury Circus, London EC2M 7JJ. Tel: 071-588 5347.

AXA Equity & Law
Amersham Road, High Wycombe, Bucks HP13 5AL. Tel: 0494-463 463 or 071-242 8644. Life company and unit trust managers.

Baillie Gifford & Co
1 Rutland Court, Edinburgh, EH3 8EY. Tel: 031-222 4000. Dealers: 031-222 4242. Unit trust managers.

Bank of Scotland
Orchard Brae House, 30 Queensferry Road, Edinburgh EH4 2UH. Tel: 031-442 7777.

Banking Ombudsman
Citadel House, 5–11 Fetter Lane, London EC4A 1BR. Tel: 071-583 1395. Fax: 071-583 5873.

Barclays Bank
Murray House, 1 Royal Mint Court, London EC3N 4HJ. Tel: 071-488 1144.

Baring Global Fund Managers
155 Bishopsgate, London EC2M 3XY. Tel: 071-628 6000.

Beneficial Bank
Beneficial Building, 28 Paradise Circus, Queensway B1 2BA. Tel: 021-633 4400.

Birmingham Midshires Building Society
PO Box 81, 35–49 Lichfield Street, Wolverhampton WV1 1EL. Tel: 0902-302 832 or 710 710.

Bradford & Bingley Building Society
PO Box 2, Bingley, W Yorkshire BD16 2LW. Tel: 0274-555 555.

Brighton Co-operative Society
94–101 London Road, Brighton, BN1 4LB. Tel: 0273-606 722.

Bristol & West Building Society
PO Box 27, Broad Quay, Bristol BS99 7AX.
Tel: 0272-294 271.

Britannia Building Society
PO Box 20, Britannia House, Leek ST13 5RG.
Tel: 0538-399 399.

Britannia (Isle of Man)
8 Victoria Street, Douglas, Isle of Man. Tel:
0624-628 512. Offshore bank, subsidiary of
UK building society.

Brown Shipley Investment Management
Founders Court, Lothbury, London EC2R 7HE.
Tel: 071-606 9833. Dealers: 0444-412 262.

Buckmaster Management
15 St Botolph Street, London, EC3A 7JJ. Tel:
071-247 4542.

Building Society Choice
Riverside House, Rattlesden, Bury St
Edmunds IP30 0SF. Tel: 0449-736 287. A
monthly newsletter. Also publishes Good
Savings Guide, Good Offshore Guide, Good
Tessa Guide, Expats and Charities Choice.

Cannon Lincoln Group
1 Olympic Way, Wembley, Middlesex HA9
0NB. Tel: 081-902 8876. Unit trust dealers:
0800 282 621. Life and unit trust company.

Capital Ventures
Rutherford Way, Cheltenham, Gloucestershire GL51 9TR. Tel: 0242-584 380. Property
enterprise zone trust and BES managers.

Carlyle Life
21 Windsor Place, Cardiff CF1 3BY. Tel: 0222-
371 726.

Charles Stanley & Co Ltd
25 Luke Street, London EC2A 4AR. Tel: 071-
739 8200. Stockbrokers.

Charterhouse Bank
1 Paternoster Row, St Pauls,
London EC4M 7DH. Tel: 071-248 4000 x2524.

Chelsea Building Society
Thirlestaine Hall, Thirlestaine Road,
Cheltenham, Glos GL53 7AL. Tel: 0242-521
391.

Cheltenham & Gloucester Building Society
Chief Office, Barnett Way, Gloucester GL4
7RL. Tel: 0452-372 372.

Cheshire Building Society
Castle Street, Macclesfeld, Cheshire SK11
6AH. Tel: 0625-613 612.

City & Metropolitan Building Society
219 High Street, Bromley, Kent BR1 1PR. Tel:
081-464 0814.

Clerical Medical
Narrow Plain, Bristol BS2 0JH. Tel: 071-930
5474 or 0272-290 566. Life company and unit
trust managers.

Close Brothers Investment
36 Great St. Helen's, London EC3A 6AP. Tel:
071-283 2241. Business Expansion Fund and
Enterprise Zone Trust sponsors.

Clydesdale Bank
PO Box 43, 150 Buchanan Street, Glasgow G1
2HL. Tel: 041-248 7070.

Collective Investments Ltd
77 London Wall EC2M 5ND. Tel: 071-628
2828. Property Enterprise Zone Trust
managers.

Co-operative Retail Services
National Investment Office, 29 Dantzic Street,
Manchester M4 4BA. Tel: 061-832 8152.

Commercial Union Assurance
Commercial Union House, 69 Park Lane,
Croydon CR9 1BG. Tel: 071-283 7500. Life
company and unit trust managers.

Coventry Building Society
Economic House, High Street, Coventry CV1
5QN. Tel: 0203-252 277.

CWS (Co-operative Wholesale Society Ltd)
Money Desk, New Century House,
Manchester M60 4ES. Tel: 061-835 2345.

Derbyshire Building Society
PO Box 1, Duffield Hall, Duffield, Derby DE6
1AG. Tel: 0332-841 791.

Derbyshire Building Society (Isle of Man)
PO Box 136, Heritage Court, 39 Athol Street,
Douglas, Isle of Man IM99 1LR. Tel: 0624-663
432. Offshore bank, subsidiary of UK building
society.

Dunedin Fund Managers
25 Ravelston Terrace, Edinburgh EH4 3EX.
Tel: 0800-838 993 or 031-315 2500.
Investment trust and unit trust managers.

Eagle Star Insurance
Eagle Star House, Bath Road, Cheltenham
GL5 7LQ. Tel: 0242-221 311.

East Mercia Co-operative Society
22 Abbey Street, Nuneaton CV11 5BU. Tel:
0203-382 331.

Edinburgh Fund Managers
Donaldson House, 97 Haymarket Terrace,
Edinburgh EH12 5HD. Tel: 031-313 1000.
Dealers: 0345-090 526.

Equitable Life
Walton Street, Aylesbury, Bucks HP21 7QW.
Tel: 071-606 6611 or 0296-391 000. Life
company, unit trust and PEP managers.

Fidelity Investment Services
Oakhill House, 130 Tonbridge Road,
Tonbridge, Kent TN11 9DZ. Tel: 0732-361 144.
Dealers: 0800-414 161 (open 7 days, 9am–
9pm).

FIMBRA
Hertsmere House, Hertsmere Road, London E14 4AB. Tel: 071-538 8860. Regulatory organisation for independent financial advisers.

Financial Times Business Publishing
Subscription Department: Tel: 081-680 3786. Editorial Tel: 071-405 6969. Publishers of Money Management Magazine, Investors Chronicle, Pensions Management Magazine, The Unit Trust Year Book, The Pension Buyer's Report.

First Direct
Arlington Business Centre, Milshaw Park Lane, Leeds LS11 0LT. Tel: 0345-100 100 (open 7 days, 24 hours). A bank, part of Midland Bank Group.

Framlington Unit Management
155 Bishopsgate, London EC2M 3FT. Tel: 071-374 4100.

Friends' Provident
United Kingdom House, Castle Street, Salisbury SP1 3SH. Tel: 0722-413 366. Life company and unit trust managers.

Furness Building Society
51–55 Duke Street, Barrow-in-Furness, Cumbria LA14 1RT. Tel: 0229-824 560.

GA Life
2 Rougier Street, York YO1 1HR. Tel: 0904-628 982. Life company and unit trust managers.

Gartmore Investment Management
Gartmore House, 16–18 Monument Street, London EC3R 8QQ. Tel: 071-623 1212. Dealers: 0277-264 421.

General Portfolio Life
General Portfolio House, Station Approach, Harlow, Essex CM20 2EW. Tel: 0279-626 262.

Girobank
Bootle, Merseyside G1R 0AA. Tel: 051-928 8181 or 071-600 6020.

Govett
See John Govett.

Greig Middleton & Co
66 Wilson Street, London EC2A 2BL. Tel: 071-247 0007. Stockbrokers and property enterprise zone trust managers.

GT Unit Trusts
8th Floor, 8 Devonshire Square, London EC2M 4YJ. Tel: 071-220 4444. Dealing: 071-626 9431.

Guinness Flight (CI)
PO Box 250, La Plaiderie, St Peter Port, Guernsey CI. Tel: 0481-710 404. Offshore fund.

Guiness Flight Unit Trusts
Lighteman's Court, 5 Gainsford Street, Tower Bridge, London SE1 2NE. Tel: 071-522 2100.

Guinness Mahon Guernsey
PO Box 188, La Vieille Court, St. Peter Port, Guernsey, CI. Tel: 0481-723 506. Offshore bank.

Halifax Building Society
Trinity Road, Halifax, West Yorkshire HX1 2RG. Tel: 0422-333 333.

Hambros Fund Managers (CI)
PO Box 255, Barfield House, St Julian's Avenue, St Peter Port Guernsey, CI. Tel: 0481-715 454. Offshore fund.

Hambros Unit Trust Managers
41 Tower Hill, London EC3N 4HA. Tel: 0800-289 895 or 071-480 5000. Dealing: 0277-261 010.

Hanley Economic Building Society
Granville House, Festival Park, Hanley, Stoke-on-Trent, Staffs ST1 5TB. Tel: 0782-208 733.

Henderson Unit Trust Management
3 Finsbury Avenue, London EC2M 2PA. Tel: 071-638 5757.

HFC Bank
North Street, Winkfield, Windsor, Berks SL4 4TD. Tel: 0344-890 000.

Hill Samuel Investment Services
NLA Tower, 12 Addiscombe Road, Croydon CR9 6BP. Tel: 081-686 4355. Unit trust managers.

Hinton & Wild (Insurance)
374 Ewell Road, Surbiton, Surrey KT6 7BB. Tel: 081-390 8166. Financial adviser specialising in home income plans.

Homeowners Friendly Society
PO Box 94, Springfield Avenue, Harrogate HG1 2HN. Tel: 0800-373 010 or 0423-567 355.

IMRO (Investment Managers Regulatory Organisation)
Broadwalk House, Appold Street, London EC2A 2AA. Tel: 071-628 6022. Regulatory organisation for investment managers including unit trusts.

Independent Schools Information Service (ISIS)
56 Buckingham Gate, London SW1E 6AG. Tel: 071-630 8793 or 8794.

Inland Revenue PAYE Enquiry Offices
Public Enquiry Room, Somerset House, London WC2R 1LB. Tel: 071-438 6622. Supplies list of local enquiry offices. Will provide leaflets listed on page 29 if you can't get them from a local office. For quicker service send a stamped addressed envelope 9″ × 6″.

Institute of Chartered Accountants
PO Box 433, Chartered Accountants' Hall, Moorgate Place, London EC2P 2BJ. Tel: 071-828 7060.

Insurance Brokers Registration Council
15 St Helen's Place, London EC3A 6DS. Tel: 071-588 4387.

Insurance Ombudsman Bureau
31 Southampton Row, London WC1B 5HJ. Tel: 071-928 7600.

Investment Ombudsman
6 Frederick's Place, London EC2R 8BT. Tel: 071-796 3065.

Investors Chronicle
A weekly magazine. See Financial Times Business Publishing.

INVESCO
11 Devonshire Square, London EC2M 4YR. Tel: 071-626 3434. Unit trust and PEP managers.

Ipswich Building Society
44 Upper Brook Street, Ipswich, Suffolk IP4 1DP. Tel: 0473-211 021.

Ivory & Sime
PO Box 189, Edinburgh EH2 4DZ. Tel: 0506-441 234 or 031-225 1357. Investment trust and PEP managers.

Jardine Fleming Bank
5 Mount Pleasant, Douglas, Isle of Man. Tel: 0624-661 880.

John Govett Unit Management
Shackleton House, 4 Battle Bridge Lane, London SE1 2HR. Tel: 071-378 7979. Dealers: 071-407 7888.

Johnson Fry
Dorland House, 20 Regent Street, London SW1Y 4PZ. Tel: 071-321 0220. Property enterprise zone trust and BES managers.

Killik & Co
45 Cadogan Street, London SW3 2QJ. Tel: 071-589 1577. Stockbrokers and PEP managers.

Kleinwort Benson
10 Fenchurch Street, London EC2M 3LB. Tel: 071-623 8000. A bank.

Lambeth Building Society
118 Westminster Bridge Road, London SE1 7XE. Tel: 071-928 1331.

Lautro Complaints Department
2–6 Sydenham Road, Croydon CR0 9XE. Tel: 081-688 8350. Regulatory organisation for life companies and unit trusts.

Law Society Compensation Fund
Portland House, Stag Place, London SW1E 5BL. Tel: 071-834 2288.

Lazard Unit Trust Managers Ltd
21 Moorfields, London EC2P 2HT. Tel: 071-588 2721. Dealers 071-374 0916.

Leeds & Holbeck Building Society
105 Albion Street, Leeds LS1 5AS. Tel: 0532-459 511.

Leeds Permanent Building Society
Permanent House, 1 Level Park Road, Leeds LS1 1NS. Tel: 0532-438 181.

Leeds Permanent Overseas
61 Strand Street, Douglas, Isle of Man. Tel: 0624-626 266. Offshore bank, subsidiary of building society.

Legal & General Assurance
Kingswood, Tadworth, Surrey KT20 6EU. Tel: 0737-370 370 Life and pensions company.

Legal & General Unit Trust Managers
Bucklesbury House, 3 Queen Victoria Street, London EC4N 8EL. Tel: 071-528 6793.

LIFFE, The London International Financial Futures and Options Exchange
Cannon Bridge, London EC4R 3XX. Tel: 071-623 0444.

Lloyds Bank
71 Lombard Street, London EC3P 3BS. Tel: 071-626 1500. Unit trust dealers: 0444-459 144. Bank and unit trust managers.

London Life
100 Temple Street, Bristol BS1 6EA. Tel: 0272-279 179.

Loughborough Building Society
6 Hill Street, Loughborough LE11 2PY. Tel: 0509-610 707.

M & G Group
Three Quays, Tower Hill, London EC3R 6BQ. Tel: 071-626 4588. Unit trust managers, PEP managers and life company.

Market Harborough Building Society
Welland House, The Square, Market Harborough, Leicestershire LE16 7PD. Tel: 0858-463 244.

Marsden Building Society
6–20 Russell Street, Nelson, Lancs BB9 7NJ. Tel: 0282-692 821.

Mercury Asset Managers
33 King William Street, London EC4R 9AS. Tel: 071-280 2800. Dealing: 071-280 2060.

Midland Bank
Poultry, London EC2P 2BX. Tel: 071-260 8000.

Midland Bank Isle of Man Branch
PO Box 20, 10 Victoria Street, Douglas Isle of Man. Tel: 0624-623 051. Offshore bank, branch of UK bank.

Money Management
A monthly magazine. Editorial tel: 071-405 6969. See Financial Times Business Publishing.

Money Observer
Chelsea Bridge House, Queens Town Road, London SW8 4NN. Tel: 071-627 0700. A monthly magazine.

Moneyfacts
Laundry Loke, Near Walsham, Norfolk NR28 0BD. Tel: 0692-500 765. An extremely useful monthly newsletter.

Moneywise
25 Berkeley Square, London, W1. Tel: 071-629 8144. A monthly magazine.

Moorgate Investment Management
49 Hay's Mews, London W1X 7RT. Tel: 071-409 3419. Investment trust managers.

Morgan Grenfell & Co
20 Finsbury Circus, London, EC2M 1UT. Tel: 071-256 7500. Dealers: 071-826 0826. Unit trust managers.

Murray Johnstone
7 West Nile Street, Glasgow G2 2PX. Tel: 0345-090 933 or 041-226 3131. Investment and unit trust managers.

National & Provincial Building Society
Provincial House, Bradford, W Yorkshire BD1 1NL. Tel: 0274-733 444.

N & P (Overseas)
56 Strand Street, Douglas, Isle of Man. Tel: 0624-662 828. Offshore bank, subsidiary of UK building society.

National Counties Building Society
147 High Street, Epsom, Surrey KT19 8EN. Tel: 0372-742 211.

National Savings
Charles House, 375 Kensington High Street, London W14 8SD. General enquiries: 071-605 9461 or 9200. For latest interest rates (24 hour recorded message) phone 071-605 9483 or 9484; Blackpool 0253-723 714; Glasgow 041-632 2766.

National Savings Bank, Capital Bond and FIRST Option Bond Office
Glasgow G58 1SB. Tel: 041-649 4555. Deals with Capital Bond, FIRST Option Bond, Investment Account and Ordinary Account.

National Savings Certificate and SAYE Office
Durham DH99 1NS. Tel: 091-386 4900. Deals with Savings Certificates, Index-Linked Certificates, Yearly Plan and SAYE.

National Savings Stock Register
Blackpool FY3 9YP. Tel: 0253-766 151. Deals with Government Stock and Income Bonds.

National Westminster Bank plc
41 Lothbury, London EC2P 2BP. Tel: 071-726 1000 or 0800-200 400.

Nationwide Building Society
Nationwide House, Pipers Way, Swindon SN38 1NW. Tel: 0793-456 800 or 071-242 8822.

New Court Unit Trusts
See Rothschild Asset Management.

Newton Fund Managers
No 2 London Bridge, London SE1 9RA. Tel: 071-407 4404.

Newcastle Building Society
Hood Street, Newcastle-upon-Tyne NE1 6JP. Tel: 091-232 6676.

NM Financial Management Ltd
Enterprise House, Isambard Brunel Road, Portsmouth PO1 2AW. Tel: 0705-827 733. Life company and unit trust managers.

North of England Building Society
50 Fawcett Street, Sunderland SR1 1SA. Tel: 091-565 6272.

Northern Bank
Donegall Square West, Belfast BT1 6JS. Tel: 0232-245 277.

Northern Rock Building Society
Northern Rock House, Gosforth, Newcastle-upon-Tyne NE3 4PL. Tel: 091-285 7191.

Norwich & Peterborough Building Society
Peterborough Business Park, Lynch Wood, Peterborough PE2 6WZ. Tel: 0733-371 371.

Norwich Union
PO Box 48, Surrey Street, Norwich NR1 3NS. Tel: 0603-622 200. Life company and unit trust managers.

Occupational Pensions Advisory Service (OPAS)
11 Belgrave Road, London SW1V 1RB. Tel: 071-233 8080.

Occupational Pensions Board
PO Box 2EE, Newcastle-upon-Tyne NE99 2EE. Tel: 091-225 6414 or 6417.

Old Court Funds (CI)
Rothschild Asset Management (CI), PO Box 242, St Julian's Court, St Peter Port, Guernsey, CI. Tel: 0481-713 713, Offshore funds.

Oxford Swindon & Gloucester Co-op
New Barclay House, Botley Road, Oxford OX2 0HP. Tel: 0865-249 241.

Pensions Ombudsman
11 Belgrave Road, London SW1V 1RB. Tel: 071-834 9144.

Pilling & Co
12 St Ann's Square, Manchester M2 7HT. Tel: 061-832 6581. Stockbrokers and PEP managers.

Portman Building Society
Portman House, Richmond Hill, Bournemouth BH2 6EP. Tel: 0800-373 176 or 0202-292 444.

Portman Channel Islands
Ollivier Court, Ollivier Street, St Anne Alderney, Cl. Tel: 0481-822 747. Offshore bank, subsidiary of building society.

Professional Life
PO Box 26, Skandia House, Portland Terrace, Southampton SO9 7RS. Tel: 071-353 5081 or 0703-334 411.

Prolific Unit Trusts
Walbrook House, 23 Walbrook, London EC4N 8LD. Tel: 071-280 3700. Dealing: 0800 262 443.

Property Enterprise Managers
2 Stratford Place, London W1N 9AE. Tel: 071-486 5267.

Provident Life
Provident Way, Basingstoke, Hants RG21 2SZ. Te!: 0256-470 707.

Prudential Unit Trust Managers
Valentine House, 51–69 Ilford Hill, Ilford, Essex IG1 TDL. Tel: 081-478 3377. Dealers: 071-911 4490.

Refuge Assurance Company
Alderley Road, Wilmslow, Cheshire SK9 1PF. Tel: 0625-535 959.

Robert Fleming (Isle of Man)
5 Mount Pleasant, Douglas Isle of Man. Tel: 0624-661 880. Offshore bank, subsidiary of UK bank.

Rothschild Asset Management
Five Arrows House, St Swithin's Lane, London EC4N 8NR. Tel: 071-280 5000. See also Old Court Funds.

Royal Bank of Scotland
42 St Andrew Square, Edinburgh EH2 2YE. Tel: 031-556 8555 or London 071-623 4356.

Royal Bank of Scotland (IOM)
Victory House, Prospect Hill, Douglas Isle of Man. Tel: 0624-629 111. Offshore bank, subsidiary of UK bank.

Royal London Group
Royal London House, 27 Middleborough, Colchester, Essex CO1 1RA. Tel: 0206-761 761. Life company.

Royal Mint
Llantrisant, Pontyclum, Mid Glamorgan CF7 8YT. Tel: 0443-222 111.

Save & Prosper Group
1 Finsbury Avenue, London EC2M 2QY. Tel: 071-588 1717 or 0800 282 101 (9am–5.30pm 7 days) or 0708-766 966. *Admin Centre:* 16–22 Western Road, Romford RM1 1TZ. Life company, unit trust managers, PEP managers, bankers (as agents for Robert Fleming & Co Ltd).

Scarborough Building Society
Prospect House, PO Box 6, 442 Scalby Road, Scarborough, N Yorkshire YO12 6EQ. Tel: 0723-368 155.

School Fees Insurance Agency
SFIA House, 15 Forlease Road, Maidenhead, Berkshire SL6 1JA. Tel: 0628-34 291.

Schroders
33 Gutter Lane, London EC2V 8AS. Tel: 0800-526 535 or 071-382 6963. Unit trust managers and bank.

Scottish Life
19 St Andrew Square, Edinburgh EH2 1YE. Tel: 031-225 2211. Life company and unit trust managers.

Scottish Provident
6 St Andrew Square, Edinburgh EH2 2YA. Tel: 031-556 9181. Life company and unit trust managers.

Scottish Widows
15 Dalkeith Road, Edinburgh EH16 5BU. Tel: 031-655 6000. Life company and unit trust managers.

Securities & Investment Board
See SIB.

Seymour Pierce Butterfields
24 Chiswell Street, London EC1Y 4TY. Tel: 071-814 8700. Booklet on shareholder perks price £5.

SIB (Securities & Investment Board)
Gavrelle House, 2–14 Bunhill Row, London EC1Y 8RA. Tel: 071-638 1240. Regulatory body.

Skipton Building Society
The Bailey, Skipton, North Yorkshire BD23 1DN. Tel: Customer services 0756-700 511. General 0756-700 500.

Spink & Son
5 King Street, St James, London SW1Y 6QS. Tel: 071-930 7888.

Standard Life
PO Box 186, 125 George Street, Edinburgh EH2 2LJ. Tel: 031-225 2552. Life company and unit trust managers.

Stock Exchange
Old Broad Street, London EC2N 1HP. Tel: 071-588 2344. Will provide list of stockbrokers willing to take new private clients. Also from Birmingham (021-236 9181), Manchester (061-833 0931), Belfast (0232-321 094), Glasgow (041-221 7060). By post write to Proshare, Library Chambers, 13–14 Basinghall Street, London EC2.

Stroud & Swindon Building Society
Rowcroft, Stroud, Gloucestershire GL5 3BG.
Tel: 0453-757 011.

Sun Life Unit Trusts
101 Cannon Street, London EC4N 5AD. Tel:
071-606 4044. Dealers: 071-606 6010.

Teachers Building Society
Allenview House, Hanham Road, Wimborne,
Dorset BH21 1AG. Tel: 0202-887 171.

Thornton Unit Trust Managers
33 Cavendish Square, London W1M 0DH. Tel:
071-493 7262. Dealers: 071-493 8545.

Tipton & Cosely Building Society
70 Owen Street, Tipton, W Midlands DY4
8HG. Tel: 021-577 2551.

TSB Bank
Victoria House, Victoria Square, Birmingham
B1 1BZ. Tel: 021-600 6000.

Unit Trust Year Book
See Financial Times Business Publishing.

Waverley Unit Trust Management
13 Charlotte Square, Edinburgh EH2 4DJ. Tel:
031-225 1551.

West Bromwich Building Society
374 High Street, West Bromwich, West
Midlands B70 8LR. Tel: 021-525 7070.

Western Trust & Savings Ltd
The Moneycentre, Plymouth PL1 1SE. Tel:
0752-224 141. A bank.

What Investment
A monthly magazine.

Woolwich Building Society
Watling Street, Bexleyheath, Kent DA6 7RR.
Tel: 081-298 5000.

Yorkshire Bank
Brunswick Point, Wades Lane, Leeds LS2
8NQ. Tel: 0532-441 244.

Yorkshire Building Society
Yorkshire House, Westgate, Bradford BD1
2AU. Tel: 0274-734 822.

Yorkshire Guernsey Ltd
PO Box 304, Canada Court, St. Peter Port,
Guernsey, CI. Tel: 0481-719 898. Offshore
bank, subsidiary of UK building society.

Appendix 2

The Retail Prices Index

The Retail Prices Index is the official measure of inflation. It is calculated once a month by the Central Statistical Office which sends people round the country to record the price of many different types of goods and services. These are averaged out according to a typical family's expenditure and summarised as an index number which is announced on the second or third Friday of the month following the month to which the index relates. All the available index numbers are listed opposite or overleaf; up to 1961 there are yearly figures; since 1962 they are monthly. From January 1987 the index has been rebased – that means the old January 1987 figure of 394.7 becomes 100.

Working out how much prices have gone up by Suppose you had £1,000 in 1955 and want to know what it should be worth today to have kept pace with inflation. Check the latest price index, say 137.9 for January 1993. Divide by the index number for 1955, 11.2 which gives 12.3125. Then multiply the answer, 12.3125 by £1,000 which gives the answer £12,312. The percentage increase in prices over that period would be 1,131% (not 1,231%). To work out percentage rise in prices over the last 12 months divide the latest index number by the one 12 months before. For instance January 1993, 137.9 divided by January 1992, 135.6 comes to 1.01696. That means prices have risen by 1.7% over 12 months.

Index-Linked Savings Certificates The index number relating to investment is the one for two months earlier. If you invest in June, it is the April index number which counts as the starting index. The April index is published in May. The same applies when you cash. The final value of your certificates relates to the index for two months earlier, published the month before.

Retail Prices Index 1914 to 1985

Figures rebased to 100 at January 1987

	1920	1921	1922	1923	1924	1925
Average	7.0	6.4	5.2	4.9	4.9	5.0

	1932	1933	1934	1935	1936	1937
Average	4.1	4.0	4.0	4.0	4.2	4.4

	1950	1951	1952	1953	1954	1955
Average	9.0	9.8	10.4	10.6	10.8	11.2

	1962	1963	1964	1965	1966	1967
Average	13.4	13.7	14.1	14.8	15.4	15.8
Jan	13.2	13.6	13.8	14.5	15.1	15.7
Feb	13.2	13.7	13.8	14.5	15.1	15.7
March	13.3	13.7	13.9	14.5	15.1	15.7
April	13.5	13.7	14.0	14.8	15.3	15.8
May	13.5	13.7	14.1	14.9	15.4	15.8
June	13.6	13.7	14.2	14.9	15.5	15.8
July	13.5	13.7	14.2	14.9	15.4	15.7
Aug	13.4	13.6	14.2	14.9	15.5	15.7
Sept	13.4	13.7	14.2	14.9	15.5	15.7
Oct	13.4	13.7	14.3	15.0	15.5	15.8
Nov	13.5	13.7	14.4	15.0	15.6	15.9
Dec	13.5	13.8	14.4	15.1	15.6	16.0

	1974	1975	1976	1977	1978	1979
Average	27.5	34.2	39.8	46.1	50.0	56.7
Jan	25.3	30.4	37.5	43.7	48.0	52.5
Feb	25.8	30.9	38.0	44.1	48.3	53.0
March	26.0	31.5	38.2	44.6	48.6	53.4
April	26.9	32.7	38.9	45.7	49.3	54.3
May	27.3	34.1	39.3	46.1	49.6	54.7
June	27.6	34.8	39.5	46.5	50.0	55.7
July	27.8	35.1	39.6	46.6	50.2	58.1
Aug	27.8	35.3	40.2	46.8	50.5	58.5
Sept	28.1	35.6	40.7	47.1	50.7	59.1
Oct	28.7	36.1	41.4	47.3	51.0	59.7
Nov	29.2	36.6	42.0	47.5	51.3	60.3
Dec	29.6	37.0	42.6	47.8	51.8	60.7

	1914	1915	1916	1917	1918	1919
Average	2.8	3.5	4.1	5.0	5.7	6.1

	1926	1927	1928	1929	1930	1931
Average	4.8	4.7	4.7	4.6	4.5	4.2

	1938	1939–45	1946	1947	1948	1949
Average	4.4	na	7.5	8.0	8.6	8.8

	1956	1957	1958	1959	1960	1961
Average	11.7	12.0	12.4	12.4	12.6	12.9

	1968	1969	1970	1971	1972	1973
Average	16.5	17.4	18.5	20.3	21.7	23.7
Jan	16.1	17.1	17.9	19.4	21.0	22.6
Feb	16.1	17.2	18.0	19.5	21.1	22.8
March	16.2	17.2	18.1	19.7	21.2	22.9
April	16.5	17.4	18.4	20.1	21.4	23.3
May	16.5	17.4	18.4	20.3	21.5	23.5
June	16.6	17.5	18.5	20.4	21.6	23.7
July	16.6	17.5	18.6	20.5	21.7	23.8
Aug	16.6	17.4	18.6	20.5	21.9	23.8
Sept	16.6	17.5	18.7	20.6	22.0	24.0
Oct	16.7	17.6	18.9	20.7	22.3	24.5
Nov	16.8	17.6	19.0	20.8	22.4	24.7
Dec	17.0	17.8	19.2	20.9	22.5	24.9

	1980	1981	1982	1983	1984	1985
Average	66.8	74.8	81.2	84.9	89.2	94.6
Jan	62.2	70.3	78.7	82.6	86.8	91.2
Feb	63.1	70.9	78.8	83.0	87.2	91.9
March	63.9	72.0	79.4	83.1	87.5	92.8
April	66.1	74.1	81.0	84.3	88.6	94.8
May	66.7	74.6	81.6	84.6	89.0	95.2
June	67.4	75.0	81.9	84.8	89.2	95.4
July	67.9	75.3	81.9	85.3	89.1	95.2
Aug	68.1	75.9	81.9	85.7	89.9	95.5
Sept	68.5	76.3	81.9	86.1	90.1	95.4
Oct	68.9	77.0	82.3	86.4	90.7	95.6
Nov	69.5	77.8	82.7	86.7	91.0	95.9
Dec	69.9	78.3	82.5	86.9	90.9	96.0

Retail Prices Index 1986–1991

	1986	1987	1988	1989	1990	1991
Average	97.8	101.9	106.8	115.2	126.1	133.5
Jan	96.2	100.0	103.3	111.0	119.5	130.2
Feb	96.6	100.4	103.7	111.8	120.2	130.9
March	96.7	100.6	104.1	112.3	121.4	131.4
April	97.7	101.8	105.8	114.3	125.1	133.1
May	97.8	101.9	106.2	115.0	126.2	133.5
June	97.8	101.9	106.6	115.4	126.7	134.1
July	97.5	101.8	106.7	115.5	126.8	133.8
Aug	97.8	102.1	107.9	115.8	128.1	134.1
Sept	98.3	102.4	108.4	116.6	129.3	134.6
Oct	98.5	102.9	109.5	117.5	130.3	135.1
Nov	99.3	103.4	110.0	118.5	130.0	135.6
Dec	99.6	103.3	110.3	118.8	129.9	135.7

Retail Prices Index 1992–1993

	1992	1993
Average	138.5	—
Jan	135.6	137.9
Feb	136.3	138.8
March	136.7	139.3
April	138.8	
May	139.3	
June	139.3	
July	138.8	
Aug	138.9	
Sept	139.4	
Oct	139.9	
Nov	139.7	
Dec	139.2	

For later numbers phone 0923-815 377 (Herts, normal charges, local for London) or 071-270 6363/4 or 0839-338 337 (24 hour recording: £1.09 for 3 minutes cheap rate; £1.49 standard).

Appendix 3

Past issues of National Savings Certificates

If you hold any of these issues you can find out what they are yielding from the following tables. If you can do better elsewhere for your tax rate, cash them in; if not hold on. Interest on all issues is tax-free.

The tables show the interest for the year *and* the average compound yearly interest you get by holding on from now until the end of the fixed term. By comparing the rate in the table with the rate on competitive investments, eg building societies, you can decide whether to cash or stay put.

After the end of the periods listed in these tables, all certificates will receive interest at a common rate which is variable; for rates turn to the table at the end of this Appendix entitled 'General extension rate: variable interest'.

If you hold certificates in the 1st to 6th issues, sold between 1916 and 1939, cash them at once; they yield less than 1.75% a year.

£1, 7th, 8th, 9th, 10th, 11th, Decimal, 14th, 16th, 18th, 19th, 21st, 23rd, 24th, 25th, 26th, 27th, 28th, 29th, 30th, 31st, 32nd Issue Savings Certificates

Interest is now variable and added every 3 months — see tables on page 205.

33rd Issue Savings Certificates

£100 investment made 1 May 1987 to 21 July 1988

Year	Value at start £	Value up each 3 months by £	Value at end £	Yield for year %	Yield if held[1] to year 6 %
5	128.65	2.90	140.26	9.03	9.03
6	140.26	Variable interest added every 3 months.			

[1] Original yield for 5 years 7% a year.

34th Issue Savings Certificates
£100 investment made 22 July 1988 to 16 June 1990

Year	Value at start £	Value up each 3 months by £	Value at end £	Yield for year %	Yield if held[1] to year 6 %
2	106.00	1.72	112.89	6.50	7.88
3	112.89	1.98	120.80	7.09	8.37
4	120.79	2.57	131.08	8.51	9.01
5	131.08	3.12	143.56	9.52	9.52

[1] Original yield for 5 years 7.5% a year.

35th Issue Savings Certificates
£100 investment made 18 June 1990 to 30 March 1991

Year	Value at start £	Value up each 3 months by £	Value at end £	Yield for year %	Yield if held[5] to year 6 %
2	106.50	1.72[1]	114.49	7.50	10.26
3	114.49	2.00[2]	125.10	9.97	11.20
4	125.10	2.44[3]	138.59	10.78	12.18
5	138.59	2.92[4]	157.42	13.59	13.59

[1] Plus £1.08 on anniversary.   [2] Plus £2.57.   [3] Plus £3.76.   [4] Plus £7.16.   [5] Original yield for 5 years 9.5% a year.

36th Issue Savings Certificates
£100 investment made 2 April 1991 to 2 May 1992

Year	Value at start £	Value up each 3 months by £	Value at end £	Yield for year %	Yield if held to year 6 %
1	100.00	Nil	105.50	5.50	8.50
2	105.50	1.71	112.36	6.50	9.26
3	112.36	2.32	121.64	8.26	10.20
4	121.64	2.98	133.56	9.80	11.18
5	133.56	4.20	150.36	12.58	12.58

37th Issue Savings Certificates
£100 investment made 13 May 1992 to 5 August 1992

Year	Value at start £	Value up each 3 months by £	Value at end £	Yield for year %	Yield if held to year 6 %
1	100.00	Nil	105.50	5.50	8.00
2	105.50	1.64	112.04	6.20	8.64
3	112.04	2.24	121.00	8.00	9.47
4	121.00	2.84	132.36	9.39	10.21
5	132.36	3.65	146.96	11.03	11.03

38th Issue Savings Certificates
£100 investment made 6 August 1992 to 4 October 1992

Year	Value at start £	Value up each 3 months by £	Value at end £	Yield for year %	Yield if held to year 6 %
1	100.00	Nil	105.25	5.25	7.50
2	105.24	1.63	111.76	6.19	8.07
3	111.76	2.01	119.80	7.19	8.70
4	119.80	2.52	129.88	8.41	9.47
5	129.88	3.42	143.56	10.53	10.53

39th Issue Savings Certificates
£100 investment made 5 October 1992 to 12 November 1992

Year	Value at start £	Value up each 3 months by £	Value at end £	Yield for year %	Yield if held to year 6 %
1	100.00	Nil	104.60	4.60	6.75
2	104.60	1.37	110.09	5.25	7.30
3	110.09	1.86	117.51	6.74	7.99
4	117.51	2.32	126.81	7.91	8.61
5	126.81	2.95	138.63	9.32	9.32

40th Issue Savings Certificates
£100 investment made on or after 13 November 1992

Year	Value at start £	Value up each 3 months by £	Value at end £	Yield for year %	Yield if held to year 6 %
1	100.00	Nil	104.00	4.00	5.75
2	104.00	1.14	108.58	4.40	6.19
3	108.58	1.56	114.82	5.75	6.79
4	114.82	1.94	122.57	6.75	7.32
5	122.57	2.42	132.25	7.90	7.90

3rd Index-Linked issue
£100 investment made 30 June 1985 to 31 July 1986

After 5 years ½% of previous anniversary value added each year plus the rise in Retail Prices Index each month.

4th Index-Linked issue
£100 investment made 1 August 1986 to 30 June 1990

Year	Value at start £	Value at end £	Yield for year %	Yield if held[2] to year 6 %
3	106.35	110.07[1]	3.50[1]	4.67[1]
4	110.07	115.03[1]	4.50[1]	5.25[1]
5	115.03	121.92[1]	6.00[1]	6.00[1]

[1] Plus rise in Retail Prices Index over the period.   [2] Original yield over 5 years 4.04% a year.

5th Index-Linked issue
£100 investment made 2 July 1990 to 4 October 1992

Year	Value at start £	Value at end £	Yield for year %	Yield if held to year 6 %
1	100.00	100.00[1]	Nil[1]	4.50[1]
2	100.00	101.00[1]	1.00[1]	5.67[1]
3	101.00	103.03[1]	2.01[1]	7.26[1]
4	103.03	108.24[1]	2.72[1]	10.00[1]
5	108.24	124.62[1]	15.13[1]	15.13[1]

[1] Plus rise in Retail Prices Index over the period.

6th Index-Linked issue
£100 investment made on or after 13 November 1992

Year	Value at start £	Value at end £	Yield for year %	Yield if held to year 6 %
1	100.00	101.50[1]	1.50[1]	3.25[1]
2	101.50	103.53[1]	2.00[1]	3.69[1]
3	103.53	106.38[1]	2.75[1]	4.27[1]
4	106.38	110.37[1]	3.75[1]	5.03[1]
5	110.37	117.35[1]	6.32[1]	6.32[1]

[1] Plus rise in Retail Prices Index over the period.

Issues past the end of fixed interest extensions

Issue	Dates when purchased	Years after purchase date	Value at end of fixed interest term £
£1	11 Jan 1943 to 3 March 1947	42	361.50
7th	22 Nov 1939 to 31 March 1947	45	558.67
8th	1 April 1947 to 31 Jan 1951	38	464
9th	1 Feb 1951 to 31 July 1956	34	434.67
10th	1 Aug 1956 to 12 March 1963	28	381.33
11th	13 May 1963 to 26 March 1966	20	290
12th	28 March 1966 to 3 Oct 1970	18	270.50
Decimal	5 Oct 1970 to 15 June 1974	13	226.50
14th	17 June 1974 to 11 Dec 1976	8	185
	1 April 1977 to 27 Jan 1979		
16th	13 Dec 1976 to 31 March 1977	6	170.30
18th	29 Jan 1979 to 2 Feb 1980	5	150
19th	4 Feb 1980 to 9 May 1981	5	163.50
21st	11 May 1981 to 7 Nov 1981	5	154
23rd	9 Nov 1981 to 10 March 1982	5	164.80
24th	19 April 1982 to 4 Nov 1982	5	138.08
25th	17 Nov 1982 to 13 Aug 1983	5	143.60
26th	14 Aug 1983 to 19 March 1984	5	134.40
27th	5 April to 7 Aug 1984	5	141.92
28th	8 Aug to 11 Sept 1984	5	153.88
29th	15 Oct 1984 to 12 Feb 1985	5	146.96
30th	13 Feb to 9 Sept 1985	5	152.84
31st	26 Sept 1985 to 11 Nov 1986	5	145.92
32nd	12 Nov 1986 to 10 March 1987	5	152.12
33rd	1 May 1987 to 21 July 1988	5	157.44

Since these dates the General extension interest rate has been applied as listed below.

General extension rate: variable interest

Added every 3 months after fixed rate term ends. The rates are   % a year.

17 June 1982 to 30 November 1982 8.4%
1 December 1982 to 31 August 1983 7.08%
1 September 1983 to 31 March 1984 7.68%
1 April 1984 to 31 July 1984 6.84%
1 August 1984 to 30 November 1984 8.52%
1 December 1984 to 31 January 1985 8.28%
1 February 1985 to 31 March 1985 9%
1 April 1985 to 31 September 1985 9.51%
1 October 1985 to 31 May 1986 8.52%
1 June 1986 to 31 October 1986 8.01%
1 November 1986 to 31 March 1987 8.7%
1 April 1987 to 30 April 1987 7.5%
1 May 1987 to 30 September 1987 7.02%
1 October 1987 to 29 February 1988 6.51%
1 March 1988 to 30 April 1988 5.76%
1 May 1988 to 30 November 1992 5.01%
1 December 1992 3.75%

The current rate can be obtained by phoning 071-605 9483 or 9484.

Appendix 4

How money grows and falls in value

This appendix contains four sets of compound interest tables which can be used for different kinds of investment arithmetic. They are as follows:

- Table 1 How lump sums grow.
- Table 2 How money invested yearly grows.
- Table 3 How much you need now to accumulate for the future or how inflation reduces the value of your money.
- Table 4 How much you need to save each year.

Each table is in terms of £1,000 invested or saved. Here are some examples of what you can work out with these tables.

Example 1A Suppose you have £1,000 and you reckon it will grow at 8% a year. How much will you have accumulated after 20 years. Look up Table 1 for 8% and 20 years and the answer is £4,661. If you are actually investing £5,000 then multiply the answer by five which gives £23,305.

Example 1B Suppose you want to know how much you will need in 10 years to buy something which costs £1,000 now and you expect prices to rise by 5% a year. Look up Table 1 for 5% and 10 years; the answer is £1,629. If what you intend to buy costs £4,500 now multiply the answer £1,629 by 4.5 which comes to just over £7,330.

Example 2 Suppose you want to invest £1,000 a year. How much will you accumulate after saving for 25 years with a return of 8% a year? Look up Table 2 for 8% and 25 years; the answer is £78,954. If you are actually investing £100 a month, an approximate estimate of what you will get is to divide the answer by ten which gives £7,895 and then multiply by 12 which gives £94,740.

Example 3A Suppose you want to accumulate £1,000 in six year's time? How much do you need now? Assume you get 7% a year interest. Look up Table 3 for 7% a year and six years; the answer is £666. If you want £3,000 in six years time at the same rate of interest, multiply the answer £666 by three which comes to £1,998.

But what about inflation? Suppose you expect inflation to average 4% a year over the next six years. Deduct from your interest rate, 7% a year, the expected rate of inflation, 7% a year, and you have the rate at which your money is accumulating in *real* terms, 3% a year. So instead look up Table 3 for 3% a year and six years; the answer is £837. So if you wanted £3,000 in today's money in six years' time, taking into account inflation you need to invest three times £837 which is £2,511.

Example 3B Suppose you reckon inflation is going to average 5% a year for the next ten years. And you reckon you will have £10,000 accumulated by then. How much in today's money will that £10,000 be worth. Look up 5% a year and 10 years in Table 3 and the answer is £614. That is the answer for £1,000. So for £10,000 multiply by ten which gives £6,140.

Example 4 Suppose you want to save regularly to accumulate £100,000 when you retire in 15 years' time and you reckon you can get a return of 8% a year on your money in a personal pension, say. Look up Table 4 for 8% a year and 15 years and you get £34.10. This is the amount you need to save each year to accumulate £1,000. So to accumulate £100,000 you multiply by 100 which gives you £3,410. If you save monthly, divide by 12 which is approximately £284 a month.

But over 15 years inflation will take its toll. Suppose you expect inflation to average 5% a year over the next 15 years. That £100,000 will not buy the same amount as £100,000 in today's money. You need to calculate how much you will need in 15 years time to have the same purchasing power as £100,000 today. Look up Table 1 for 5% and 15 years and the answer is £2,079. Multiply by 100 to get the answer for £100,000 instead of £1,000; you get £207,900. Now that's a real shame because you've got to save over twice as much with inflation only at 5% a year.

So multiply £34.10 by 207.9 and you get £7,089 which is how much you need to save a year to accumulate £100,000 in todays money value in 15 years time. If you save monthly the amount is approximately £7,089 divided by 12 which is £591 a month.

Table 1   How lump sums grow

This table shows how much £1,000 will grow to at 2% a year to 7% a year over different time periods.

| Years | Interest or growth rate | | | | | |
	2% £	3% £	4% £	5% £	6% £	7% £
1	1,020	1,030	1,040	1,050	1,060	1,070
2	1,040	1,061	1,082	1,103	1,124	1,145
3	1,061	1,093	1,125	1,158	1,191	1,225
4	1,082	1,126	1,170	1,216	1,262	1,311
5	1,104	1,159	1,217	1,276	1,338	1,403
6	1,126	1,194	1,265	1,340	1,419	1,501
7	1,149	1,230	1,316	1,407	1,504	1,606
8	1,172	1,267	1,369	1,477	1,594	1,718
9	1,195	1,305	1,423	1,551	1,689	1,838
10	1,219	1,344	1,480	1,629	1,791	1,967
11	1,243	1,384	1,539	1,710	1,898	2,105
12	1,268	1,426	1,601	1,796	2,012	2,252
13	1,294	1,469	1,665	1,886	2,133	2,410
14	1,319	1,513	1,732	1,980	2,261	2,579
15	1,346	1,558	1,801	2,079	2,397	2,759
16	1,373	1,605	1,873	2,183	2,540	2,952
17	1,400	1,653	1,948	2,292	2,693	3,159
18	1,428	1,702	2,026	2,407	2,854	3,380
19	1,457	1,754	2,107	2,527	3,026	3,617
20	1,486	1,806	2,191	2,653	3,207	3,870
21	1,516	1,860	2,279	2,791	3,400	4,141
22	1,546	1,916	2,370	2,925	3,604	4,430
23	1,577	1,974	2,465	3,072	3,820	4,741
24	1,608	2,033	2,563	3,225	4,049	5,072
25	1,641	2,094	2,666	3,386	4,292	5,427
30	1,811	2,427	3,243	4,322	5,743	7,612
35	2,000	2,814	3,946	5,516	7,686	10,677
40	2,208	3,262	4,801	7,040	10,286	14,974

This table shows how much £1,000 will grow to at 8% to 13% a year over different time periods.

Interest or growth rate						Years
8% £	9% £	10% £	11% £	12% £	13% £	
1,080	1,090	1,100	1,110	1,120	1,130	1
1,166	1,188	1,210	1,232	1,254	1,277	2
1,260	1,295	1,331	1,368	1,405	1,443	3
1,360	1,412	1,464	1,518	1,574	1,630	4
1,469	1,539	1,611	1,685	1,762	1,842	5
1,587	1,677	1,772	1,870	1,974	2,082	6
1,714	1,828	1,949	2,076	2,211	2,353	7
1,851	1,993	2,144	2,305	2,476	2,658	8
1,999	2,172	2,358	2,558	2,773	3,004	9
2,159	2,367	2,594	2,839	3,106	3,395	10
2,332	2,580	2,853	3,152	3,479	3,836	11
2,518	2,813	3,138	3,498	3,896	4,335	12
2,720	3,066	3,452	3,883	4,363	4,898	13
2,937	3,342	3,797	4,310	4,887	5,535	14
3,172	3,642	4,177	4,785	5,474	6,254	15
3,426	3,975	4,595	5,311	6,130	7,067	16
3,700	4,328	5,054	5,895	6,866	7,986	17
3,996	4,717	5,560	6,544	7,690	9,024	18
4,316	5,142	6,116	7,263	8,613	10,197	19
4,661	5,604	6,727	8,062	9,646	11,523	20
5,034	6,109	7,400	8,949	10,804	13,021	21
5,437	6,659	8,140	9,934	12,100	14,714	22
5,871	7,258	8,954	11,026	13,552	16,627	23
6,341	7,911	9,850	12,239	15,179	18,788	24
6,848	8,623	10,835	13,585	17,000	21,231	25
10,063	13,268	17,449	22,892	29,960	39,116	30
14,785	20,414	28,102	38,575	52,800	72,069	35
21,725	31,409	45,259	65,001	93,051	132,782	40

Table 2   How money invested yearly grows

This table shows how much £1,000 invested yearly grows to at 2% to 7% a year over different time periods.

| Years | Interest or growth rate | | | | | |
	2% £	3% £	4% £	5% £	6% £	7% £
1	1,020	1,030	1,040	1,050	1,060	1,070
2	2,060	2,091	2,122	2,153	2,184	2,215
3	3,122	3,184	3,246	3,310	3,375	3,440
4	4,204	4,309	4,416	4,526	4,637	4,751
5	5,308	5,468	5,633	5,802	5,975	6,153
6	6,434	6,662	6,898	7,142	7,394	7,654
7	7,583	7,892	8,214	8,549	8,897	9,260
8	8,755	9,159	9,583	10,027	10,491	10,978
9	9,950	10,464	11,006	11,578	12,181	12,816
10	11,169	11,808	12,486	13,207	13,972	14,784
11	12,412	13,192	14,026	14,917	15,870	16,888
12	13,680	14,618	15,627	16,713	17,882	19,141
13	14,974	16,086	17,292	18,598	20,015	21,550
14	16,293	17,599	19,024	20,578	22,276	24,129
15	17,639	19,157	20,825	22,657	24,673	26,888
16	19,012	20,762	22,698	24,840	27,213	29,840
17	20,412	22,414	24,645	27,132	29,906	32,999
18	21,841	24,117	26,671	29,539	32,760	36,379
19	23,297	25,870	28,778	32,066	35,786	39,995
20	24,783	27,676	30,969	34,719	38,993	43,861
21	26,299	29,537	33,248	37,510	42,392	48,006
22	27,845	31,453	35,618	40,430	45,996	52,436
23	29,422	33,426	38,083	43,502	49,816	57,177
24	31,030	35,459	40,646	46,727	53,865	62,249
25	32,671	37,553	43,312	50,113	58,156	67,677
30	41,379	49,003	58,328	69,761	83,802	101,073
35	50,994	62,276	76,598	94,836	118,121	147,913
40	61,610	77,663	98,827	126,840	164,048	213,610

This table shows how much £1,000 a year grows to at 8% to 13% a year over different time periods.

Interest or growth rate						Years
8% £	9% £	10% £	11% £	12% £	13% £	
1,080	1,090	1,100	1,110	1,120	1,130	1
2,246	2,278	2,310	2,342	2,374	2,407	2
3,506	3,573	3,641	3,710	3,779	3,850	3
4,867	4,985	5,105	5,228	5,353	5,480	4
6,336	6,523	6,716	6,913	7,115	7,323	5
7,923	8,200	8,487	8,783	9,089	9,405	6
9,637	10,028	10,436	10,859	11,300	11,757	7
11,488	12,021	12,579	13,164	13,776	14,416	8
13,487	14,193	14,937	15,722	16,549	17,420	9
15,645	16,560	17,531	18,561	19,665	20,814	10
17,977	19,141	20,384	21,713	23,133	24,650	11
20,495	21,953	23,523	25,212	27,029	28,985	12
23,215	25,019	26,975	29,095	31,393	33,883	13
26,152	28,361	30,772	33,405	36,280	39,417	14
29,324	32,003	34,950	38,190	41,753	45,672	15
32,750	35,979	39,545	43,501	47,884	52,739	16
36,450	40,301	44,599	49,396	54,750	60,725	17
40,446	45,018	50,159	55,939	62,440	69,749	18
44,762	50,160	56,275	63,203	71,052	79,947	19
49,423	55,765	63,002	71,265	80,699	91,470	20
54,457	61,873	70,403	80,214	91,503	104,491	21
59,893	68,532	78,543	90,148	103,603	119,205	22
65,765	75,790	87,497	101,174	117,155	135,831	23
72,106	83,701	97,347	113,413	132,334	154,620	24
78,954	92,324	108,182	126,999	149,334	175,850	25
122,346	148,575	180,943	220,913	270,293	331,315	30
186,102	235,125	298,127	379,164	483,463	617,749	35
279,781	368,292	486,852	645,827	859,142	1,145,486	40

Table 3   How much you need now to accumulate for the future

This table shows the lump sum you need now to accumulate £1,000 at 2% to 7% a year growth over different time periods. It also shows how much £1,000 at the end of different periods of time is worth in today's money at 2% to 7% a year inflation.

Years	Interest or growth rate or inflation rate					
	2% £	3% £	4% £	5% £	6% £	7% £
1	980	971	962	952	943	935
2	961	943	925	907	890	873
3	942	915	889	864	840	816
4	924	888	855	823	792	763
5	906	863	822	784	747	713
6	888	837	790	746	705	666
7	871	813	760	711	665	623
8	853	789	731	677	627	582
9	837	766	703	645	592	544
10	820	744	676	614	558	508
11	804	722	650	585	527	475
12	788	701	625	557	497	444
13	773	681	601	530	469	415
14	758	661	577	505	442	388
15	743	642	555	481	417	362
16	728	623	534	458	394	339
17	714	605	513	436	371	317
18	700	587	494	416	350	296
19	686	570	475	396	331	277
20	673	554	456	377	312	258
21	660	538	439	364	294	242
22	647	522	422	342	278	226
23	634	507	406	326	262	211
24	622	492	390	310	247	197
25	610	478	375	295	233	184
30	552	412	308	231	174	131
35	500	355	253	181	130	94
40	453	307	208	142	97	67

or how inflation reduces the value of your money

This table shows the lump sum you need now to accumulate £1,000 at
8% to 13% a year over different time periods. It also shows how much
£1,000 at the end of different periods of time is worth in today's money
at 8% to 13% a year inflation.

Interest or growth rate or inflation rate						Years
8% £	9% £	10% £	11% £	12% £	13% £	
926	917	909	901	893	885	1
857	842	826	812	797	783	2
794	772	751	731	712	693	3
735	708	683	659	636	613	4
681	650	621	593	567	543	5
630	596	564	535	507	480	6
583	547	513	482	452	425	7
540	502	467	434	404	376	8
500	460	424	391	361	333	9
463	422	386	352	322	295	10
429	388	350	317	287	261	11
397	356	319	286	257	231	12
368	326	290	258	229	204	13
340	299	263	232	205	181	14
315	275	239	209	183	160	15
292	257	218	188	163	141	16
270	231	198	170	146	125	17
250	212	180	153	130	111	18
232	194	164	138	116	98	19
215	178	149	124	104	87	20
199	164	135	112	93	77	21
184	150	123	101	83	68	22
170	138	112	91	74	60	23
158	126	102	82	66	53	24
146	116	92	74	59	47	25
99	75	57	44	33	26	30
68	49	36	26	19	14	35
46	32	22	15	11	8	40

Table 4   How much you need to invest each year

This table shows how much you need to invest each year to accumulate £1,000 if your money grows from 2% to 7% a year over different time periods.

| Years | Interest or growth rate | | | | | |
	2% £	3% £	4% £	5% £	6% £	7% £
1	980.39	970.87	961.54	952.38	943.40	934.58
2	485.34	478.26	471.34	464.58	457.96	451.49
3	320.35	314.11	308.03	302.10	296.33	290.70
4	237.87	232.07	226.43	177.53	220.96	215.65
5	188.39	182.87	177.53	172.36	167.36	162.51
6	155.42	150.09	144.96	140.02	135.25	130.65
7	131.87	126.71	121.74	116.97	112.39	107.99
8	114.23	109.18	104.35	99.74	95.32	91.09
9	100.51	95.57	90.86	86.37	82.10	78.02
10	89.54	84.69	80.09	75.72	71.57	67.64
11	80.57	75.80	71.30	67.04	63.01	59.21
12	73.10	68.41	63.99	59.83	55.92	52.24
13	66.78	62.16	57.83	53.77	49.96	46.40
14	61.37	56.82	52.57	48.59	44.89	41.44
15	56.69	52.20	48.02	44.14	40.53	37.19
16	52.60	48.17	44.06	40.26	36.75	33.51
17	48.99	44.61	40.58	36.86	33.44	30.30
18	45.79	41.46	37.49	33.85	30.53	27.49
19	42.92	38.65	34.75	31.19	27.94	25.00
20	40.35	36.13	32.39	28.80	25.65	22.80
21	38.02	33.86	30.08	26.96	23.59	20.83
22	35.91	31.79	28.08	24.73	21.74	19.07
23	33.99	29.92	26.26	22.99	20.07	17.49
24	32.23	28.20	24.60	21.40	18.57	16.06
25	30.61	26.63	23.09	19.95	17.20	14.78
30	24.17	20.41	17.14	14.33	11.93	9.89
35	19.61	16.06	13.06	10.54	8.47	6.76
40	16.23	12.88	10.12	7.88	6.10	4.68

This table shows how much you need to invest each year to accumulate £1,000 at 8% to 13% a year over different time periods.

Interest or growth rate						Years
8% £	9% £	10% £	11% £	12% £	13% £	
925.93	917.43	909.09	900.90	892.86	884.96	1
445.16	438.96	432.90	426.97	421.16	415.47	2
285.22	279.87	274.65	269.56	264.60	259.75	3
205.48	200.61	195.88	191.29	186.82	182.47	4
157.83	153.30	148.91	144.66	140.54	136.56	5
126.22	121.94	117.82	113.85	110.02	106.33	6
103.77	99.72	95.82	92.09	88.50	85.05	7
87.05	83.19	79.49	75.96	72.59	69.37	8
74.15	70.46	66.95	63.61	60.43	57.41	9
63.92	60.39	57.04	53.88	50.88	48.04	10
55.63	52.24	49.06	46.05	43.23	40.57	11
48.79	45.55	42.51	39.66	37.00	34.50	12
43.08	39.97	37.07	34.37	31.85	29.51	13
38.24	35.26	32.50	29.94	27.56	25.37	14
34.10	31.25	28.61	26.18	23.95	21.90	15
30.53	28.10	25.29	22.99	20.88	18.96	16
27.43	24.81	22.44	20.24	18.26	16.47	17
24.72	22.21	19.94	17.88	16.02	14.34	18
22.34	19.94	17.77	15.82	14.07	12.51	19
20.23	17.93	15.87	14.03	12.39	10.93	20
18.36	16.16	14.20	12.47	10.93	9.57	21
16.70	14.59	12.73	11.09	9.65	8.39	22
15.21	13.19	11.43	9.88	8.54	7.36	23
13.87	11.95	10.27	8.82	7.56	6.47	24
12.67	10.83	9.24	7.87	6.70	5.69	25
8.17	6.73	5.53	4.53	3.70	3.02	30
5.37	4.25	3.35	2.64	2.07	1.62	35
3.57	2.72	2.05	1.55	1.16	0.87	40

Index

Other Popular Titles

SHARES A BEGINNERS' GUIDE TO MAKING MONEY
112 PAGES. £2.95.

The Guardian said: 'How to pick a winning share and how to ditch a loser . . . the guide explains how to speculate without losing your shirt and describes how to profit by judging the right time to buy and sell.'

HEALTHY EATING   ISABEL SKYPALA
240 pages. £3.95.

The nutritional breakdown of over 300 foods in everyday portions, in terms of calories, fat, salt, sugar and fibre, as well as the essential vitamins and minerals. *Today* said: **'It must be the most useful and down-to-earth guide I have ever read'.** The author is Chief Dietitian at London's Brompton Hospital.

BANISH STRESS AND PAIN   ROSS VALENTINE
240 pages. £4.95.

Relaxation and massage for every body. This book teaches you how to relieve backache, headache, pains in your neck, shoulders, arms and legs; and how to alleviate the tiredness at the end of a hard day.

ALLERGY? THINK ABOUT FOOD   SUSAN LEWIS
224 pages. £2.95.

This book explains **how natural foods and additives can cause allergic reactions like asthma, eczema, migraine, hyper-activity, bedwetting, aches and pains and even depression.** *The Daily Telegraph* said: "One of the major problems with many additives is that they are known to cause allergies. If you do have one which you cannot trace, **it would be worth investing in a paperback called ALLERGY? THINK ABOUT FOOD."**

CRYING BABY HOW TO COPE   PAT GRAY
144 pages. £3.50.

Pat Gray helped start CRY-SIS, the national support group for parents with crying babies. *The Guardian* said: **"Full of tips on the problems of yelling infants including how to help yourself survive."** With a foreword by Dr Miriam Stoppard.

ASK YOUR BOOKSHOP FOR COPIES OR USE THE FORM OVERLEAF

SHARES
A BEGINNERS' GUIDE
TO MAKING MONEY

'Describes how people can make
the most profit by judging the right
time to buy and sell'
Daily Telegraph

'A very useful book'
Ideal Home

'. . . easy to read, jargon free'
The Scotsman

'The book includes sections on how to
select shares, when to sell and how to get
a good deal from a stockbroker . . .'
The Times

ASK YOUR BOOKSHOP FOR COPIES OR USE THE FORM BELOW

To: **Wisebuy Publications, 25 West Cottages, London NW6 1RJ**

Please send me _____ copies of SHARES – A BEGINNERS' GUIDE TO MAKING MONEY
at £2.95 per copy plus 60p p&p or £6 airmail including p&p.

Please send me _____ copies of BANISH STRESS & PAIN
at £4.95 a copy plus 65p p&p or £8 airmail including p&p.

Please send me _____ copies of HEALTHY EATING
at £3.95 a copy plus 60p p&p or £8 airmail including p&p.

Please send me _____ copies of ALLERGY? THINK ABOUT FOOD
at £2.95 a copy plus 60p p&p or £7 airmail including p&p.

Please send me _____ copies of CRYING BABY HOW TO COPE
at £3.50 a copy plus 60p p&p or £6 airmail including p&p.

I enclose cheque/PO for £ _____ payable to Wisebuy Publications

Name _____
Block letters please

Address _____

_____

_____ Post code _____